THE AVANT-GARDE
AND GEOPOLITICS IN LATIN AMERICA

ILLUMINATIONS:
CULTURAL FORMATIONS
OF THE AMERICAS

John Beverley and
Sara Castro-Klarén,
Editors

THE AVANT-GARDE and Geopolitics in Latin America

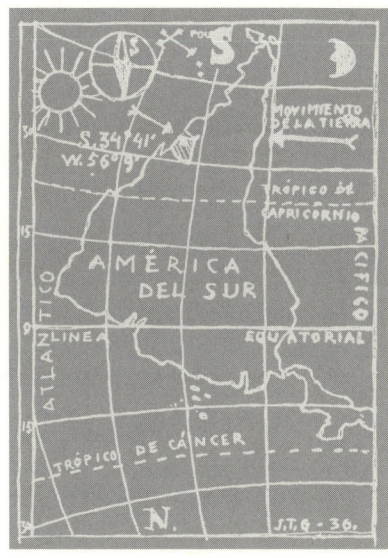

UNIVERSITY OF PITTSBURGH PRESS

FERNANDO J. ROSENBERG

Published by the University of Pittsburgh Press, Pittsburgh, PA 15260
Copyright © 2006, University of Pittsburgh Press
All rights reserved
Manufactured in the United States of America
Printed on acid-free paper
10 9 8 7 6 5 4 3 2 1

Library of Congress Cataloging-in-Publication Data

Rosenberg, Fernando J.
  The avant-garde and geopolitics in Latin America / Fernando J. Rosenberg.
    p. cm. — (Illuminations)
  Includes bibliographical references and index.
  ISBN 0-8229-4279-8 (cloth : alk. paper) — ISBN 0-8229-5916-x (pbk. : alk. paper)
  1. Latin American literature—20th century—History and criticism. 2. Literature, Experimental—Latin America—History and criticism. 3. Politics and literature—Latin America. 4. Arlt, Roberto, 1900–1942—Criticism and interpretation. 5. Andrade, Mário de, 1893–1945—Criticism and interpretation. I. Title. II. Illuminations (Pittsburgh, Pa.)
  PQ7081.R664 2006
  860.9'358098—dc22
                                                            2005034017

Physical Processing

Order Type: NTAS

Sel ID/Seq No: **67739** /32

Cust/Add: 228470005/01 JFGC   FLORIDA GULF COAST UNIVERSITY
Cust PO No. P0012361   **Cust Ord Date:** 01-May-2006
BBS Order No: C514360 Ln:61 Del:1 **BBS Ord Date:** 01-May-2006
0822942798-27005334
(9780822942795) **Sales Qty:** 1   **#Vols:** 001

The avant-garde and geopolitics in Latin America

Subtitle: Stmt of Resp: Fernando J. Rosenberg.

HARDBACK   **Pub Year:** 2006   **Vol No.:** _____ Edition:

Rosenberg, Fernando J.   **Ser. Title:**

University of Pittsburgh Press

Acc Mat:

Tech Services Charges:
PromptCat Barcode US   Property Stamp US   CD ROM US
Barcode Label   Security Device US   Spine Label PromptCat
Barcode Label Protector TechPro Cataloging US
Base Charge Processing Spine Label Protector US

Cust Fund Code: LIT-2006   **Cust Location:**
Stock Category: **Cust Dept:** FGAA

Order Line Notes

Notes to Vendor

221002

Blackwell's Book Services

Contents

    Acknowledgments   vii
1. Locating the Avant-Garde   1
2. A Case for Geopolitics   12
3. Locating the Future in *Los siete locos*   49
4. *Macunaíma* in the Mouth of the Cannibal   77
5. Leaving Home: Cosmopolitanism and Travel   106
6. Cosmopolitanism and Repentance: The Homecoming of the Avant-Garde Poet   136
7. Epilogue   161
    Notes   169
    Works Cited   193
    Index   205

Acknowledgments

Many of our intellectual adventures start when we try to understand the origins of our passions, and this book is no exception. The book concludes, though, that, more than origins, there is an iterative desire to understand that is no less passionate and no less intriguing. My own desire brought me to some early readings in my native Buenos Aires that have informed my practice of critical reading over what now seems a scandalous number of years. My interest in the avant-gardes of Latin America (and in so many other things) started as a teenager and was fostered by more artists, writers, and intellectuals than I could possibly enumerate and to whom I will always be grateful, from whom I am always inspired to learn, to teach, to write, to move around, and to think collectively.

Over the course of recent years in the United States, my engagement with the arts and literature was enriched by conversations that make my writing, and sometimes my very existence, less solitary. Fernando Degiovanni, Moira Fradinger, Cecilia Enjuto-Rangel, Pedro Caro, Ana Merino, Diana Bellessi, Dorit Naaman, Eliot Tretter, Christopher Powers, Arto Clerc, Michael Garral, Denise Corte, Nicole Asquit, Curtis Wasson, Marilyn Miller, Jacqueline Loss, Horacio Legrás, Sarli Mercado, Alicia Borinksy, Ellen Curry, Guillermo Irizarry, Lúcia Costigan, Luiza Moreira, Maria Negroni, Seth Fein, Eduardo González, and Frances Ferguson were, at different points, among my inspiring interlocutors. To be continued. Special thanks to Pablo Boczkowski and Irina Konstantinovsky for their bright vision that helped me to see beyond myself, and their joyful, warm hearts. Rolena Adorno, Nöel Valis, María Rosa Menocal, Roberto González Echevarría, David K. Jackson, Lidia Santos, and Oscar Martin, my colleagues at the Department of Spanish and Portuguese at Yale University, questioned and welcomed some of these ideas. More fundamentally, they provided me with a community of exemplary scholarship from which I have benefited tremendously and from which I draw inspiration daily. I am particularly grateful to Josefina Ludmer, for her passionate intellectual honesty (evident, for example, in her insistence that the vanguards were a dead topic), and for caring to honor my disagreement.

Sara Castro-Klarén had faith in this project from its very first stages and listened to my initial ruminations and well beyond. She facilitated my work with critical encouragement at every stage. Jorge Schwartz's careful reading of a first draft helped me to delineate it further along a very idiosyncratic path. John Beverley rightfully challenged some of my assumptions and gave me invaluable methodological and theoretical suggestions. Walter Mignolo's rare intellectual generosity was a high point for these ideas to come together. Vincent "Bud" Bynack and Tobias Hecht proved to be superb copyeditors, and without their input my ideas would have appeared far less lucid. Nathan McBrien, Kendra Stokes, and Deborah Meade at University of Pittsburgh Press lent me their full editorial support. The staff at Biblioteca Nacional in Argentina and at the Instituto de Estudos Brasileiros at the University of São Paulo in Brazil were as patient as my impatience allowed.

At different stages of this project I benefited from the institutional support of Johns Hopkins University, SUNY-Binghamton, and Yale University. This book received generous support from the Hilles Publication Fund from the Whitney Humanities Center at Yale University.

This book is dedicated to my parents, Sima Danon and Jorge Rosenberg, with profound gratitude for their constant gift of what remains impossible to fully appreciate.

THE AVANT-GARDE
AND GEOPOLITICS IN LATIN AMERICA

■ Chapter 1

Locating the Avant-Garde

THIS BOOK is about the avant-gardes of Latin America and their critique of modernity.[1] Rather than engaging in the construction of an alternative modernity or attempting to renegotiate the modern in relation to the traditional, these vanguardists, I contend, sought to produce a critique of the modern as a global project.

From the perspective of a narrative of progress, Latin America seems to be cast either as a relic from the primitive past or as an unrealized but promising future. The linear temporality of the Judeo-Christian tradition—"ascending, descending, progressive or regressive," as Gianni Vattimo (1992, 87) characterizes it—and its modern varieties—evolution, decadence, revolution, and novelty—were as deeply embedded in the Latin American discourses of emancipation as they were in every project of modernity. But the difference that the avant-gardes opened to inquiry, a difference that cannot be reduced to the contours of "cultural difference" in the traditional anthropological sense, is that at both ends of the foundational narrative—the promise of the future and redemption through and of the past—Latin

American discourse reencountered itself as subject to a larger order. It is as if the various futurisms and primitivisms that European movements displayed in an attempt to articulate a reaction against a bourgeois, conservative order (to express it in blatantly vanguardistic terms) were untenable from the Latin American position. For the Latin American avant-gardes, these alternatives kept referring back to the subaltern situation of Latin Americans themselves vis-à-vis the idea of the West, a concept that neither clearly included nor excluded Latin America.[2]

From this position, Latin American avant-gardes could undertake a critique of modernity and its narratives, including those of "international"[3] modernism and its avant-gardes, but along a different axis, not through rushing the temporalities of progress forward or through a return to primitive origins. Instead, they developed narratives of space that articulated the Latin American situation in a shifting world order. Some European avant-gardes movements (cubism, dadaism, surrealism, etc.) attempted to undermine the legacy of the Enlightenment and its foundation in the white man as the model of rationality and historical agency under the direction of universal, abstract progress. Because of their investment in modernity and their peripheral position in its foundational narratives, however, Latin Americans were forced to level their criticism through and with a particular attentiveness to spatial issues that addressed this problematic inclusion but that were repressed by the same idea of progress that they embraced.

This is not to say that Latin American avant-gardes were at any point more "advanced" than their European counterparts. While they tried to unravel European cultural supremacy, European avant-gardes usually remained attached to an assumption of their own universality. Artistic flights overseas were one way in which this was expressed, as the search for non-Western ways of life and perception became an exploration into the repressed soul of the universal human. For Latin American avant-gardists, (many times, no doubt, inspired by the Europeans), that position was untenable because the process of "discovery" was carried out under the suspicion of reproducing colonial dynamics. Therefore, tracking down influences and assessing the degree to which Latin American movements followed or did not follow European movements, as has been done repeatedly, misses the point and reproduces a colonial logic of unilinear development that, as we will see, Latin American avant-gardes tried to destabilize.

Vicky Unruh rightly argues in her seminal book *Latin American Vanguards* (1994) that these movements overcame an idea of national and/or continental identity as rooted in an original nature and landscape.[4] What Peter Bürger in his *Theory of the Avant-Garde* (1984) called the nonorganic character of the work of art, that is, the possibility of assembling different components with no final resolution of the internal tensions, is akin to this moment in which identity was conceived as a collage (Unruh, chapter 3). The connection Unruh makes between the collagelike constitution of the work of art and issues of national and continental identity is compelling, since ideas of hybridism, transculturation, and cultural anthropophagy or cannibalization—conceptual tools that the avant-gardes favored—traversed the twentieth-century Latin American discussion. But to what degree did the vanguards represent only another step in the constitution of national or regional identities? No doubt, the different movements and writers are inevitably embedded in national traditions. But some texts of the vanguards, I propose, suggest that the question of identity is intertwined with a redefinition of the location of discourses about it in the context of a global negotiation. In these texts, the problem of loci of enunciation—that is, the conditions of possibility for Latin American artists and writers to intervene in the larger debate about modernity—takes precedence and redefines the problem of identity.

As part of a geopolitical shift that, with the advent of World War I, shook loose the assumptions of nineteenth-century liberal culture, the avant-gardists in Latin America explored the limits of a national, culturalist response to crisis of the universality of civilization. The concern of the national creole elite in the constitution of its hegemony—namely, how to organize the nation (or Latin America, for that matter) so as to inscribe its culture more firmly in the annals of universal history—was for the first time left in suspense, owing to the war that put an end to the nineteenth century's faith in the rationality of European history and the worldwide projection.

Since literary criticism in Latin America was by and large engaged in the travails of the national cultural elite, I intend to open up the vanguard texts to this different set of concerns, shedding light by the same token on the makeup of that critical tradition. I am interested in the moments of interruption when vanguard experiments called attention to contemporary places of identification and symbolic production that were neither national cultures nor reducible to them. Such interruptions occurred as literary discourses exhibited an openness to planetary concerns that resulted in an exploration of vanguardistic ambition. As a result, the vanguards were led to recognize the indebtedness of literary discourses to the reproduction of colonial perspectives and to occupy positions of utterance that they imagined to dislodge this coloniality.

"From 1922 (the date is tentative, it is a situation of consciousness that has been defining itself little by little) all that has ended," writes Jorge Luis Borges (1926, 15), the vanguardist, in reference to the sea change that set in motion a Latin American artistic and intellectual field that would no longer voice "our longing for Europe."[5] Without attempting to reduce cultural production to a set of contextual conditions, I want to point out certain major historical trends that framed this alternative imaginary. The 1920s and 1930s were decades when the political order was reconfigured as the consequence of an ongoing change in the global geopolitical balance following World War I. It was a time of increasing democratization in the Latin American social space, but it was also an era of new pacts between conservative forces in different national arenas. The upheavals and revolutions that provoked regime changes in more than one national context at the end of the 1920s differed in character, yet they shared a common soil, as historian Tulio Halperin Donghi (1996, 371) makes clear:

> The world crises that erupted in 1929 had an immediate and devastating impact in Latin America, the loudest sign of which was the collapse, between 1930 and 1933, of the majority of the political situations that had consolidated during the good times that came before. What was not immediately evident was that the crash differed from previous complications along the way not only in terms of its unprecedented intensity; this crisis ushered in a new era in which the painful solutions that had allowed the continent to incorporate itself into an increasingly global economy proved ineffectual.[6]

We are not referring to a discrete event but to a broad historical pattern that subtly undermined faith in the viability of national autonomy as a way to frame, understand, and localize the production of culture. The question of what might constitute Latin America's possibilities, its conditions of cultural production in this "increasingly global economy," was at stake in many avant-garde texts of the early 1920s.

A parallel demographic change touched on the imaginary of positive modernity and its inception in foundational national narratives. The rural-urban balance of power on which modernity as spatial conquest was carried out (that is, the city as a model of governmentality whose effects were to be projected onto the rest of the territory) was unsettled with the formation of what the historian José Luis Romero (1986, chapter 7) called the "massified city." Major demographic changes were already occurring in many Latin American cities and had produced an overall change in the cultural landscape at the end of the nineteenth century. But the vanguard movements were the first artistic enterprises of the cultural elite that didn't react to this shift with strategies of domination, separation, or rejection. Instead, in an effort to cross the "great divide" between mass culture and elite culture, they integrated with and accommodated themselves to the logic of mass production and consumption.[7] The well-studied phenomena of unabashed promotion of artistic movements, the circulation of ideas through magazines, the interest in new media, and the political engagement with increasingly visible nonelite subjects can all be traced back to the vanguards' attempts to break through the narrowly conceived boundaries of literary culture.

This change of cultural practices entailed a broader concern with what I will call positionality. At a time when the hierarchies embedded in a notion of a progress that promised to spread from center to periphery and from city to countryside were being questioned, some cultural actors found themselves needing to gauge new configurations of production, circulation, and consumption within an expanded horizon, a world-system of attribution of cultural value and meaning. Countering modernity as a merely expansionist force, to the unilinearity of universal history, Latin American artistic movements would continue to posit places of resistance to anchor their identities in the midst of historical flows. Consequently, the elemental refuge of the baroque rain forest that magically eschews Western categories or the boundary-less hinterlands that haunt the gaze of the observer, though refractory of positivist discourse, would continue to be revamped (by early travelers of the nineteenth century, regional writers of the early twentieth century, and practitioners of magic realism) as a cornerstone of cultural formation. But the avant-gardes opened the possibility of a different strategy. Amid so much praise and condemnation of speed and transportation as icons of the universalized, homogeneously modern abolition of spatial constraints, the vanguards elaborated, for the first time, their own loci of enunciation imbricated in the circulation of goods, discourses, and peoples. Two seminal manifestos of the early 1920s—one Argentinean, the other Brazilian—are exemplary in that regard:

> A single struggle—the struggle for the way. Let's divide it up: poetry for import. And Brazilwood poetry for export. (Schwartz 1991, 138)

> *Martin Fierro* accepts the consequences and responsibilities of situating oneself. . . . Instructed on his antecedents, his anatomy, the meridian on which he walks, he consults the barometer, the calendar, before stepping into the street in order to live it with the nerves and mentality of nowadays. . . .[8] To accentuate and to expand to the rest of the intellectual activities, the independent movement in language initiated by [poet] Rubén Darío doesn't mean . . . that we will renounce, much less pretend not to recognize, that every morning we use Swiss tooth paste, French towels, and English soap (Schwartz 1991, 113–14).[9]

Two native, national products, one commercial ("Brazilwood," the first Brazilian export to the metropolis and the source of the region's name) and one cultural (Martín Fierro, the mythic character in the epic poem about an autochthonous gaucho as a founder of Argentinean nationality) are not only the anchor for a renewed nationalism, as has been argued widely, but also become vantage points from which to understand an expanded geopolitics. The map projected to elaborate this position needs to be altogether different from the one inherited from the period of nation-state formation. The modern and the new, so the "Manifesto Martín Fierro" seems to claim, necessarily come from an elsewhere that also has the power to define modernity and its others, whereas the "Brazilwood manifesto" foregrounds the fact that what stands as artistically new also depends on a sort of validation that is not at all foreign to a global circulation of commodities.

If, as Perry Anderson (1984, 105) affirms, "the market as an organizing principle of culture and society" was "uniformly detested by every species of [Euro-American] modernism," what are we to make of these seemingly conformist attitudes of the Latin Americans? It is a critical consensus that the reabsorption by advertisement and the market of the avant-garde aesthetic of the fragmentary, the shocking, and, of course, the appeal of the new and permanent change is one of the factors, if not the main one, that emptied some aesthetic techniques of any revolutionary potential. "The modern today is not in the hands of the poets. It is in the hands of the cops," affirmed Louis Aragon as early as in 1925 (Meschonnic 1992, 413). The avant-gardes from everywhere are conventionally referred to as propounding an aesthetic of rupture and resistance, an oppositional stance that these sections of the manifestos don't seem to honor. Were the Latin Americans envisioning that development—the "mass-mediafication" of avant-garde aesthetics—*avant la lettre*, and thus accommodating it—working it out, as it were—from within? Immediately after the Spanish-American war of 1898, an earlier form of modernism, Hispanic American *modernismo*, constructed itself and the Latin America that it was meant to represent as a spiritual enclave that rejected the materialistic, massified world. *Modernismo* in turn fashioned this rejection into a theory of a spiritually oriented Hispanic identity—a moment emblematically captured by the antithesis proposed by Uruguayan critic José Enrique Rodó, of the idealistic Ariel and the utilitarian, materialistic Caliban.[10] The avant-gardes, no doubt, distanced themselves from that position. They were especially attuned to the reverberations between the new art and the logic of the commodity because both shared, from the standpoint of the peripheries of capitalism, the affective aura of modernity as identified with an elsewhere. They triggered, to use Benedict Anderson's phrase, the "specter of comparison" that lies at the peripheries in their relation to modernity.[11]

I contend that the Latin American avant-gardes therefore understood "the new" spatially, not temporally—along a horizontal axis, not a vertical one. This is underscored, for example, by the Nicaraguan movement, which in one manifesto strove to differentiate between two senses of the new: on the one hand the genuine sense that opposed the conservative values of the literature and politics of the past and, on the other, the "evil and fake novelty" supported by interventionist and neocolonialist U.S. policy (Schwartz 1991, 215). Although the strict separation between these two senses of the new might strike us as too simplistic, it nevertheless calls attention to the effort to sort out the category of the new in geopolitical terms. Cognitive mappings were the only possibility for imagining the contours of modernity, its lines of circulation and re-creation, its impossible demands and the limits on its utopian projects, without rejecting modernity altogether, thus leaving its promises open.[12]

In chapter 2, "A Case for Geopolitics," I examine the problem of Latin American literary historiography and the place of the idea of modernity within it. I argue that the avant-garde is not only a privileged example around which Latin American modernity was debated but that it also provides some of the major trends that characterized this debate. This partially accounts for the continuing appeal of the avant-gardes in the cultural and artistic landscape of the continent, I contend. The avant-gardes took issue with the philosophical foundations of modernity and the place assigned to Latin Americans by the narrative of progress, a critique that becomes apparent from our (post)postcolonial and (post)postmodern situation.[13] Drawing on Walter Mignolo's understanding of modernity (2000a) as always already colonial, I reframe the reading of avant-garde texts as engaged in a discussion that transcended (although often by including) the constitution of national modern cultures. In my debate with the more convincing theoretical efforts to gauge the global geopolitics of the avant-gardes, namely those of George Yúdice, Nestor García Canclini, Fredric Jameson, and Perry Anderson, I point out the different impasses that their critical readings fail to overcome. Throughout this theoretical chapter, I also elaborate on concepts that are more or less canonical in modernist studies, such as simultaneity, cosmopolitanism, and artistic autonomy, to make them speak the language of the geopolitical problems that I contend they often echo.

Chapter 3 focuses on Roberto Arlt's novelistic diptych *Los siete locos/Los lanzallamas* (The seven madmen/The firethrowers) (1986 [1929–1931]).[14] Written in Buenos Aires at the end of the 1920s, the novels addressed a number of the topics that the avant-gardes understood as constituting the new landscape of cultural production, such as the immersion of the subject in the conditions of urban life, the possibility of revolutionary change, and the inception of film and mass media. The main argument of the novels could be said to be geopolitically charged: It concerns a revolutionary cell that plans a sudden change in the global balance of power, achieved from a peripheral position (the outskirts of a South American city) and position of social abjection (the characters are outcasts). This tour de force can be read as an attempt to bring closure to the conditions of cultural production and political change that were still prevalent in the 1920s and as an attempt to map out and propose new ones. The role in this novelistic diptych of the epistemological enterprise of mapping a new world order is far from metaphorical. It is a continually pending quest that is at the base of every one of its intellectual, aesthetic, and political concerns. From the map present in the novels, a mysterious emblem, I read this narrative as an investigation into the possibilities of a mapping that, from different and movable peripheral positions, is unable to claim any mimetic authority, but is nevertheless necessary in order to imagine alternative political possibilities.

From here I turn, in chapter 4, to a completely different intellectual trend introduced by the avant-garde: the ethnological inquiry that is at the base of Mário de Andrade's attempt to address the constitution of a distinctive culture in his 1928 novel *Macunaíma, o herói sem nenhum caráter* (Macunaíma, the hero with no character).[15] Anthropological knowledge was a discursive tool that modernist intellectuals used in their critique of modernity, and many in Latin America had recourse to it as a token for the constitution of a differential cultural identity. Miguel Angel Asturias's surrealist recreation of Mayan texts in *Leyendas de Guatemala* (Guatemala legends, 1930) and the representation of the indigenous in the production of Mexican muralists are cases in point. The ethnological object, the native antihero Macunaíma, enacts the mediation between traditional and modern, popular and elite, in the construction of a national culture by traversing a multifarious Brazilian territory and negotiating between different temporalities, pushing to the extremes the ethnological quest for identity. But *Macunaíma* also bears witness to the impossible closure of the quest, which through this ethnological pursuit keeps referring back to the afterlife of the colonial enterprise, an afterlife that resists being placed under the banner of national culture—not even the carnavalesque, multitemporal, anthropophagic one in which the Brazilian avant-garde (the *movimento modernista*) was invested. Under the pretense of ethnography, the geography of the nation is the stage for questioning the colonial makeup of modern knowledge.

In chapter 5, I come back to the works of Roberto Arlt and Mário de

Andrade in order to elaborate on vanguardist travel writing. The writers appear as figures of the artistic voyager that are part of the culture of modernism at large—on the one hand, the urban traveler as a master of ironic detachment, a painter of the modern life, on the other, an interpreter, admirer, expert, performer, and reinscriber of those cultures displaced and subordinated by different "civilizing missions" (colonial, national). In their writing practice, however, as they interact with places and people, they confront their own role as traveler-writers by unpacking the discursive traditions and systems of value that sustained them. Travel writing, as much celebrated by postmodernists for its deterritorialization as accused by postcolonial thinkers of reproducing and expanding power structures, becomes a practice that confronts and examines established regimes of representation while pointing to subjects and practices occluded under those regimes.

In chapter 6, I analyze the cultural phenomenon of artistic repentance that many participants of the vanguard movements seemed to experience in the 1930s and 1940s with respect to their own earlier artistic pursuits, which they suddenly regarded as foreign and too "cosmopolitan." The importance of this moment becomes apparent in the iterative aspect pointed out by several cultural critics: that is, throughout the twentieth century, many Latin American artists and intellectuals reencountered their Latin American ties in a kind of a posteriori reaction against their own European affiliations (Asturias, Carpentier, Cortázar, etc.). Primary in the intellectual stance of the avant-gardes in the 1920s was a criticism of any vernacular ontology in favor of more dynamic and cross-cultural notions, but some repentant artists intended a later recuperation—destined to remain inevitably ironic—of the organic notion of identity. I trace the poetic development of, among others, Oliverio Girondo, Vicente Huidobro, and Oswald de Andrade, three of the most "cosmopolitan" writers, if cosmopolitism is to be understood as the power of detachment of the well-traveled. But ultimately, my purpose is to take issue with this notion of cosmopolitanism in order to call attention, in analyzing texts by César Vallejo, to a different understanding of the concept. Another, alternative cosmopolitanism unsettles binary oppositions between authenticity and irony, nativism and elite cosmopolitanism, particularism and universalism.

Even though I claim that some of my arguments can be used to revamp the discussion of Latin American avant-gardes, my texts are not selected under the assumption of representation—neither at the national nor the continental level nor in terms of artistic movements. I take inspiration, here and elsewhere, from Walter Benjamin, who wrote that "to encompass both Breton and Le Corbusier—that would mean drawing the spirit of contemporary France like a bow, with which knowledge shoots the moment in the heart" (2003, 459). This book doesn't intend a cataloguing of different trends, and thus three of its five substantive chapters focus on the writings of Mário de Andrade and Roberto Arlt. The intellectual projects of these two writers differ radically, yet what might be akin to idiosyncratic primitivisms and futurisms—if we are to give their endeavors familiar labels—ultimately become critical explorations of the geopolitical assumptions presented in these trends. I am attracted to this corpus not so much because of their potential as case studies but because they do not embrace the international vanguard aesthetic of which they uncomfortably partake as a new universal, but actively open and problematize it from a particular locus of enunciation. This strategy highlights a whole period of cultural production, not in terms of its proclaimed rupture and aesthetic battles, but in its somewhat reluctant figuration of a culture to come.

■ **Chapter 2**

A Case for Geopolitics

IN HIS influential and widely reprinted 1927 article "Contra el secreto profesional" (Against the professional secret), Peruvian poet César Vallejo dismissed Latin American vanguard trends as so much "aping" of foreign aesthetics (Schwartz 1991, 513–16). The ensuing decades of cultural analysis have either echoed this accusatory stance or reversed Vallejo's argument and taken up a defense of the vanguard by highlighting the movement's originality. In sketching the major trends of this debate, I aim not to conduct an exhaustive historical survey but rather to foreground different agendas for Latin American modernity as they are set in critical readings of the vanguards.

Until fairly recently, it was common in the field of Latin American literary historiography to redeem the vanguard movements of the first part of the twentieth century by locating them within a narrative of increasing historical consciousness and identity formation. Many avant-garde artists, critics argued, expressed a new sense of social commitment, a democratic fall or a step forward on the inevitable road from cosmopolitan high-cultural grace to increasingly social, localized allegiances. It is hardly a coincidence that such an evolutionary framing also seemed to offer a conceptual window onto the trajectory of the preceding literary movement in Spanish America—the fin-de-siècle *modernismo*. The shift from the cosmopolitan to the particular and the local was seen as both a mechanism inside the movement and a force breaking it apart. Thus Rubén Darío's rejection of the ideal of supreme beauty of the swan in favor of the culturally specific "buey que vi en mi niñez [ox that I saw in my childhood]" was emblematic of this larger shift from the ivory tower of *modernismo* to the more prosaic *postmodernismo*.[1] The vanguards would cap this development, so this narrative of progression goes, and point toward a heightened sociohistorical consciousness that would lead to subsequent achievements, especially to the "boom" in Latin American literature of the 1960s and its first generation of internationally recognized Latin American authors.

Early literary critics of the avant-gardes tended to align themselves with one side of the spectrum or the other: with cosmopolitanism and modernity as a moveable feast (as it was for Girondo, Huidobro, Oswald de Andrade, Maples Arce, and others) or the articulation of social struggles in artistic polemics (as was the case for Vallejo, Neruda, Mariátegui, and the Mexican muralists); with an international or a national language; with modernity or tradition; with the 1920s or the 1930s; with the city or the countryside; with elite culture or that of the masses, and so on. For the late romantic, proto-surrealist Neruda of the 1920s or for his later Latin Americanist reincarnation in the 1940s, the critical scheme often frames the reading of a single author's trajectory as a progressive maturation. Thus, the paradigmatic journey from artistic adventures in Paris to the native land—which many artists of this time followed and in some cases used to launch their careers as vanguardists—represented to artists and critics alike an allegory of discovery and self-discovery, a dialectical sublation of the antagonisms sketched above, a step in the direction of a higher realization of Latin American self-consciousness.

No doubt the change of perspective performed by several studies since the 1970s represented an important step toward a more complex understanding.[2] Against the tradition of a critical search for literary autochthony—with its inevitable accusations that the vanguards were insufficiently rooted, and a parallel reaction of safeguarding the autonomy of the aesthetics—a critical trend developed that demonstrates the role of avant-gardes in the formation of modern local cultures. But these studies were nevertheless entrapped, as Carlos Alonso (1998, 25) put it, in "a dialectics of restoration through the affirmation of the opposite,"[3] with the obligation to demonstrate the sociohistorical pertinence of the movements for a national or Latin American historical frame of analysis or their originality vis-à-vis the European counterparts. Typically, a theory of the critical reception of European currents complements one of the national cultural field, producing the aforementioned legitimation.

The reading I propose here is intended to transcend the deadlock in Latin American literary criticism between the accusation that the vanguards had a purely cosmopolitan allegiance and opposing efforts to demonstrate their relationship to a more autochthonous historical problematic. The geopolitical reading I am suggesting brackets the question of the origins (native or foreign) and the mimicking of cultural production to emphasize a remarkable simultaneity that cannot be explained away by any account of the specific influences and European journeys of individual artists. In the flow of transnational and transatlantic vanguard creative forces, I intend to highlight a grammar in which the artistic expressions of the periphery issued statements about global positionality.

It has always seemed remarkable to me that even today, among the ruins of the national or continental projects of emancipation and autonomy, the production of the vanguard movements is nevertheless a constant reference within the Latin American cultural scene—and not merely as an object of academic study. In fact, critical and artistic works of the avant-gardes are often called upon and made relevant in current intellectual debates and artistic endeavors, a re-enactment that differs from the paradigm of aesthetic autonomy of art through which Anglo-European modernism has been canonized by museums and teaching institutions.[4] Part of the production of the vanguard movements of the 1920s and 1930s retains currency nowadays when most of the assumptions about the role of territorially defined notions like "region" and "nation" as the principal component of cultural identity and as the horizon of any social struggle have been questioned on various fronts (through globalization from below and above, to put it schematically).

Because it is the fate of literary and cultural studies to be anachronistic, inasmuch as they always tread behind the object of study, I find it productive to make my own anachronism more explicit. I believe that many critical perspectives on the avant-gardes are based on a nostalgic quest for the lost place of art as the master arbiter of cultural value or for the social forces unleashed in the golden age of avant-garde activity. (Paradoxically, the avant-gardes themselves faced and to some degree responded with nostalgia and relief to a sense of loss of art's valued place.) I want to demonstrate instead that some discussions that seem to have acquired prevalence in the last twenty years (e.g., regarding postcolonialism, globalization, and, lately, Latin Americanism) were posited and worked out in the production of the vanguards; the debates around these critical viewpoints are in fact significant, but partly because they illuminate issues that were in place long before the reinvention of their intellectual and academic novelty. What is more, they were left aside in the hegemonic efforts to create a modern, national culture. Thus, this study attempts to read the vanguards through a set of problems that may, rightly, seem to be defined in hindsight but that does so in order to reclaim the vanguard productions for the present theoretical and cultural discussion. By the same token, it tries to understand the Latin American vanguards' continuous currency as a means to resignify the present while transcending the specificity of literary culture.

How does this relate to the title of this book, *The Avant-Garde and Geopolitics in Latin America*? By recasting avant-gardes in terms of geopolitics, I want to take to task the pervasive inclination to reduce spatial position to stages of temporal progress in discussions of modernity. The term "geopolitics" has been a conceptual key to understanding the global distribution of symbolic power and the possible ways to locate folds or niches of resistance in it and to it: from the inception of the notion of geopolitics as a way for the nineteenth-century imperial sciences to identify location and physical environment as variables in the struggle for global power;[5] to its use as a way of viewing discrete entities—nations—in their mutual interconnectedness; to the more recent world-system analysis, in which the predominance of the nation as the only privileged agent in the global power game is challenged and new actors and new ways to gain cultural agency emerge. To analyze the world as a system is a logical consequence of a closed world divided, effectively or potentially, into nations with imaginarily equal footing in the global order and in which development and progress are the models proposed to understand their inequality. For my purposes, geopolitics refers to these designs to reproduce and legitimize power at the larger scale, but in order to better highlight strategies of contestation, alternative productions of knowledge and aesthetic interventions meant to disrupt this reproduction.

During the nineteenth century, from the military to the political and then to the artistic arena, the movement forward implied by the term "avant-garde" acquired a chronological dimension: one of progressive advances against values and forces identified as regressive or conservative. The term thus not only changed its fields of application but also came to signify something temporal, not spatial. Matei Calinescu (1977, 95) has made this connection clearly: "It was modernity's own alliance with time and long-lasting reliance on the concept of progress that made possible the myth of a self-conscious and heroic avant-garde in the struggle for futurity." Progress and futurity reveal their own colonial logic when considered in light of what Mary Louise Pratt (1992, 7) has identified as "diffusionist accounts": modernity envisaged as a discretely European invention that reaches the peripheries as so many hand-me-down ideas.[6]

But if we are to aspire to dismantle all sorts of diffusionist accounts that leave Latin America in an epistemologically subrogate position, vanguardism must not be read as part of a single line of progress that only belatedly catches up with Latin America. Neither can it be considered native offspring, a new attempt to unveil a local nucleus of identity that remained untouched by, or that at least decelerated, the wave of modernization or that selectively and cogently consumed its products. Instead, I invite the reader to recognize the modernity of the Latin American avant-gardes as enunciations from and about a global, simultaneous dynamic. This concern with positionality implies that the division between margins and centers, although unavoidable, is always in the making, continually reformulated, reinforced, and contested, a constitutive tension more than a fetishized temporal or spatial partition.

ON MODERNITY AND TEMPORALITY

The shift of critical emphasis away from notions of progress and backwardness, identity and alienation to what I am calling the geopolitical—to issues of spatialization within a global order—is an effort to foreground aspects of the artistic production of this period that have been occluded by the master narratives of modernity that have tinged our critical approaches. The discussion of what falls under the label "avant-garde" and of how to conceptualize this artistic production is often paradigmatic of how Latin American modernity has been assessed. In fact, it has been said that the avant-garde has defined not only the later Latin American literary field (Unruh 1994, 1–2), but, more dramatically, the terms in which Latin American ways of existence were elaborated in the twentieth century (Yúdice 1999, 63). Artistic manifestos and essays from the period readily suggest how different positions that marked twentieth-century polemics regarding modernity in Latin America are already sketched out by these movements. It is also possible to begin to see that these are not the only positions inscribed in them.

Let us examine, in some programmatic texts of the 1920s, the possibilities opened up by the avant-gardes. In them, the avant-gardes inquired into their own legitimacy—that is, the paradoxical possibility of their own existence as vanguard movements far from the centers of modernism. This self-examination asks us to pay attention to their effort to dismantle the epistemological location that the modern/colonial order assigned them and to interrogate how they named the deadlock. The avant-gardists perceived themselves, no doubt, as agents of modernity. Yet in rewriting modernity from their particular location, their travails often placed them at junctures where modernity's own process of self-confirmation, the continuous reinforcement of the narratives of universal progress, came to a halt.

First, there is the claim that Latin American modernity is derivative, mimetic, dependent: "the avant-garde has reached America with great delay, like the old colonial couriers. . . . It is nothing but a vague mistake of Chronos, but a mistake very much on target for South America" (Osorio T. 1988, 372). The idea of belatedness here, which puts everything on a single temporal line, is obvious. As I will demonstrate, however, the avant-gardes in Latin America indeed brought to the fore the problem of temporality, but they did so by confronting how production in the peripheries is conditioned by a geopolitical position—by the intervals and simultaneities occurring at a global level. Therefore, the key aspect of the statement that "the avant-garde has arrived late to America" is not so much the perception of belatedness but rather the "mistake very much on target" that shifts the linear temporal dimension into a simultaneous dynamic, which suggests the pertinence of a spatial reading. This idea of global modernity could likewise entail the affirmation that Latin America's belated arrival can't be voluntarily counterbalanced; it must be radically overturned—"the first positions [in capitalist competitions] are already assigned. And the opposition in linguistic, racial, spiritual terms has no decisive role" (Osorio T. 1988, 318).

From the Latin American position as unavoidably backward, we might seize a somewhat contrary affirmation that could also be found in these foundational avant-garde texts—that the idea of modernity is tied to the idea of the New World and, consequently, literary modernity is of the Americas first and foremost, the heritage of Poe, Whitman, Lautremont, and Laforgue (Uruguayans the last two): "the boomerang that fecundated European poetry is now back in the New World" (Osorio T. 1988, 235). Despite their differences, this reversal of high culture universalism has in common with the sense of belatedness that they all urge us to understand modernity from a trans-Atlantic negotiation of values. America, referred to without qualifiers in many manifestos (neither Latin, Hispanic, nor Portuguese) is a predicament that points back to the colonial encounter.

The desire to be modern also might represent an embrace of the forward-looking dictum *il faut être absolument moderne* (Rimbaud) in a nationalistic key—"Puerto Rico can't stay behind this movement that puts the world in a state of expectation" (Osorio T. 1988, 147). What this recommendation highlights is not modernity's accomplishments, which would make it universal, although uneven, but its promises, equally distributed around the globe. Complimentarily, modernity can also be conceptualized in these foundational texts as an idealistic framing device of an inclusive Western universalism, conceived precisely in the "Latin boiling pot," in which Latin America participates in its own right (Osorio T. 1988, 272).[7] This was the position also maintained by Borges from his vanguard years on, although his embrace of the Western cannon was by the same token an interrogation of its embedded hierarchies.

Finally, Latin American modernity might be proposed as a reevaluation of the indigenous legacy that inevitably contains an ironic distance from its native self, a perspective majestically put forward by Oswald de Andrade's

"Tupi or not Tupi: that is the question" (Schwartz 1991: 143).[8] The encounter of these different trends flourishing on avant-garde soil can be explained as culturally specific, but only if these particularities are understood as positions within a global order rather than as expressive manifestations of pre-existing culture.

The avant-gardists were, in different ways, modernizers. City dwellers, they enjoyed a certain level of sophistication in consumption; they were culturally and, in numerous cases, materially privileged, many of them embracing a world of technology and the commodification of a secularized daily life. But it is exactly this basic disposition toward novelty and its artistic representation, even when some artists and movements constructed their stance in partial opposition to it (e.g., Borges's mythical Buenos Aires or Asturias's recreation of Mayan legends), that made their production sensitive to their historical position of enunciation—that is, to the place they occupied in the assigning of cultural values, such as novelty and backwardness, within a world of shifting hegemonies. Although many avant-gardists hardly abandoned the more or less updated role of the Latin American national intellectual as a mediator between heterogeneous histories and cultural experiences for the constitution of national identity, many of the impasses they encountered bear witness to an acute awareness of their position in the modern/colonial order and its reproduction via the nation-state. None of the available intellectual strategies to make sense of the role of their art—national or cultural difference, the autonomy of art, or a total submission to the logic of homogeneous progress (advanced by liberals and socialists alike)—provided them a locus of enunciation to articulate aesthetically their position after the First (imperial) World War.

My reading does not celebrate the Latin American avant-gardes as already postmodern but rather attempts to mobilize them to unsettle the modern/postmodern division. The prevalent consensus now is that modernity has been superseded and conveniently periodized, which permits us to measure our distance from its naiveté, its longing for totality, its utopian impulse, or whatever our epistemological superiority allegedly overcame. This new common sense confirms the idea that historical change has a preset direction that allows every turn to be understood in terms of an advance or a setback. However, modernity's main narrative of progress returns to the scene at the very moment its death is declared.[9] The advent of something that can be named "postmodern" is supposed to signal the end of this basic narrative. The discourse in which this "new" cultural logic and the phenomena associated with it are labeled, though, starts by denouncing the difficulty of this perspectival change. Modernity is reconfirmed when "postmodern" takes the place of "the new," which in its turn acquires its allure and the symbolic value associated with it.

With the putative dissolution of the modernity-versus-tradition dialectic said to define postmodernity, the terms are no longer agonistically posited but converted into signs with market value. Tradition becomes marketable, and its agents become producers and consumers. That is the logic that allows for the diversification of temporalities characteristic of the postmodern and not, as becomes more and more obvious, a new spirit of worldwide tolerance on the verge of the final demise of the *grand récit*. That is why the celebrated idea of the postmodernity *avant la lettre* of the Latin American situation is unsustainable, especially when predicated on the convivial existence of different temporalities as *the* characteristic of the Latin American cultural space before it became acceptable everywhere else. Postmodernity in Latin America is sometimes narrated as a new philosophical ground that will permit subaltern subjects to finally make it on time to a new global socius (e.g., Carlos Rincón [1995]). My intention in pointing to the pervasive modern narratives of postmodernist emancipation is to underscore the critical potential of some paradigmatically modern Latin American texts. That critical potential consists precisely in upsetting this notion of temporality.

It has been argued that the Enlightenment is not the pivotal narrative in relation to which Latin American modernity needs to be conceptualized.[10] From the perspective of the study of the avant-gardes, however, it remains important to emphasize modernity's own self-understanding: that modernity has declared itself to be a temporal structure that, although it has inherited Christian, lineal, irreversible temporality, it has also constituted itself as a negation of the theological order. Modernity emerged as a project by ordering existence in terms of temporal determinants, imposing standards of advancement or belatedness which confirm its (always already) colonial dominance. This construction, the kind of subjectivities that it forms and the mappings that it projects, is a product of the Enlightenment.

However, I am not championing the long-standing promotion of modernity as self-consciousness, a state of maturity to which all humankind would eventually aspire.[11] Instead, I am referring to the constant writing over of modernity's own definition by the act of disavowing what becomes, through this act, obsolete. As Henri Meschonnic (1992, 413) suggested, discussions about modernity's origins—whether it started at the "end of the Middle Ages" or with a "Charlie Chaplin movie," as he puts it—are to be read as a consequence of the performativity unleashed by the idea of modernity, that is, the kind of division that immediately sets in motion and constitutes its performative aspect, that decides what moves to modernity's tempo and what is left behind.[12]

The Enlightenment reformulation of the place of Europe in the geopolitical world order set modern temporality in motion—which is not the same as to say that it emerged in one region only to appear elsewhere later. This was achieved by disavowing the role of the rest of the world in the constitution of modernity. What this construction of the world of traditional cultures—and the idea of culture itself—contains is a spatialization of modernity's own temporal order that entails a submission to space by time. Therefore, a set of temporal hierarchies maps out the whole territory (and modernity's territory is necessarily no other than the globe) and confers on different places and practices a different mark on a scale that passes for common ground.

"Progress" is, of course, the most powerful organizational principle in this development. The idea of national independence with which the Latin American republics were created entails the will to adjust to the coordinates of modern, universal history. At most, tradition is reintegrated as a cultural value that will endow and define the local as vernacular, devoid of any oppositional stance, any value for organizing political alternatives, any heterogeneous assembling of common experience. This version of modernity is capitalist, but modernity transcends a particular economic order. Marxism constituted for many Latin American intellectuals of the twentieth century a way to advance further into modernity, perhaps in a more orderly fashion. Moreover, for the left avant-garde of the 1920s and 1930s, modernity also first delivered its promises elsewhere, and political engagement strove to bring them about locally.

In this sense, it is useful to mention Carlos Alonso's conceptualization (1998, 5–10) of two master discourses in Latin America that partake in the temporality of modernity on a global scale. What Alonso pointed out are the discourses of futurity (the perpetual promise that the "new" continent represents for the "Old World") and of novelty (the never-ending chance for discovery). Two temporal narratives are inseparable from a dialectic that was set in motion with the colonial encounter, narratives that the avant-gardes pushed to the limit. They are particular not because they spring from a localized culture, but rather because they partake of a particular position in the universal problematic of coloniality. The avant-gardes are, in part, an investigation of the conditions of these discourses and the possibilities of unlocking them.

How was it possible for the Latin Americans to criticize the modern project from a location that is often perceived to lack the material and cultural resources promised by the project of modernity, resources that are projected as already existing elsewhere and desired at home? Would this challenge not lead to taking up the obscurantism of the decadent or the purportedly circular temporality of the primitive, thus disavowing modernity in its entirety by rejecting its claim to rationality? It is necessary to recall that Latin American intellectuals in the 1920s and 1930s had appropriated the diagnosis of European decline from Oswald Spengler's influential book *The Decline of the West* (1962), first published in 1918.[13] Alternative responses to the narrative of hegemonic European modernity, other prophetic philosophers à la mode such as Herman Keyserling, were no less enthusiastic in proclaiming a new era for South American civilization. But Spengler's organic idea of cultural development in which civilizations grow, fulfill their mission, and disappear by their own internal undoing, disavowed every possibility of thinking about cultures in inevitable connection with one another. Keyserling, for his part, attempted a compromise between a Latin American reservoir of telluric impulses and a futurist regard for modern technology—for the conception of a newborn human who would replace European exhaustion with organic vitality. In other words, these philosophies, seductive as they were in their prophetic optimism in the midst of a worldwide sense of crisis, also revealed themselves to be too embedded in a metaphysical restitution of autochthonous originality with no place to articulate the paradoxical position on the map of modernity. They encountered Latin American readers and critics, but not followers.

The primary difference between the literary enterprises of the avant-gardes and contemporaneous efforts such as the regional novel is not necessarily a difference of style (realist or antimimetic, linear or open-ended, wholesome or fragmented, and so on) but rather a matter of how each one of these intellectual projects responded to the interrelated narratives of futurity, novelty, discovery, organic growth, etc. Regional writers fed on the tradition of writing about vast American spaces open to exploration (from the *selva* (the jungle) to the pampas to the *sertão* (the rugged, dry backlands of Northeast Brazil) that appeared in the Latin American canon from the chronicles of the conquest onward. A romantic paradigm permeates the regional novel. Redemption is sought (and whether it is ultimately found or lost doesn't change its ontological premise) through a cultural or natural remnant that sublates some perennial arcadia into a reconstitution of national culture. A parallel might be drawn between the *novela de la tierra* (novel of the land) and the work of reactionary European modernists (such as Heidegger) who intended a reinscription of being in place, a geopolitics of local destiny, as a response to a crisis of universals. But paradoxically, this movement back to local truths is complicit with the coloniality of the modern: In the tradition of portraying the American space as an untamable openness, nationalist ideologies are often cast in terms of the territorial logic of conquest, along with the march of progress. The writers I examine as a model of an overall appraisal of the Latin American avant-garde movements do not eschew completely this project of understanding and reconstituting national culture. Rather, the national territory is frequently comprehended in avant-garde texts as the arena of present flows (cultural, commercial, financial, demographic, economic, etc.) without necessary attachments, flows that exert pressure on the self-understanding of localized cultures.

Latin American avant-gardes questioned the romantic comprehension of culture as always anchored in an "anthropological place," to use Marc Augé's (1995) evocative expression, by their increasing challenge to the notion of culture as locale, a discrete entity in space and time. Although this dis-location of culture is usually related to the supposedly recent phenomenon of globalization, it is also true that globalization has a long history, particularly from the perspective of the Third World, the ex-colonies, or "developing nations." The teleology involved in globalization's narrative is a refashioning of the colonial/modern world history on which the history of nations, their foundation, is supported. If the constitution of national space is an internal reproduction and continuation of the colonial logic both in the center and on the peripheries, there are nevertheless many colonial differences to take into account.[14] Eduardo Mendieta (1998) and others have argued that, in the Latin American case, the ideology of progress embedded in nation-states inherits and redeploys the chronotope of evangelization, with its linearity and the two temporal poles on which understanding national history is performed: future redemption and decadence and fall.[15]

The projection of a primitive state of being, preserved from the colonization of space and subjectivity, has always been a common way of attempting to think against the grain of universal linear history. Continuing developments that in their modern expressions stem from the Romantics, European avant-gardes produced their own versions of the primitive, by way of the raw, the unconscious, or the native other. The fascination with primitivism that refashioned for the avant-gardes a long-standing European tradition was now advanced as an enchanted token to counter the empire of the secular, a critique of bourgeois values in which the primitive other was approached as the repository of some forgotten or hidden truth. Just as the Enlightenment made the achievement of a higher place on the ladder of modernity tangible through a comparison with those whom this mapping designated as traditional or undeveloped, primitivism constituted a response that nevertheless left intact the basic historicist assumption. Needless to say, Latin American intellectuals had resorted to different uses of native, ahistorical cultural markers (e.g., José Martí's *hombre natural*, in his seminal essay "Nuestra América") as an instrument of an overall reassessment of their own Western alliances. Primitivism participated in what Johannes Fabian (1983) considers the principal strategy of anthropology, arguably one of the foundational grounds of Western superiority, which he has famously dubbed the "denial of coevalness" that proceeds by treating the time of the other as "encapsulated in cultural gardens" (153). Latin American vanguardists did not attempt to avoid this vantage point altogether. It can be easily demonstrated, for example, that the Brazilian *modernistas* (a prominent case that will be investigated in depth) displayed primitivist strategies when they traveled through the state of Minas Gerais to rediscover the riches of the native land or that the Argentinean Oliverio Girondo (1994, 71) resorted to worn-out clichés of an orientalist gaze when strolling the streets of Dakar. The modern values that most Latin American intellectuals embraced implied temporal narratives in which primitivism was only a logical consequence, a resource seemingly available for contestation, albeit ironically implemented in the most diverse situations.

But primitivism needs to be examined in a comparative context in order to understand that it was sometimes reworked and sometimes challenged as an epistemological strategy complicit with colonization. The seduction of primitivism left Latin American primitivists ensnared in a backwardness dangerously close to what had led them to declare their vanguardism in the first place. That is why in other instances the primitive did not merely serve as a basis for an identity that would be a refuge against the forces of modernization; instead, as Roberto Schwarz (1992, 8) put it in a statement that makes reference to Brazilian *modernistas* but that holds true for the rest of the continent, "for the first time the processes under way . . . were weighed in the context of the present-day world, as having something to offer in that larger context." That is, primitivism was not just predicated on an archaic remnant—necessarily expelled from the national cultural field and later recovered, only to enshrine it in its state of abjection and justify current domination—but was projected back into a global negotiation of cultural value, reworked through a postcolonial mapping.

The conceptualization of a nonsynchronous Latin America, the differential product of its own heterogeneous historical time, fell into a comparable deadlock; the discord could be possible only within the anthropological mapping of discrete cultures, a humanistic byproduct of Western expansion. Both primitivism and nonsynchronicity, although challenging the linear historicity of modernization as homogenization, fed the same monster they tried to defeat. The assessment of temporal difference was made through the modern narrative of history as a continuing abolition, sublation, or overcoming of the past whose persistent survival through cultural practices and objects was treated as a remnant on the verge of extinction or as marks of a character to be put in the account of the cultural whole. Although both Latin American and European avant-gardes might be regarded as collapsing spatial and temporal differences, the Latin Americans were, by virtue of the loci of enunciation, more sensitive to the backward place that the master narrative of lineal modernization, through its surrogates primitivism and nonsynchronicity, assigned to their own cultural production. Peruvian philosopher José Carlos Mariátegui pointed this out in 1927: "Native themes and indigenous motives are asked of all the artists that have lately emigrated to Europe" (Schwartz 1991, 597). Hence the reversal offered by Brazilian Oswald de Andrade, who called for a mockingly performative display of "the pre-logic mentality, so [the French anthropologist] Mr. Lévy-Bruhl can study it" (Schwartz 1991, 145).

Thus, the avant-gardes combined an investment in modern temporality with a sensibility for the paradoxical loci of enunciation from which these texts examine the consequences of different temporal narratives. A poem-manifesto by Chilean avant-garde artist and activist Vicente Huidobro, "Aviso a los turistas" (Tourist advisory), might be read as illustrating the conundrum of a (peripheral) subjectivity in a permanent state of lack, ill adjustment, or delay, despite its good-intentioned forwardness.

TOURIST ADVISORY

I arrived too late to take the train I had set in motion.

I had time to catch the last car, though it was already moving, and each time the train started to jump the tracks I signaled the conductor, showing him from afar what adjustments to make. In the third, second, and even first class cars, there crept through the vestibules several traveling salesmen from the great corporate headquarters. Arriving at the station, I perceived that the train had changed itinerary and destination. I got off and, all alone, took another route: the one that runs through polar dreams. (Huidobro 1999, 101)

The engineer vaguely resembled me but he wasn't.

The text is composed as a calligram to resemble train tracks: two vertical lines to be read upward and downward recall the movement of the train along the tracks, while the central corpus between these tracks is formatted as a rectangle to recall a train car. The linearity of reading moves the eyes forward down the page. But the "progression" of reading is also disturbed by the two lines that, at the margins of the "main" body of text, or the train itself, can be read only in a different direction. Although the elements signaling a direction and the operators (trains, travelers, engineers, the corporation executives) figure the modern self, nothing seems to be set at the right pace for the subject to recognize his own image, for reality to match expectations, for traveling that is full of unpredictable movements off-track to march toward the correct destination. I read this text as an allegory of a peripheral subject trying to untie the knots of his own positions within, or his own attachments to, the march of universal history that he wants to halt, a history from which he needs to disengage, that he knows cannot accommodate him, from which he needs to deviate. This out-of-sync train wends through the production of the avant-gardes, and it will appear in different sections of this book.

THEORIES OF THE GLOBAL AVANT-GARDE

Let us turn toward other critics of the avant-gardes who are particularly attuned to geopolitical loci of enunciation. In an article that attempts a "Rethinking [of] the Theory of the Avant-Garde from the Periphery," George Yúdice (1999, 54) has argued that the avant-garde "is the first global expression, in the field of culture, of the struggles to 'integrate,' that is, to dominate the world on the part of several competing imperial and industrialized powers and, also, to resist these attempts locally." However, integration into global modernity and resistance to it cannot be pinned down geographically in a dichotomy that tends to reify the local as a site of a negative resistance, something the manifestos of the Latin American avant-garde strove not to do. Indeed these two tendencies coexist in the avant-garde texts, which are simultaneously agents and resistant subjects of colonial modernization.[16] That is also to say that resistances, if they want to remain effective, should be articulated as interior to the system, not the configuration of a vantage point preserved from global flows of various kinds. Every cultural actor that constructs its enunciation assuming a regional or national exteriority, as the regional novel did, does so by denying and aestheticizing its own struggle to gain hegemony at that regional or national level.

On the matter of resistance, Yúdice privileges hybridism through cannibalization, the selective consumption of metropolitan products and creative mixes of local breeds, a line that traverses twentieth-century thought in Latin America (from Brazilian *antropofagia*, to José María Arguedas's *transculturación*, to ulterior reconceptualizations by Néstor García Canclini). And he adds that "It should be stressed, however, that for the intertextual, intercultural cannibalism to be socially effective, it had to emerge as a national perspective" (68). The critic arrives here at the impasse that Brazilian anthropophagic *modernismo* rarely overcomes, for it always falls too close to the traditional stance of the Latin American lettered man as the privileged agent of an ironic transculturation: a translator and administrator of cultural differences for the construction of the national whole—the master cook of the culturalist diet. To conceptualize the avant-gardes in these terms leads to an anthropophagic impulse of a different kind, one that shatters every heterogeneous story that is incongruous with the narrative of the nation as self-realization, anthropophagic, or otherwise.

What is at stake, entwined with the possibility of a critical position within global modernity, is the production of cultural subordination within the very universalist agenda of the nation. The language of temporality is again pervasive. Latin Americans did not embrace the forward temporality of perpetual novelty, and this, Yúdice points out, is a major difference between them and their European counterparts. More than a rupture, Yúdice argues that the Latin American avant-gardes represented an effort to rearticulate traditions. But to conceptualize the avant-gardes in these terms entails a reconfirmation of modernity's own schematic divisions between modernity and tradition, producing both an abjection of the traditions it sets itself up to save and a dismissal of the future-oriented aspirations dear to these Latin American intellectuals.

Futurism, no doubt, is archetypical of a vanguardist impulse toward the active rejection of the history of artistic forms through a rhetoric of total recursive beginnings. Futurism, it is true, and its promoters (including Marinetti himself, ambassador of his own movement) received a cold and sometimes sarcastic reception among Latin American artists.[17] However, although no Latin American manifesto is comparable to Marinetti's first aggressive gesture (the 1909 manifesto calling for the outright abolition of tradition), there is nevertheless a corpus of poetry (often repudiated in criticism for the lack of any local quality) that can be called futurist for the poems' perception of historical acceleration and celebration of modern technology. Guatemalan poet Luis Cardoza y Aragón, for example, states boldly in the 1924 poem that opens *Luna Park: Poema instantánea del siglo XX* (Luna Park: Poem-snapshot of the twentieth century): "Whoever is not in the Future doesn't exist. / The Future started yesterday," to which he adds, switching time for space as a snapshot of the present, "The compass no longer wants to point North" (Borges, Hidalgo, and Hidobro 1926, 52).

But it is important to remember that apart from the declared intentions of the Italian futurists, no avant-garde movement can be reduced to a total dismissal of the past. To reduce what falls under the label "avant-garde" to a drive toward total newness amounts to neglecting its many complex trends—Ezra Pound's search for world traditions in the engulfing impulse of the *Cantos* or Federico García Lorca's recourse to Andalusian archetypes, to mention only two prominent examples. Temporalities other than an always renewed future and total erasure of the past are present in the European and North American artistic enterprises as well, in the form of the cyclical, the eternal, the primitive, and the outmoded.

The rearticulation of tradition, the democratizing practice that Yúdice reads in the avant-garde of Latin America, is hardly unique to the exponents of this movement. It is actually the principal strategy of a disciplinary national project that proclaims as tradition heterogeneous communal bonds and practices in order to reabsorb these cultural practices as relics of the past, elements that fall under the banner of (national, regional) cultural difference.[18] In other words, to call certain practices "traditional" is to subscribe to the labeling effected by the unilinear logic of modernization as homogeneous desacralization, as a movement that leaves these cultural remains behind. It is no surprise that the task of the intellectual, as Yúdice reads it, is to save these cultural vestiges from oblivion. As I said before, modernity has always defined itself against tradition, and the invention of the notion of progress gave direction to the continuing movement that would ultimately sweep up the burden of tradition.

Latin American avant-gardes presented anew what, to avoid historicist descriptions of the traditional and the mythical, can be called alternative narratives of community—for example, of African slave descendants (in the work of Nicolás Guillén) and of indigenous peoples (Miguel Angel Asturias, Mário de Andrade, and others). Insisting on the canonical reading of their work as projects of creation of a differentiated creole national culture through the appropriation of traditions only redoubles an historical suppression of authority; instead I propose to read in these alternative narratives the promises not kept by modernity—thus doing justice to both their impetus identifiable as modern and their other-than-modern subjects, not falling prey to the narrative of modernity as a progressive overcoming.

García Canclini also aims to overcome this impasse in *Culturas Híbridas* (1989) when he resorts to the vanguards as a pivotal point of his ambitious theorization of Latin America's peripheral modernity. For García Canclini, the vanguards were early examples of his performative notion of cultural identity: "the way in which the elites take issue with the intersection of different historical temporalities and try to elaborate with them a global project" (71). But the idea of different temporalities is in itself permeated by the early anthropological gaze that located cultures outside history.[19] Or, seen through a different lens, the rearticulation of traditions that Yúdice highlights requires practices that are not "traditional" at all, but very much of the present: Even if from the historicist perspective, they are remnants, disposable or in need of conservation. Moreover, in focusing exclusively on the problem of tradition and differential temporalities, instead of on positions that are already a response to modernity, both Yúdice and García Canclini overlook the power of the new, of what has no foundation in the past, which they ascribe to the futurist tendencies of the Europeans. Not only do they credit the vanguards with no genuinely revolutionary potential, or even with potential for the unexpected, they also dismiss the inassimilable heterogeneity of what passes for "tradition."

This is perhaps the reason why Yúdice tries to reinvigorate academic discussions of the avant-garde, bringing these movements closer to *testimonio* literature. However, if *testimonio* is a radical revision of lettered cultural practices, as Yúdice seems to believe, it is because it implies a sea change in the understanding of cultural identity, calling into question the constitution of the modern nation.[20] A democratization of lettered practices such as the one advanced by *testimonio* is not predicated upon the territorial boundaries of the nation-state, it represents a displacement of the nation-state's sovereignty as the sole site of cultural identification and the sole arena for political allegiances. In fact, in another brilliant and related article on postmodernism, Yúdice (1992, 24) acknowledges that *testimonio*—a genre through which he defines Latin American postmodernity— "no longer operates solely within the framework of the nation." But neither does the avant-garde, something Yúdice doesn't recognize, despite his intent to open the movement to a larger geopolitical framework. Taking issue with Fredric Jameson's much-discussed proposition that the Third World is condemned to produce national allegories whereas the First World is more capable of projecting cognitive mappings, Yúdice replies that "in Latin America the mappings are different; they correlate to different sets of conditions imposed by transnational capitalism" (20). Fair enough. However, if these cognitive mappings, as Yúdice's argument seems to imply, are necessarily projected from a nation-state's vantage point, we cannot expect any cognition but a confirmation of the status quo as an international order.

Trying to situate their cultural practices as world hegemonies were being reconfigured during the world wars and the United States was actively pursuing the consolidation of its cultural and economic dominance in the Americas (Halperin Donghi, 1996, 288–308), artists and intellectuals had an acute awareness of global designs (to use Mignolo's striking concept [2000a]). It is in this context that the Latin American vanguards sometimes expressed how national difference doesn't resolve the problem of global positionality, except to confirm a linear historicism in which (national) culture is a sublimated but subordinated byproduct. From the viewpoint of the nation, we are forced to understand global dynamics either in terms of an inscription that is always pending or subordinated or in terms of a purely cultural difference, thus leaving the solidarity of the national form within the global design unquestioned and hindering the potential of mapping to construct an alternative position. Argentinean poet Oliverio Girondo (1994, 139) acknowledges this dynamic of assigned "traditional" roles and mismatched simultaneity while looking for a different loci of enunciation: "Europe starts to be interested in us. Disguised with the feathers or the peasant garment that she attributes us, we would achieve smashing success! It's a shame that our sincerity obliges us to disappoint her . . . to present ourselves as we are; although she would be incapable to differentiate us . . . although we are certain of her disapproval!"[21] In the global design, peripheries are inscribed in what Dipesh Chakrabarty (2000, 9) calls "the waiting room of history," the time of unaccomplished, belated but consequently always-to-be-desired modernity.

This desire to be modern is what Fredric Jameson has acutely described at the beginning of *A Singular Modernity* (2002) as an affective charge that made modernity a desirable object that someone else possesses.[22] This is of course a properly colonial structure of feelings. The effectiveness of such a modernity, which Jameson takes up only in the conclusion to this contradictory book, is the capacity for creating the illusion of this elsewhere as the realm of its accomplishment, which puts in place a historicist worldwide stage of progress and backwardness. But if modernity is a concept of otherness—as Jameson (211) states toward the end, "a modernity for other peoples, an optical illusion nourished by envy and hope, by inferiority feelings and the need of emulation"—this coda only renders problematic what he declares is his main thesis regarding modernism. That is, the idea that modernism is about incomplete modernization (part 2). To make sense, that proposal needs to be connected to an oppositional dynamic at work in a given, possibly national, geographic setting "organized around two distinct temporalities: that of the new industrial big city and that of the peasant countryside," in which artist and intellectuals "still live in two distinct worlds simultaneously" (142). However, his main theorization seems limited to Europe, not located within the broader scope suggested before—the perspective in which one can locate his passing remark that among the different beginnings that can be proposed for modernity and modernism, the Nicaraguan Rubén Darío's labeling, in the 1900s, of his own intellectual enterprise as *modernista* is scandalous. Darío's daring gesture of declaring a radical simultaneity testifies that the mapping implicitly performed by this other-than-central intellectual is not that of different worlds centered on different temporalities but of only one world with differentially assigned positions in it.

Jameson draws on a groundbreaking article by Perry Anderson (1984) that is also extensively quoted by García Canclini and Yúdice. Taking issue with Marshall Berman's *All That Is Solid Melts into Air* (1982), Anderson introduced the thesis that, contrary to the common belief that modernism is the cultural expression of modernization (social, technological, economic, etc.), an uneven state of modernity is one of the prerequisites for modernism to develop—that is, modernism requires a modernity that can be characterized as yet unaccomplished but that is nevertheless promised and promising. One of the main consequences of Anderson's thesis is that it allows a break with the idea that modernism in general in the Latin American context is necessarily out of place and merely compensatory—a symbolic counterpoint to an inadequate modernization. The three factors that Anderson highlights in modernism are the persistence of an old regime (academicism upheld by an aristocratic class), the novelty of new technology and mass production, and the perspective of a revolution.

In a modernism thus conceived, the global unevenness that Anderson highlights must be articulated with the colonial imagination that understands unevenness as different levels of accomplishment along a single line of modernization. Anderson's scheme would be immensely enriched if the frame of analysis in which the aforementioned factors converge were not the classical divide between city and countryside, which was no longer the geography of the avant-gardes. In this case, it is possible to go back to Yúdice's interesting addition to Anderson's tripartite scheme—that the imperial crisis that set off the first global war was a fourth condition for the avant-gardes' emergence—and to note that it is not truly an addition to that scheme but an overall restructuring of it. I understand, however, that Yúdice doesn't fully pursue the consequences of his own contribution. This crisis spread immensely and left the physical boundaries of everything that counts permanently unstable.

What counts for Perry Anderson is the novelty of change and the memory of what is being left behind, the experience of the present as containing remnants. However, what seems to count in peripheral modernism is the assessment of what is at stake globally when these peripheries are what remain behind. Technological novelty and mass production might certainly be diagramed on the city-countryside axis, because some Latin American countries experienced in their own right an immense growth of the urban and industrialized sectors. This is, in fact, how García Canclini applies Anderson in order to read the Latin American avant-garde movement as a way to cope with the "different temporalities" of the cultural context (city and countryside, indigenous and European, etc.). I argue that in the Latin

American context technological novelty and mass production, with the fundamental reference to the elsewhere that modernization promises to bring closer, is principally a factor of what constitutes colonial modernity. This, and not simply the affective charge of tradition, explains more fully the reason why Futurism as such was never embraced in Latin America: The avant-gardes questioned the desirability of what was promoted as new, since novelty so obviously reinforced the old story of being left behind in the waiting room of history.

With respect to the aristocratic class representing a stagnant academicism in Anderson's explanatory scheme, no obvious animosity existed in Latin America between the avant-gardes and an old regime. Avant-gardist's investment in modern values granted them the occasional support of the wealthiest, as was the case with Brazilian *modernistas* and Argentinean *martinfierristas,* while some exponents of the movement, such as Chilean avant-gardist Vicente Huidobro, themselves belonged to the landowning aristocracy. Although the promotion of a modern, sometimes revolutionary art can be said to be opposed to the class interests of this economic elite, the gesture can be better explained within a global framework and a colonial structure of feelings. The modernization of the cultural field did not imply a disavowal of the upper classes' place in the power structure, but was capitalized as a further step into their own colonial admiration for an administration of European culture as cultural capital in their possession. The easy acceptance by part of the more conservative elite of all sorts of shocking artistic innovations from Europe and their violent rejection when comparable innovations were enacted locally (e.g., the early exhibitions by painters Anita Malfatti in São Paulo and Emilio Pettoruti in Buenos Aires) illustrate how a paradoxically modernizing aesthetic signified different things for different cultural actors.[23] This does not, however, imply a questioning of the disruptive value of the political and cultural vision of the avant-gardes, unless we want to portray the conservative elite as the privileged agents of history.

The simultaneous constellation of avant-garde production on both sides of the Atlantic remains a curiosity that usually leaves scholars who have focused on European modernism staggered. But the perspective of a social revolution posited by Anderson was certainly not solely a European phenomenon. Despite the emphasis of traditional modernist studies on new means of communication and mass transportation, which have been regarded as an incentive for avant-garde aesthetic concerns, it is remarkable how cultural and political climates are perceived as transcending only some well-defined, contiguous frontiers. The expectancy of a revolution was of course internationalized, as entangled in the web of mass migration, communication, transportation, and so on as world wars and capitalism itself. As Peruvian poet Magda Portal put it in 1927 in reference to the art represented by *Amauta*, the cultural magazine directed by Peruvian Marxist philosopher José Carlos Mariátegui, "the new Art—heir to an epoch of formidable blasts, the European war, the Russian Revolution, the German, the Chinese, and the Russian famine, and lastly, the Chinese Revolution—of big scientific achievements that have multiplied the activity of life, erasing all the kilometers of the map, disconcerting common sense and creating a new philosophy, the new Art was an unavoidable, fatal, nonpostponable result" (Osorio T. 1988, 206). It is noteworthy that Portal fails to mention any equally "formidable blast" in Latin America, such as the Mexican Revolution or the ongoing political movements throughout the region. But it can be said that by pointing out the most distant phenomena, she is underlining their interconnectedness and the inviability of separating local from global dynamics.

In that sense it is curious that even someone as attuned to the geopolitical conditions of avant-garde production as Perry Anderson encounters an impasse when dealing with what he argues is the foreclosing of the historical conditions of avant-gardes after World War II (the disappearance of a sense of the unpredictable march of history that characterized the cultural climate of modernism due to the geopolitical organization of the world in two super-power blocks that mirrored one another). He traces the differential position of the peripheries in terms of "societies still at definite historical cross-roads" and therefore still able to produce great modernist works—as well as great historical shifts that societies at the center of capitalism, Anderson's reader is forced to conclude, would no longer be able to produce (Anderson 1984, 109). No doubt the vicissitudes of this sense of historical possibility is part of the international appeal of the so-called boom in Latin American literature (Anderson doesn't fail to mention García Márquez), and we can certainly speculate that this sense of crisis is at the bottom of the creative impulse of its writers, too. But the way Anderson organizes his exposition into two distinctive and unrelated blocks—where the First World and the Third don't seem to be part of the same world—falls short of making sense of the global conditions of the avant-garde, to say the least.[24] If, as Jameson (2002, 134) has remarked, Perry Anderson's argument was "not that the artists of the modern occupy the same space as these social forces [of the tripartite scheme above], nor even manifest any ideological sympathy for or existential knowledge of them, but rather that they feel the force of gravity at a distance," it is clear that both Jameson and Anderson have dismissed not only the wide arc of cosmopolitan distance within which these forces can be felt and be effective but also the extent of the intervention advanced by peripheral intellectuals. That is the task we take up here by beginning to elaborate the spatial, rather than temporal, characteristics of the discourses of the Latin American avant-gardes.

SIMULTANEITY AND COSMOPOLITANISM

The spatializing tendency of modernist writing has become a classic topic in literary analyses. Features of modernist poetics such as a cosmopolitan sensibility and the emphasis on simultaneity were often recast by Latin American avant-gardes as attempts to map out some pressing (historical) issues: how colonial expansion and the ways of being that were wiped out as a consequence affect the temporality of the present and how location, the way of being in the present, is shaped by what is not present, by those forces that cannot be located or discerned in the positivistic mappings of the world.

It is useful to recall Bakhtin's introduction (1981, 84) in the 1930s of chronotopic criticism—the "intrinsic connectedness of temporal and spatial relationships that are artistically expressed in literature"—which was no doubt sensitive to modernist literature's reorganization of the naturalized space-time coordinates of realism.[25] Despite Bakhtin's intent to open a new frame of literary analysis, the concept of the chronotope, as he elaborated it, remained loyal to a teleological view of literary history. The chronotope of the novel embodies the openness of modern history and human agency: the novel is increasingly dialogical and heteroglossic, whereas the epic is monologic. But hitting closer to the narratives we will touch upon in the next two chapters, Franco Moretti has demonstrated convincingly that heteroglossia is the model for incorporative imperial domination present in what he calls the modern epic or "world-text" (a concept that paraphrases Immanuel Wallerstein's "world system"): "a sign of a 'neutralized' cultural sphere, in which everything is possible—*pol*ysemy, *pol*yphony—because nothing is important any longer" (Moretti, 1996, 90, emphasis in the original). The "strengthening of capitalism," continues Moretti, "doesn't require any longer an alignment of the cultural sphere" (90, n. 14).

Joseph Frank (1963) pointed out more explicitly the link between spatialization and modernism when he called attention to how European literature used spatial configurations to question the linear causality of plot. According to Frank, the different modes of spatialization (among which we find the spatialization of the poem as a performance of temporal simultaneity typical of avant-garde writing both in Europe and the Americas) reveal a nostalgia for perennial, transhistorical values pursued, paradoxically, by way of compressing time into speed and simultaneity. Space would be a way to escape from the nightmare of history (to paraphrase Joyce's *Ulysses*). Frank was part of a North American critical movement in the 1950s that implemented the canonization of modernism in the U.S. academy, a pursuit this kind of reading fit only too well.

The emphasis on simultaneity long attributed to avant-garde poetics shows the differential and contextual value of any particular space-time organization. Simultaneity—that is, the compression of time that becomes space—has also been regarded as an instance of democratic multiperspectivism (to put it in the terms of a facile interpretation of cubism) and as a way to coordinate national space (as Benedict Anderson [1996] has argued in relation to the realist novel). I read the simultaneous and polyphonic displays of avant-garde poetics in an altogether different way: not as a democratic achievement (Bakhtin) or as a quest for transcendence (Frank), and not as a neutralization of differential positions (Moretti), but as a means to account for an increasingly unified global logic that nevertheless escapes representation as such because this simultaneity is spatially discontinuous. My contention is that, in certain cases, simultaneity is better understood as a paradoxical way to map a totality. "For if what we call a paradox is the simultaneous presence of two contradictory terms, it follows logically that a historiographic perspective of simultaneity engenders multiple paradoxes," affirms Hans Ulrich Gumbrecht (1997, 432) in his study on historical simultaneity in the year 1926. Rather than as a way to revive transhistorical or universal literary values, simultaneity can be mobilized as a cognitive instrument to map out historical forces that can't be accounted for within local or national narratives. One might say that simultaneity is a way to understand what appears to be nonsynchronous, that it is about coping spatially with a time lag. The "simultaneity of the radically disparate," with which Peter Bürger (1984, 63) qualifies the availability and consequent mix of different styles from different eras in avant-garde artistic experiments, acquires in this geopolitical view a completely different meaning. In fact, paradox is implied from the beginning in the project of mapping a totality whose different, simultaneous histories "are coeval but do not necessarily add up to a single or coherent picture" (Chambers 1994, 30). They simply can't, since local history always happens in reference to an elsewhere, and it is from a concrete position, not from an abstract universality, that this act of mapping is performed. Vicente Huidobro's affirmation (1963, 366) in his poetic masterpiece *Altazor* that "the three cardinal points are two: North and South" acquires new meaning in relation to this set of preoccupations, not only as an abstract defiance of logic but as a very situated way to understand the shifting world hegemony and, simultaneously, to declare the impossibility of achieving a coherent picture.

The urban reality that seems to be expressed in the deployment of multifarious, chaotic perspectives typical of avant-garde poetry is an incarnation of concrete urban experiences, but not in a purely mimetic or expressive way. Rather, this poetry echoes such experiences in the sense in which Raymond Williams (1997) characterized urban life. According to Williams, "the metropolis of the . . . first half of the twentieth century moved into a quite new cultural dimension. It was now much more than the very large city, or even the capital city of an important nation. It was the place where new social and economic and cultural relations, beyond both city and nation in their old senses, were beginning to be formed" (44). Symptomatically not taken into account in Williams's argument, however, despite his investment in a decentralization of modernist studies, is that the effects of an unstable incorporation into a larger order were always more present on the periphery than in the centers of capitalist accumulation (see King 1995).

This affirmation differs from the common argument, deployed in critical approaches to the avant-gardes, that focuses on the Latin American city as the embodiment of a fetishized, "alternative" modernity, the realm of demonstrable progress and innovation (often São Paulo, Buenos Aires, and Mexico City are emblematic of this approach). Following Williams's insights—which he doesn't push beyond Europe—the most relevant critical strategy would be to trace how these urban spaces are frequently interrupted and crisscrossed by global flows that point to the formation of an expanded horizon beyond both city and nation and make problematic the presentation of urban modernity as a token of (national) progress.

So much for the old but often refurbished idea of Latin American modernism without modernization, which partakes in the temporality of "not yet"—the argument that Latin Americans were dreaming with a modernity that was not yet there, making it happen, as it were, through their compensatory literary imagination. Although this argument has been counted many times in praise of this literary imagination (which was, once upon a time, worth millions in the cultural market), the same argument is nevertheless reproduced to discredit the literary field now that this imagination has fallen into disgrace.

Other important consequences might be extracted from this reading of Raymond Williams that are not exactly figured in his text. The historical and economic factors that created spaces of hope and hopelessness around the world brought about both European immigration to some areas of Latin America (Argentina, Uruguay, Brazil, Chile, Peru, Mexico, and Cuba) and internal waves of migration from the countryside to the cities. These movements shaped the Latin American cultural and political life of the first part of the twentieth century, accentuating their sense of immersion in the turmoil of the modern world. According to Williams (chapter 4), displacement was the historical base for the defamiliarization, or *ostranenie*, that Shlovsky and the Russian formalists related to literariness. However, while Williams decentralizes the modernist metaphysics of the artist as perennial émigré (most notably advanced in Terry Eagleton's *Exiles and Émigrés* [1970] and Malcolm Bradbury and James Walter McFarlane's *Modernism* [1976]) through a historicization of the convulsed background of a European city that is linguistically and demographically unstable, he pays little attention to the broader map of cultural production that I have been trying to address.[26]

Instead of merely applying Williams's insight to Latin America (by showing the defamiliarization wrought by internal or external migration to Latin American cities), I find it more productive to introduce a critical notion of cosmopolitanism to discuss the connection between such displacements and avant-garde poetics. In accordance with European cosmopolitanism since Kant's early formulation, which is grounded in the vantage point of a teleological historicism, Latin American intellectuals since independence have exercised their privileged cosmopolitan stance to advance their project of national development toward modernity. Avant-garde cosmopolitanism in Latin America often brings to mind an exercise of mundane privileges, a mere refashioning of the nineteenth-century Latin American patriarchal *homme de lettres*, sometimes enriched with a fashionable air of parody that only extended the life of this literary figure—in, for example, Oswald de Andrade's 1924 novel *Memorias sentimentais de João Miramar* (Sentimental memoirs of João Miramar). There was certainly the presence of this predominantly male perspective exercising a power of detachment in crossing borders and assessing difference. It is possible to read a tactical counternarrative,[27] however, in the spatial features of some Latin American texts from the period—to read how the texts exercise a critique of progressive reason while they also look for ways out of the position of the master of ironic detachment. The "discrepant cosmopolitanism" (to use James Clifford's expression [1992, 108]) that was opened by and to some of these writers (who will be the object of chapters 5 and 6) moved away from reproducing cosmopolitan privileges. The reappropriation of the idea of "cosmopolis" to name practices not obviously self-defined as such entails shaking the philosophical ground where the concept is based. It means acknowledging the historicist frame that linked cosmopolitanism to a level of abstraction purportedly attained by northern European societies and the concomitant evolutionary narrative and geopolitical division between Europe and the rest of the peoples—always imagined as attached to localized identities, still caught in their provincial, primary allegiances.

The notion of a critical cosmopolitanism, breaking simultaneously with the idea of a self-contained (Anglo-European) modernity and discrete (other) cultures, points to the ethical ideal of a non-Eurocentric, always-situated universalism. It is a cosmopolitanism that transcends individualist strategies of ironic detachment but is equally suspicious of the claims of communitarian autochthony. It eschews the negativity of cultural critiques that equate cosmopolitanism with Eurocentric distancing from local loyalties and political alliances.[28] Discrepant cosmopolitanisms are positive but complex cultural standpoints that can help to conceptualize the different strategies of the avant-gardists. Amanda Anderson (1998, 289) very elegantly sums up my own perspective on the subject: "cosmopolitanism is an ethico-political ideal as well as a description of global positioning, and thus is open to appropriation by those situated more specifically as postcolonial."

GEOPOLITICS, SUBJECTIVITY, AND THE SCENE OF WRITING

Seen as "a description of global positioning," cosmopolitanism is an ethos that interrogates the position of the subject as a geopolitical question. The purpose of this section is to locate, in programmatic texts surrounding the novels central to this book (Roberto Arlt's *Los siete locos/Los lanzallamas* and Mário de Andrade's *Macunaíma*) a number of categories mediating between a broad global concern and subjectivity, categories that are undergoing an epochal transformation, such as the place of the author, the public, and the conformation of the literary field. But these transformations of the cultural sphere cannot be described simply through a nationally framed sociology of literature (à la Bourdieu).[29] The prologues of both novels are, indeed, directed toward the local literary systems, but are interventions intended to question the constitutional fabric of those systems and how value is assigned within them.

Arlt throws his darts at the duplicity of the educated elite (who might consider his novels vulgar, whereas Joyce's obscenities are celebrated as haute culture, given their more prestigious origins—even Ireland might have represented the metropolis, from a non-European perspective). Mário de Andrade, on the other hand, takes issue with the accusation—made, as he shows with sarcasm, by European-influenced national intellectuals— that his "spirit" has not been "regimented in the legitimate [Brazilian] culture" (Lopez 1974, 92–93). These two arguments already give a very accurate picture of how differently organized their respective national literary cultures were at approximately the same time, but my critical intention doesn't stop at describing them in their autonomy.[30] Instead, I want to point out, in the midst of these polemical and circumstantial texts, where the writers portray themselves in the private scene of writing, how they register the conformation of the national literary field itself as a site of cosmopolitan practices and global resonance. The scenes of writing are the stage of geopolitical anxieties. While Mário de Andrade sustains his scene by repressing the anxiety wrought by the metropolitan library that he tries both to master and disregard, Roberto Arlt manages his own anxiety over the depersonalizing acceleration of modernity by resorting to the compensatory ego of a contentious literary persona.[31]

Andrade drafted two different prologues for *Macunaíma*, but he published neither of them. Taken together as part of the same effort to state his position and his novel's stance in the spirit of national renovation that he himself helped to put forward in the 1922 launching of the Week of Modern Art, the authorial viewpoint is as difficult to pin down in the prologues as it is in the novel itself. The prologues are the scenarios of converging tensions that can be categorized as the aesthetic, the geographical, and the popular.

The aesthetic tension points to the construction of aesthetic autonomy, and autonomy of national culture under the guise of aesthetics. "This book is simple playfulness, written in a single stroke of six uninterrupted days of hammock, cigars and crickets while on the Pio Lourenço farm, near that nest of light called the Araquara River." But in spite of its alleged lightheartedness, "I never had as I do in its [his book's] presence the impossibility to assess the value of my own work" (Lopez 1974, 90). Andrade stages his own scene of writing as the privileged scenario in an idyllic landscape, "among mango trees, pineapples and crickets . . . where people don't pay attention to prohibitions, fears and frights of science or reality," where he is able to rescue "those treasures about which no one thinks anymore" (87)—rescue them, that is, from the work of voyagers, naturalists, ethnographers, and historians who, from colonial times on, have written about Brazil. The role of the modern artist that Mário de Andrade seems to cast for himself intends the reactualization of a "sleeping and awakening" library to be "reframed, re-read, re-made" (Rancière 2002, 143) while portraying himself as leisurely immersed in natural surroundings. Aesthetic distance and autonomy are called forth by the romantic recreation of the playful subject of aesthetic inquiry[32] guaranteed by the writer's withdrawal from the time and place of daily business, the city of São Paulo. This fundamental operation of the aesthetic subject merging the national archive and nature is at the same time denounced as highly troubling when the writer recognizes the failure to guarantee aesthetic distance when his product comes back to haunt his aesthetic judgment.

The geographical tension refers to the construction, as much embraced as abhorred by the national intellectual, of a territorial border for culture. To "degeographize" (*desgeograficar*, a neologism in Portuguese) is Mário de Andrade's collagelike strategy for giving the whole picture unity: "a legendry disrespect for the geography, the fauna and the flora. In this manner I degeographized as much as possible the creation at the same time that I managed to conceive of a homogenous Brazil by literary means" (Lopez 1974, 89). But by the same token, the boundaries of this unity become blurry and the parts dissociate: "Even the hero that I draw from the German [Theodor] Koch-Grünberg, we can't say he is from Brazil. He is as much Venezuelan as ours, and he dismisses the stupidity of boundaries. . . . I like it as what it is, this circumstance of the hero not being absolutely Brazilian" (91).

Finally, the popular tension concerns the notion of a people as a sedimented unity. Macunaíma is characterized from the subtitle of the novel as "the hero without any character." Different peoples around the world, Mário sustains, have achieved a "traditional consciousness" through "their own civilization, eminent danger, or centennial consciousness" (Lopez 1974, 87), and therefore they have, as opposed to Brazilians, a so-called character. Nevertheless, the novel is a narrative of this lack, presenting the paradox of the historical continuity of a national character defined by the lack of any characteristic whatsoever.

Mário narrates the scene of encounter with the legend of Macunaíma in Koch-Grünberg travelogue *Von Roraima zum Orinoco* [From Roraima to Orinoco] as the groundbreaking moment in a personal quest.

> Brazilians don't have character because we have neither our own civilization nor traditional consciousness. . . . They are like a twenty-year-old. . . . From this lack of psychological character derives, I optimistically believe, the lack of moral character . . . and moreover a very improvised kind of existence as the imaginative illusion of a Columbus-like figurehead searching with eloquent eyes for an El

Dorado that can't possibly exist. . . . As I was mulling this stuff over, I came across [the myth of] Macunaíma in the [work of] the German [ethnographer] Koch-Grünberg. And Macunaíma is a hero surprisingly without character. (87–88)

What De Andrade finds in ethnology is the stuff of his own ruminations, full of colonial references, from Columbus to the sheer diagnosis of the lack of maturity of the native, as confirmed by European science.

In response to the accusation that Mário plagiarized from Koch-Grünberg's study, which certainly figures prominently as a source for the novel, Brazilian writer Raimundo Moraes published an article in defense of Mário's undisputable originality and individual artistic imagination. Although the two prologues to the novel remained unpublished, Mário did decide to publish an open letter that appeared in a major Brazilian newspaper, the *Diário Nacional*, on September 20, 1931, in which he, ironically, defends himself from his defender. Mário makes clear how far he is from aligning himself with Moraes and claims that his act of appropriating sources is in fact much more widespread. Not only did he take from the German ethnographer but also from Brazilian ethnographers and historians, from different Amerindian narratives, from Portuguese colonial chronicles, and so on. Originality is not his game, Mário argues, resorting to his folkloric and ethnomusicological knowledge, nor is it the artistic method of folk singers of Northeast Brazil, who never hesitate to draw from different sources. His argument thus aligns his work both with a popular Brazilian tradition and the theory of cultural consumption delineated under the label of *antropofagia*.

Between the writing of the troubled prologues and the cheerfully self-assured open letter, Oswald de Andrade advanced an overall interpretation of the location of culture in his groundbreaking "Manifesto antropófago" of May 1928—in which he champions the cannibalization of the European as the inaugural operation of native agency. Mário complained just after the manifesto appeared about how the novel was said in retrospect to have "anthropophagic" qualities: "I lament all these coincidences. . . . To complicate my book with this anthropophagic business is prejudicial for it. But let's be patient. Of all my works, it is the most dreadful; it even scares me"

(Lopez 1974, 96). Despite his complaints, however, the impact of anthropophagy as a cultural topic lent a certain solidity to his own intellectual pursuits. Now he was able to pronounce publicly for the first time on his uncanny novel. And instead of a single, ground-shaking reading of the German ethnographer, he provided a web of various sources whose cultural hierarchy is put into question by his self-portrait as an active, iconoclastic, irreverently anthropophagic reader. Variety assures levity, and the weight of the cultural sources diminishes. Ironic distance becomes a handy tool allowing for the recovery of control over his writing and legitimizes the semantic openness of his book.

What Mário de Andrade had encountered in the German book was his own subjectivity already inscribed as a token of the metropolitan archive. His own elaborations on the Brazilian lack of character were revealed to be already informed, if unconsciously, by European knowledge. His own literary space, identified with the freedom from constraints and the fresh air of Brazilian nature, appears to be already shaped by ethnology. And the futurity assigned to Brazil in virtue of its immaturity, the seemingly open temporality of the not-yet, irrupts as a condition of the country's inscription in universal history. Although these problems are performed in the novel, they were subsequently muffled by decades of anthropophagic readings, as anthropophagy became a master discourse of Brazilian cultural self-understanding. *Antropofagia* domesticates and makes more digestible, so to speak, the malaise of a European intellectual heritage that sometimes revealed itself as weighty and monolithic, threatening the creative space of the modernist writer, his critical distance, and his playful aesthetics.

The inception of *antropofagia*, which has acquired almost iconic value as a tool of postcolonial emancipation, would condition the critical approaches to the novel. With this concept, colonial modernity is narrated as a road toward the acquisition of self-consciousness through a culturalist diet, the selective synthesis of elements of various origins. As such, the author acquires a role in the management of distances, mediating between the new and the old; the regional, the national, and the continental; the native and the metropolitan; the elite and the people, appeasing the tensions outlined above. The modern autonomous aesthetic and its subject are threatened when the aesthetic object comes back to shatter the capacity for analysis, but *antropofagia* allows for a repositioning of the aesthetic subject through a theory of cultural mediation. However, the novel and the two unpublished prologues cannot be easily read as illustrating the archive (national and foreign) through which the Latin American intellectual comfortably strolls, selecting what suits his purposes. *Antropofagia* suggests the need and attempts a strategy for restoring agency to the native national. But by the same token, it displaces the focus onto the problem of what can be consumed from the European archive, thus dislodging the more fundamental question of how this archive constructs itself as the center by producing the peripheries as the site of a lack (of aesthetic autonomy, of character, of unity of history).

Negotiations between proximity and distance, between the national and the foreign, are also staged by Arlt in his prologue to the second part of his novel *Los lanzallamas*, but in an altogether different manner. In contrast to Mário de Andrade's scene of literary production as extended leisure time, Arlt makes a case for the speed of labor time: Literature is cooked up in the interstices allowed by journalism, which is the sign of the times. The stolen time and space from his labor as a reporter does not make for a clear-cut separation between the discourses of journalism and literature, as is apparent in the footnote at the end of the novel: "This work was finished in such a hurry," Arlt states impersonally, "that the publisher printed the first proofs while the author was writing the last chapters" (394). In the prologue, he declares himself to be in the opposite camp from those who enjoy "comfort, profits, the good life" (189), an accumulated time that can be slowly savored because it is not subject to the need to earn a living.[33]

But it is precisely this constriction that is the basis of Arlt's epistemological, political, and aesthetic position. Arlt's depiction of himself in the "noisy newspaper office," with the vertiginous speed of writing, printing, and ringing telephones is not the expected frame for the self-portrait of the artist or the intellectual. A reporter is a rather different figure, a thinker involved in action, a participant who is both the object and subject of thinking. In the writing room, the boundaries between outside and inside are repeatedly breached: In its turbulence, the newspaper office embodies "the noises of an inevitably collapsing social edifice" (189). He finds (or loses) himself in the midst of time "rushing forward" or "in advance of itself" where "the future becomes present" (Harvey 1990, 225). This perspective lacks the exteriority where time accompanies the process of cogitation: "Those times are bygone. The future is ours, by prepotency of work" (190).

The intellectual bourgeoisie with which the prologue contends, with its availability of "solitude and retirement," projects an image of subjective depth in which patiently woven tribulations are given shape. All of these, Arlt claims, he lacks, as much as he despises. His nemesis is the figure of the modernizing intellectual, the mediator between selected products of European high culture who reproduces internally a system of distinctions and exclusions that traditionally delineated the map of the Argentinean literary field. Instead, the fast, chaotic, energetic pace of production strikes the appropriate chords for current times: "Writing, in proud solitude, books that contain the violence of a hook to the jaw. Yes, one after the other, and let the eunuch snort" (190).

The potential lack of individuation brought about by his position inside the writing machine is unsettling for the writer and thus is counterpointed in this prologue, quite pathetically, by this affirmation of force and stubborn macho energy. Because his literature is produced in the interstices, it needs the fervent acceleration that threatens to annihilate it. This social condition is the very material on which this literature feeds, not as the object of analysis, not as thematic input, but as a model for the articulation of truth. Literature is a truth that embodies the conditions of its own articulation, and the lack of abstraction and separation between production and product is the sign of its scandalous contemporaneity, the pure simultaneity of a total present that doesn't allow for contemplative distance. Not a "panoramic canvas" (189) where the observer is the privileged, authoritative, spanning eye, Arlt's writing lacks the material conditions of reflection, the possibility of separation between subject and object. It nevertheless produces a diagnosis of which he is himself a subject and that is possible only from within the potentially liberating conditions of thought in the era of mass production and communication. It is not just faith in futurity and an alignment with social revolution. It is not just a technocratic ethos, a futuristic praise for mass communication. We have to hear Arlt's cry for his diminished self and the paradox of an entrapment that is also a source of strength in order to realize to what extent that transformation is an epistemological standpoint in its own right. The transformation doesn't find a solution in the realm of subjectivity, planting there an aesthetic refuge, because subjectivity is the thermometer of changes that do not occur at that level or at the level of the national cultural field whose battles he only appears to be fighting. Instead, it points to a change in the air that cannot be situated in the local but that is echoed in his writing. It will be our task to understand this body of literature as divergent attempts to make sense of those changes.

■ **Chapter 3**

Locating the Future in *Los siete locos*

Because the Far West encircles the planet
and is mirrored in the dreams of men
who have never been there.

Jorge Luis Borges, "The Outsider"

ROBERTO ARLT'S position in the Argentinean avant-garde is always a contested topic. The way he fashioned his literary persona does not fit easily with an ostensibly avant-garde group or with a clear-cut declaration of an historical or literary break with the past. He was anomalous in the main avant-garde circles: too much of a plebeian for the aristocratic and worldly intellectuals of the magazine *Martín Fierro*, who dismissed his unpolished prose, and too disconcertingly metaphysical and morally ambiguous for the politically engaged intelligentsia of the Boedo group, cultivators of hard-core social realism.[1] If avant-garde narrative is reduced to a list of more or less identifiable stylistic resources considered "transgressions" of a realist model (stream of consciousness, discontinuous or fragmentary prose, the dislocation of time/space narrative variables, authorial or character unity and consistency, etc.), Arlt doesn't belong in the literary pantheon of those who, in the consideration of literary historiography, "modernized" literary prose. Nevertheless, his writing can be ascribed to the cultural milieu in which the vanguards flourished. Moreover, to investigate assumptions and geopolitical consequences, he pushed to the limit the avant-garde's future-oriented ethos, its political rhetoric, its fascination with means of transport and communication, its questioning of authorial perspective.

The novelistic sequence comprising *Los siete locos* (1929) and *Los lanzallamas* (1931) was written at a juncture in history marked by the global crisis of capitalism, with the stock market crash of 1929. At the local level was the first military coup in Argentina (against the democratic, mildly reformist regime of Hipólito Yrigoyen). This context is omnipresent in Arlt's narrative, not in a thematic or a circumstantial way, but in the sense of historical urgency: a pervasive sense of imminent change that shapes the moral backdrop of the argument. The novelistic diptych's epistemological drive to understand times of uncertainty is posited from the beginning, and the narrative can be read as a thermometer announcing a radical shift in intermingling notions of subjectivity, nationhood, and global politics.

The novels demand the reader gain awareness of a changing geopolitical and geocultural condition in which novels and readers participate and that allow new political alternatives to be envisaged. Modernist interpreters (e.g., Amícola 1994) read the novels as getting closer to the need for real socialist revolution, but never achieving full clarity in that regard, whereas postmodern critics (e.g., González 1996), have emphasized how the novels nihilistically reveal the lack of foundation for every social association or communitarian bond. Indeed, the novels work through a set of questions, rather than providing answers to pressing sociocultural problems. However, through a constant recombination of elements present or at least insinuated at the time (including the possibility of world-spanning political movements, the shifting geopolitical alliances, the transformation of the public sphere through the mass media, etc.), they delineate the contours of "a space that is now ours and that today is reaching its limits, the limits of the earth and the limits of the political," as Derrida (1994, 38) pointed out in reference to Marx.

The main elements of the plot can be summarized as follows. A heterogeneous group of characters headed by the Astrologer—a sometimes communist, sometimes fascist charismatic leader—get together in a suburb of Buenos Aires in order to forge a plan to take over not merely a single state but the imagination and subjectivities of the inhabitants of the whole planet.

Many chapters of this tale about a scheme that is by turns totalitarian, by turns libertarian are centered on the archetypically alienated Erdosain—a low-ranking employee, a money collector for the fictional multinational corporation Limited Azucarer Company. Accused of stealing money from the company and anguished by the prospect of losing his position, he resorts to his acquaintance the Astrologer for a loan. Erdosain feels immediately compelled to participate in the Astrologer's plans for a revolutionary secret society whose final aim is to be achieved through a series of shocking interventions involving mass-media-constructed events and chemical weapons. Other members of the society include Haffner, alias the Rufián Melancólico (Melancholic Thug, an experienced pimp who would be in charge of the administration of a chain of brothels, the envisaged financial base for the revolutionary plot), and the Buscador de Oro (Gold Prospector), who poses as a pioneer seemingly skilled in the activity that gave him his name. Erdosain enters the group as a gloomy, inventive, solitary genius responsible for the design of a chemical plant. In addition, he comes up with the idea of kidnapping his wife's cousin and personal enemy, Barsut, in order to expropriate his recently acquired small fortune.

The Astrologer is a master operator whose uncanny manipulative ability is based partially on making everyone believe a different version of his plan while nevertheless keeping the cell together through the appeal of his own slippery personality and an endless series of simulacra. The whole point is, in fact, that everything that surrounds the Astrologer smacks of forgery. Not only his speech but also the secret reunions and characters he invites to participate (a military man, a communist lawyer) have a certain degree of affectation and suspicious theatricality. Paradoxically, this might prove his genius. One of his most consequence-laden acts is the staging of the assassination of Barsut (letting him escape) in order to hold sway over Erdosain.[2]

In the sequel *Los lanzallamas*, the Astrologer entices another acquaintance of Erdosain's, Hipólita (who at first had the intention of blackmailing the Astrologer, only to be seduced by him later), to join the group. Barsut is liberated by the Astrologer and endowed with a sum of counterfeit money, for which he will be arrested. Erdosain enters into a period of supreme anguish mixed with revolutionary zeal while he comes up with the plan of the homemade chemical plant, a sketch of which is reproduced in the novel. Meanwhile, he murders his young lover in an act of gratuitous and planned violence, precipitating his own end and that of the society.

The first-person narrator identifies himself as a journalist to whom Erdosain, a fugitive from the police, confesses his deeds and declares his moral pain before committing suicide on a train. The events are exploited by the newspaper as one more spectacle—despoiled of any revolutionary content and reduced to a twisted criminal plot. The fugitive Astrologer disappears from sight, and Barsut, dreaming of Hollywood, launches a career as a film actor when he is hired to play himself in a movie about the suddenly spectacular events.

THE MAP

From the start, cartography has a prominent role in the novels. The Astrologer's den contains not a map of Buenos Aires, the city where the revolt was to have initiated, but one of the United States of America. "Indeed geopolitical arguments were image-driven, illustrated by means of powerful cartographics" assures Denis Cosgrove (2001, 234) with respect to the imperial struggles of the early twentieth century. More than illustrating the expansion of an empire whose shape can be projected, explained, or figured out, this map points to the fictional fabric of any representation.[3] The United States is not only a particular country in these novels, nor is it just a very powerful or expansionist one, it is rather the synecdoche of possibilities and menaces of the contemporary world that eschew the totalizing representation of ideology. The United States is, alternately and simultaneously, an imperialist threat to Latin American countries, the incarnation of moral decay associated with mass culture, the promise represented by mass culture as a common dream factory, the international power of individual supermen represented by the fortunes of J. P. Morgan and John D. Rockefeller,[4] and a model for underworld political associations of different signs (the Mafia and the Ku Klux Klan).

This kaleidoscopic image, the map hanging from a wall, captures the imagination of anyone who visits the Astrologer's room, addressing their subjectivities directly and projecting on them a common goal. Signaling the articulation of geography and the order of desire, the Astrologer works alternatively on an astrological chart and on this projective geography (56).

Arlt critics haven't given much thought to the Astrologer's occupation, except as an example of the author's fascination with and condemnation of the occult sciences (Sarlo 1992) or as another manifestation of the irrationalism of the interwar years (Amícola 1994).[5] But the universe offered by the Astrologer is one in which individual destiny and world revolution are intimately tied. When Erdosain asks himself "When will there be maps for the pain that spreads all over our poor bodies?" (220), the only responses that soothe his tortured, solipsistic mind by anchoring it in the social are the phantasmatic images of totality offered by the Astrologer's powerful projections and, prominent among them, the map of the United States.

Arlt's novels thus register a change in geopolitics that is a change in the realm of subjectivity. "Cartesian monadism, Enlightenment individualism, or autonomous egoism"—the various names of the subject of modernity as summarized by Kathleen Kirby (1996, 46)—each organizes and is organized by "invariable boundaries, an atemporal, objective, transparent space," with cartography certifying the mastery of this subject over its territory. From this mirroring objectification, the hanging map draws the power that it exerts on each of the characters of the novels. And the map's magnetism is a consequence of acknowledging the failure of this same mimetic quality, a symptom that satisfies the desire for total representation while recognizing its lack of realization. While acknowledging the demise of the centered subject of rationality and effectively shattering the capacity to think, the map draws upon itself the promise of its restitution and thus supplements the Astrologer's hypnotic strategies.

> Erdosain thought, gazing absent-mindedly at the map of the United Sates and going over what he had heard the Astrologer say that afternoon as he pointed out the different states to the Thug.
> "The Ku-Klux-Klan is powerful in Texas, Ohio, Indianapolis, Oklahoma, Oregon. . . ." (73)

The Lawyer [sic] occupied the same spot where Barsut had been. But as soon as he sat down and looked at the map of the United States tattooed with black flags, he got up and, approaching the desk, closely examined the work of the Astrologer.
"What is this?" he mumbled.

"The Ku Klux Klan dominated territories...."
"Ah..." he said, and went back to his seat. (1986, 241)

Why are the flags piercing the map in the territories where the Klan, according to the Astrologer, "controls" and "dominates" (1998, 27; 73), if nothing in his plan calls for racial supremacy? The conjugation of map and flags seems to bring up something from deep inside everyone, as much as the reign of the visible is ruled from what the Astrologer calls its "caves" (21). As Jacques Rancière (1994, 35) has pointed out, "[the United States of] America is the land that conjures up the theatre of democratic visibility. It is the land of *mimesis*." The map proposes on the one hand an embodiment of the mimetic principle of total representation while, on the other, it attempts to figure out what escapes mapping, voicing its own limits. The United States's power of fascination over the Astrologer can be attributed to the conjugation of its might and its impotence—or unwillingness—to subsume all power under its spell, given the ostensibly transparent democracy of the states of the union, its failure or reluctance to make visible what falls between the cracks of representational politics. But because the United States takes on different meanings in the novels, because it is both a point of reference and its displacement, both territory and flux, the pinned map is the figuration of contradictory claims: The United States (not the United Kingdom, whose presence is also everywhere in the novels) is now the center of power in the modern world; the center of power of the modern world is always displaced, fluctuating, everywhere and nowhere.

With his antidemocratic babbling, the Astrologer scandalizes the well-intentioned, left-wing lawyer that he brings to the group. But before presenting his Machiavellian solutions (which would lead the majority of the population to a state of ignorant bliss) the Astrologer's arguments draw on very specific and arguably sound historical knowledge of the more or less direct intervention of the United States in affairs south of its borders and in the Middle East that facilitated its control over the financial system and its influence in the rise and fall of governments around the world (241–55). The map and the flags also speak to the fact that, because of its identification with transnational capital, U.S. hegemony challenges the very idea of national autonomy as a place for a differential standpoint, by a worldwide order than can be defied only from within.[6] The presence of the flags, rendering visible the immense power of the invisible in the union of the states, has an allegoric potential and is posited as a strategic model for achieving power. The model for political association and for a sudden shift in the political order ominously suggested by the Ku Klux Klan is a subterranean, defiant, disarming navigation of what is presented as already mapped out, wholly represented political space and its institutionalized trajectories.

The Astrologer combines in the polysemic device of the map two theories of geopolitics: the paranoid, territorial struggle of the nation-state and its borders with the always flexible, continuously movable strategy of capitalist expansions that deterritorialize only to dominate more effectively.[7] The map consequently figures competing representations, but also their failure, power, and ways of overthrowing it. It points to the importance of a new mapping, which the novels—in order to display the possibility of a political strategy that would effect a total transformation of the world from the outskirts of the outskirts of the planetary order—carry out. The narrative as a mapping device is, no doubt, oblique, multilayered, and polyvalent. It can never guarantee a clear-cut final result. Instead of the master version by which the Astrologer posits himself as a guarantor of order—stitching together the known and the unknown in a dreadful although well-disciplined new totality—the novels suggest the need for and present the provisional fragments of an open-ended new mapping of decentralized, diffuse sovereignty.

TIME: THE TIMETABLE

As soon as the Astrologer incorporates Erdosain into the secret society as an inventive chemical-weapons genius, the leader performs one of his many speeches. The epochal topic à la Spengler of the decadence of the West where the secularized eschatology of progress is turned around, is here related to the malaise wrought by the abolition of distances that has put an end to the heroic era of exploration and geographical quests. In this diagnosis, the ground is cleared for the appearance of reactionary modernisms and all-encompassing new social totalities.

> In days gone by we would at least have had the chance to take refuge in a convent or to go on a journey to distant, magical lands. Nowa-

days you can eat an ice cream in Patagonia in the morning and bananas in Brazil in the afternoon. What is to be done? I read a lot, and believe me, all the books from Europe are full of the same current of bitterness and despair you speak of in your own life. Just look at the United States. Movie stars have platinum ovary implants; and there are murderers trying to beat the record for the most horrible crime. You've been around, you've seen it. House after house, different faces but the same hearts. Humanity has lost its ability to celebrate, to feel joy. Mankind is so unhappy it's even lost God! Even a 300-horsepower engine is only fun when driven by a madman who is likely to smash himself in a ditch. (1998, 76)

This sort of diagnosis captures the cultural climate in which the avant-garde flourished, when the main arguments of nineteenth-century positivist modernity were crumbling. Some artists and intellectuals turned reactively to the balm of some form of authenticity left in the self or in a local culture threatened by the precipitous advent of modernity. The Argentinean *martinfierristas*, for example, presented their art as a ground where modernity and tradition, universality and locality, existed in convivial good measure.[8] *Los siete locos/Los lanzallamas*, on the other hand, makes its geopolitical claims and investigates the cracks in the system through the complete embrace of the accelerated, forward temporality of modernity, not through an attempt at countering it or slowing it down locally.

But means of transportation and communication do not stand in these novels for fetishistic icons of the future, utopic or dystopic. They are not the symbolic resolution of an uneven modernity to which the avant-gardes (especially in the peripheries) have been related—the allure of a recently acquired or coveted technology whose mere presence announces the overcoming of historical delay.[9] They neither carry out nor symbolically embody the new mores of modern life. Clearly related to the coordinated time of a unified world, transportation and communication technologies are instruments of diagnosis as well as tools for a potentially revolutionary change. It is through this world-spanning system that revolutionary action finds a place to be imagined first and eventually executed.

The omnipresence of the train in the novels represents a convergence of different narratives of modernity shaping public and private life. The train stands as a symbol of the order of daily life, the modern organization that reticulates the space of the city and its outskirts and administers their interconnection. Historically, the railroad system constituted a symbolic and material instrument, a means to achieve national unity, as has been the case in many Latin American countries. Indeed, the train displays and nationalizes the achievements of modernity in its administration of time-space. The realist novel is said to employ the time of "the meanwhile" in an effort to reinforce the territorial sovereignty of the nation-state and naturalize its boundaries.[10] But the simultaneity that we are confronting in Arlt's sequence doesn't stop at national borders. It is projected onto the entire globe, making the case not for the achievement of well-defined national boundaries, but underscoring the political logic that demands the reproduction of nation-state defined territories in the first place.

The train was indeed considered an enlightening device when the modern nation-states of Latin America were consolidating—facilitating communication and commerce, helping to overcome barbarism, and ultimately establishing national time at a pace commensurate with that of the rest of the civilized world.[11] The train carries within it the geopolitical argument of the nineteenth century, and this is hardly a metaphor. Stephen Kern (1983) shows convincingly how the coordination of the clock around the world, in other words the sublation of autonomous local time by a universal one, was made possible and necessary in Europe at the end of the nineteenth century through the coordination of rail travel. This was extended to the globe via telegraphic transmission: The decision to establish Greenwich as the reference point for global time occurred by an imperial diplomatic contest in its own right. The triumph of homogeneous public time, Kern concludes, was never seriously challenged by the reveries of interior time (of which the character Erdosain is a prime practitioner) or by the cultural time of myth with which philosophers, writers, and sociologists were trying to carve an alternative time. Only Einstein's relativity "challenged the irreversibility of public time" (Kern 1983, 34).

Kern focuses on the fin-de-siècle spirit that came to an end with World War I. Interestingly, he doesn't elaborate on revolutionary time as a possible interruption of public, homogeneous time, but maybe this is because revolutionary time was more often than not a further embrace of unidirectional linear time, an acceleration of irreversible progress that was the touchstone of modernity's main geopolitical argument.[12] However, what is presented in our novels is the possibility of an event that disrupts the order of the visible—something that, as Rancière (1999) would note, constitutes the definition of the political as not limited to the administration of the already defined public space—an event that can define, by accommodating the scattered elements of the new cultural landscape, the shape of a different geopolitics.[13]

Despite the fact that from a historicist viewpoint the arrival of universal modernity to the peripheries is ineluctably delayed, our novels take as a given a time of simultaneity on a global scale. With the planet always already the ultimate horizon of this expansion, position in the world system becomes crucial while the evolutionary scales and cultural differences through which the world is imagined are mere dependent variables. The revolutionary, explosive time that the cell intends to enact would pose a challenge to the homogeneous, irreversible, atomistic, and quantifiable notion of modern time, at least in the beginning. The Astrologer is the philosophical mastermind of the extent to which the globe is only mapped through the administration of time, and its disruption is possible only from within. The final stage of his plan entails the total recuperation of control over public time through worldwide media campaigns that would engulf private time in their wake. "The revolutionary movement will rise up simultaneously in every town in Argentina" (1998, 218), and then "the telegraphic agencies spread the news all throughout the roundness of the planet" (1986, 234). The revolution will then run for just a short span, because otherwise it "would be a failure" (1986, 217). In one of the versions of the Astrologer's final solutions (a "solution" for the crisis of the present, and an extermination of the revolutionary impetus), the communications network spanning the globe will be instrumental in that revolutionary instant, only to form part of a much more hierarchical, but well-surveilled and centralized, order later, when shock and oblivion are to be woven together through mass media.

Unlike the anarchist plan at the heart of Conrad's *The Secret Agent* (1907), the plan fabricated in *Los siete locos/Los lanzallamas* pushes to the extreme both the emancipatory and the enslaving possibilities of the homogenization of public time. In Conrad's novel, the Russian anarchist plans to blow up the Greenwich Observatory, symbolically destroying public time on a global scale. The railroad infrastructure was built and functioned in Argentina, as in most other Latin American countries, under British supervision and in the interests of economic ties with Britain. But twenty years after the publication of Conrad's novel, in the aftermath of the first imperialist war, control of public time in this periphery no longer seemed directly tied to the British Empire. Its strength was diffuse, its monitors everywhere.[14]

One of the fascinating features of *Los siete locos/Los lanzallamas* is the unstable imbrication of divergent focal points: the self-involved angst of modernist alienation (archetypically represented by Erdosain) is combined with an impulse to understand the fabric of the social. On the side of the self, the iconography of the railroad has been charged with a dialectics of desire and prohibition, openness and restriction—the experience of a train trip falls somewhere between a vacation and incarceration, between randomness and synchronization.[15] The train is at once representative of the alienating homogenization of the quotidian and of the possibility of escape. The train provides the movable locale for this paradox, not just for dreamy reveries and fluxes of consciousness—for the "private time" explored by modernist writers and pointed out by Kern as a deadlock.

The novels are crisscrossed by train trips between the suburban Temperley station (paradigmatic, by the way, of economic and cultural ties to Great Britain)[16] and the center of Buenos Aires, a trajectory where we can see the national simultaneity of the realist novel both displayed and threatened. The sign of the exceptional appears in the first of these trips to the Astrologer's house in Temperley, triggered by Erdosain's intention to borrow six hundred pesos from him in order to return the money he had purloined and thus avoid being dismissed from the company. The sum represents the chance of restoring the order of a miserable life, something that Erdosain abhors and strives for. But present in the room and deliberating the revolutionary plans with the Astrologer is Arturo Haffner, alias the Melancholic Thug, who, without knowing Erdosain, furnishes him with the money as a gift.

Erdosain is at first oblivious of the conversation that he had rudely interrupted. Although the Astrologer, before Erdosain's sudden request, had announced, "We will also welcome all those who have some grandiose scheme for reshaping the universe, all those clerks who dream of becoming millionaires, all the failed inventors—don't take it personally, Erdosain—all those who have lost their job, whatever it might have been" (28). Erdosain, of course, does take it personally and makes this overheard conversation into his most intimate passion: private suffering and public affairs will be woven together. On the train back to Buenos Aires, Haffner narrates to Erdosain the only extraordinary event of his life, a romantic and adventurous encounter with a prostitute that transformed him from obscure math teacher into a pimp.[17] And it is on the railway platform, after being abandoned by his wife and slapped in the face by Barsut, that Erdosain's idea of kidnapping, extorting, and murdering Barsut in order to foster the revolutionary plans—toward a simultaneous transformation of his life and the totality of the social field—is fleshed out. The redemption promised by the revolutionary plan is likened to the abolition of distance at a planetary level, thus overcoming the alienation by which: "these words [kidnapping and extorting Barsut] don't give me the feeling of a crime, in the same way that a telegram of a catastrophe in China doesn't convey any catastrophic feelings" (1998, 71). The plan would eventually close this gap between representation and event, reunifying affect and catastrophe, subjectivity and history.

The abduction of Barsut, whom Erdosain convinces to accompany him by train to the Astrologer's abode, allows Erdosain to picture himself as the protagonist of extraordinary deeds of far-reaching impact. He contemplates the landscape through the car window while speculating on what the other passengers, still inhabiting the ordinary, would think if they knew he was an assassin-to-be and his companion the victim. As a possible reminder of the material base of the passenger's reveries, the train traverses "Awful spectacle of Remedios de Escalada" (107), an industrial wasteland (built, by the way, at the end of the nineteenth century under British supervision) dedicated to the maintenance of the railroad system—"with its ghastly redbrick roundhouses and their blackened openings, where locomotives shunted to and fro under the arches, while in the distance, between the tracks, gangs of poor wretches were shoveling ballast or hauling railroad sleepers" (107–8).[18] The space of the railroad, inextricably woven in the imagination of social change, shows its share of human misery, which paradoxically can be seen only through the train windows. The premeditated act of changing the regime of human misery cannot be mounted outside of the regulatory order of the railway

The train seems at first to incarnate a protected bubble for daydreaming. But whenever an immersion in the subjective as compensation for the modern reticulation of time and space is suggested—a Bergsonian moment of flux and duration—it is revealed as shortsighted. On the train, Erdosain plans intimate, secret redemptions, as when he stares at a fifteen-year-old girl and imagines her as the embodiment of some lost purity, or when he speculates on the possibility of breaking out of his alienation by committing a gratuitous murder, only to fall into an even more dreadfully alienating fantasy: "Anyway, what would I do all alone on earth? Watch dynamos in workshops go rusty, or the skeletons perched astride the furnaces crumble into dust?" (1998, 70). The division of public and private time, work and leisure, are unaltered by Erdosain's deeds or even by the desperate act that sets the narrative in motion, his stealing company money and squandering it—an attempt to break with the time of labor, public time's grip on the individual, and the daily, painstaking accumulation of savings.

By the end of the sequel, nevertheless, with the revolutionary society dissolved and Erdosain pursued by the police for his act of petty theft, the division between public and private that the revolutionary plan had lifted closes up again, and only individual correctives remain. Erdosain commits suicide on the train—marking his final engulfment by the continuum of public space and public time. Neither daydreaming, interior monologue, crime, or punishment seem to offer a way out for this modern character. And public time keeps coming back in his dreams, and his nightmares are the dark side of any notion of achieved modernity represented by the train and of any dream of cultivating an individual imagination inside the protective niche of the train car: "although he wants to stop, he can't. He collapses vertiginously toward a horrendous civilization: terrible cities on whose decks stardust falls and in whose basements triple webs of overlapping train tracks drag a pale humanity toward an infinite progress of useless mechanisms" (207). Although modernity is assumed to have been achieved on the surface, its travails for the conquest of new spaces of realization are in the making, digging into cavernous undergrounds and deep inside everyone's subjectivity.

In the revolutionary moment, a redoubling of both speed and public spectacle would bring a sudden shift of the present forces, if only to accommodate a new distribution of world power in new hands. Whereas it is suggested that transnational forces are implicitly operating in the chronotope of the railroad, the novel simultaneously foregrounds the increasing role of mass media in shaping the private imagination and its potential for re-articulating it with the political on a global scale.

THE EXTRAORDINARY

The prestige of the extraordinary appeals to a certain epistemological superiority of the exceptional over the regular in the tragic tradition that Franco Moretti (1986) called "the moment of truth." Much thinking on the Left partakes in this tradition, insofar as it holds the exceptional, revolutionary moment as revelatory of the underpinning logic of history. Despite revolutionary time's prevalence throughout the diptych, the text ultimately puts in doubt the idea of the authenticity of the explosive event, since the exceptional depends not only on careful planning but also on flagrant manipulation. The moment can't be measured in terms of veracity; it must be measured in terms of effectiveness, its capacity to convince regarding its truly revelatory status . Moreover, authenticity, as the novels seem to point out, is always a dubious notion for any revolution, inasmuch as the figure of the specialized, even professional, revolutionary is there to stir up the rebellious spirit, as Reinhart Koselleck (1997) argues. Thus, the novels interrogate the relation between the construction of a revolutionary moment and the production of a consumptive spectacle. By dismantling the ontological claims of a revolutionary political change, the novels point to a different way of conceiving of political action.

It is easy to read in the novels a critique of the spectacular in political life—a trend that Arlt envisions like no one else in Latin America and that would acquire prominence in every mass movement of the period throughout the world. In fact, the messianic time of revolution (planned to be carried out in part through, and later sublated in, the media) is submerged by the end in the prosaic time of newspapers, radio, and film, that is, in business as usual, the circulation and cyclical renewal of novelty. Parallel to the anxiety about the power of mass media to construct reality, an anxiety that is passively incorporated by Erdosain or actively manipulated by the Astrologer, the narrative develops a trend that incorporates mass media in the novels' core, turning away from the poles of consumers and manipulators, objects and subjects, victims and victimizers. The narrative voice qualified as that of the "commentator," for example, partially identified with the journalist who at the end takes Erdosain's deposition, appears in footnotes and marginalia also as promoter of the second part of the "present study" (in a footnote at the end of *Los siete locos*), promising to deliver "extraordinary episodes as: 'The Blind Prostitute,' 'Elsa's Adventures,' 'The Man Who Walked with Jesus,' and 'The Poison Gas Factory'" (1998, 103). These titles are nowhere to be found in the sequel *Los lanzallamas*, which didn't prevent the narrator from borrowing from the strategies of advertisement. (Whether this absence denounces a lack of a writer's master plan or of control over the edition, it doesn't really matter.) Arlt's novels are indebted to the model of the serial novel, which was conditioned by the mass media, not only in terms of its distribution but in its very structure. Serial novels could never afford the luxury of setting itself apart as an object independent of its means of circulation. Instead of keeping a protected, autonomous realm for artistic creation by simply "thematizing" the inception of mass media while differentiating itself against them, the novels incorporate them into their very structure.

Subjectivity is woven in a mass mediatic environment that provides the raw material of social imagination. While living only "endless empty hours," Erdosain awaits "an existence in which tomorrow wouldn't be the continuation of today, with its measure of time." The way out is imagined as "something different and totally unexpected, like in the plots of North American films, where yesterday's tramp suddenly becomes today's secret society boss, and the gold-digging secretary turns out to be a multimillionairess in disguise" (1998, 6). Erdosain's subjectivity is shaped by this material, which combines the expectation of life-changing marvels with their mediatic realization—not unlike Guy Debord's notion of the spectacular as "a moment of authentic life whose cyclical return we are supposed to look for" (1994, 112). No doubt a negative critique of media consumption is present in the novels, but this pessimistic assessment of media spectacle as the pinnacle of commodity fetishization converges with a recognition of new cultural landscape and political agency opened up by mass media. Jesús Martín-Barbero's reading (1993, 225) of melodrama's appeal in Latin America as the fable of recognition whose subtext is the relationship of the state to the people might be employed to interpret Erdosain's attachment to pulp fiction. Indeed, his love of melodramas, adventure novels, and Hollywood icons seems to encode a utopia of its own, entailing a reversal of fortunes or positions in a social hierarchy that transcends national/popular sovereignty, a matter between state and the people, to embrace the whole world.

Far from being the barren truth, every extraordinary event posited in the novels ends up uncovering its highly mediatic nature. Adventure novels give material for Erdosain's imaginative fugues: "I saw myself sailing through the Malaysian archipelago, or on a ship in the Indian Ocean. I had changed my name, I growled out English; my sadness might have been the same, but now I had powerful arms, and a calm gaze" (1998, 106). Not surprisingly, since a heroic longing for adventure and the colonial enterprise intersect, this imagination is constantly challenged by the anxiety wrought by a world in which local specificity has vanished. The discovery of gold as narrated by the Gold Prospector is so self-consciously and carefully crafted that it ironically sets itself apart from any narrative of discovery in an exotic locale. Erdosain expects this character to be endowed with the features of a mythical hero and, despite the character's travel in Patagonia, more in tune with Western genre characters than with ordinary Argentineans ("According to the idea the cinema had given him of this kind of character, he had imagined a giant of a man, with a bushy blond beard, who stank of drink" [1998, 145]). In fact, when the naïve Erdosain wants to hear more, the Gold Prospector confesses—perhaps covering up the truth, whatever it might be—that the whole story was made up and that the majesty of the act of lying consists in passing it off as truth. Nothing in *Los siete locos/ Los lanzallamas* escapes a certain degree of influence by the mass-mediatic. The novels' interest in the circulation of fictions and the construction of belief, even the belief in an extraordinary event, is applied in the revolutionary society as an ethics of the "eloquent, enormous, transcendental lie" that trumps the "niggardly and stupid" lies "that run our society," in the eloquent words of the Gold Prospector (1998, 150). But for this singular lie to take the place of the multifarious and chaotic, petty ones, an analysis of the later is needed, and the novels provide one.

The overarching lie, or extraordinary event, is, of course, total revolution. "Great times are just around the corner. I don't have the time or the inclination to tell you of all the wonders that are about to happen. There's no doubt a new age is dawning" (1998, 118), says the Astrologer, voicing the prophetic theme that is everywhere in the novels, and that intersects with the structure of promise and suspended fulfillment characteristic of advertisement. This intersection of the mechanics of mass media and a messianic message that announces the destruction and overturn of the world order becomes apparent at the very moment of revolutionary action.

This revolution is indeed doubly staged: terrorist action and the disruption of daily life through poisonous gases and bacteriological attacks, on the one hand, and the controlled stagnation of human society through the continuous production and spectacular display of "apocryphal miracles" (94) that feed upon culturally charged icons of the distant and exotic, on the other. "And if we can get a newspaper to back us, we can perform miracles. There are lots of them desperate for something sensational like this to sell . . . we can have photos taken of the god of the jungle . . . we could make a film with our cardboard temple in the middle of the jungle, and show the god talking to the spirit of the earth. . . . We'll chose someone in between Krishnamurti and Rudolph Valentino, but more mystical" (1998, 128).

Arlt's critics seem to agree on the fact that the Astrologer is a big impostor. This argument is as irrefutable as it is fruitless. The structure of the novels challenges the epistemology of big lies or big truths and leaves us with uncomfortable half-truths that we, as readers, must rearrange. The extraordinary in time and space—the secularized prophecy of revolution, the promised lands—is clothed in mass media, clueing the reader to a skeptical interpretation of the extraordinary, while preserving the reasons for a radical change. But this is not the Astrologer's position, who relies upon the prestige of a tragic discovery and an enlightening event. On the other hand, he assigns the achievement of the second stage of the revolution to the tactic of total ignorance and misinformation, of which he would be, among other privileged illuminati, the mastermind.

But the Astrologer's idea of a final stage of history is grounded on a theory of the media that the novels undermine. That is, the Astrologer's dystopian vision of a total split between consumers of images in a complete state of ignorance and the producers of them—endowed with a cynical instrumental reason—relies on the mimesis of total mapping available only to some. But this majestic stroke only reveals the same dispersion of viewpoints that he strives to conjure up, where the border between consumers and producers is suggested to be much more porous and where trust in authenticity is suspended.

Gianni Vattimo (1988, 5) may be overly optimistic when he affirms that, "These means [of communication] have been decisive in bringing about the dissolution of centralized perspectives. . . . This view of the effect of the mass media seems to be the very contrary of that taken by the philosopher Theodor Adorno. . . . Instead, what actually happened, in spite of the efforts of the monopolies and major centers of capital, was that radio, television and newspapers became elements in a general explosion and proliferation of *Weltanschauungen*, of world views." Guy Debord (1994) would contest this idea by showing how capitalist ideology is actually confirmed by these proliferations and how in fact mass media enters into a whole new stage that he calls diffuse[19]—a thesis akin to Franco Moretti's perspective (1996) on the constitution of the modern epic (with which our novels share a world-spanning impetus) as a multifarious display of voices whose perspectives are posited only insofar as they are in no position to seriously threaten the established order. In this vein, we might conclude that our novels stage the passage from (Astrologer-like) concentrated societies to diffuse societies of spectacle, anticipating both the concentration in an individual as "the guarantor of the system's totalitarian cohesiveness" (Debord, 42) under fascism and Stalinism, and the diffusion of spectacle in market economies. But more importantly, the novels challenge the tragic moment of truth as the only epistemological basis for social change and suggest a permanent, open-ended strategic action from within streams of information that become sites of contestation. But for this to happen, we would still have to account for the revolutionary potential, the promise of emancipation, that haunts the narrative and that is neither co-opted nor weakened by the diffusion of simulacra.

INVENTING AS MAPPING

The figure of the inventor is paramount in Arlt's novelistic production (particularly in his 1926 *El juguete rabioso* [The rabid toy]), and this has been noted by many Arlt critics.[20] But different forms of invention imagine different worlds in which they intervene. For Erdosain, the magic of invention infuses the disenchanted world of mass production with an extraordinary aura of individual power and sheer magic. He dreams of marketing applications as bizarre as a dry-cleaning service for dogs, but his attempts at invention fail to produce any positive outcome. On the contrary, they draw him deeper into bankruptcy, while also further impoverishing a poor family he puts in charge of the production of one of his inventions, a copper rose. He is invited by the Astrologer to abandon his attempt at individualistic salvation through the alchemy of capitalist entrepreneurship in favor of a more far-reaching enterprise of turning the system around. The Astrologer's inventive talent is invested in providing a unifying narrative to that portion of everyone's subjectivity that feels unfit, thus attracting the disenfranchised, transitory identities of the odd group and, potentially, of the rest of the world. Despite his proposal to do away with the small lies of the modern world and to replace them with a formidable, unifying lie, his method of association is based on catering to each individual's private imagination, a flexibility rather in keeping with the market economy and its petty lies that he claims to be fighting. From revolutionary leader to criminal fugitive by the end of the sequel, his failure is due to his ambition to monopolize control over everyone's imagination (even if we agree with the argument that all was a calculated scheme, and that the Astrologer had no revolutionary intentions, as some Arlt critics have second-guessed). Paradoxically, it is the kidnapped Barsut, a character portrayed as despicable and who remains a prisoner for most of the narrative, who ends up with a certain degree of success when he fulfills his dream of acting in a movie. It is not by chance that his character is endowed with traits that the macho ideology of some avant-gardes attributed to mass-media consumerism (an ideology to which Arlt, no doubt, subscribed): femininity, passivity, a capacity to be molded and easily attracted to different messages.[21] Barsut, a frivolous fake, reflects the dangerous, illusory nature of the other characters in their paranoid or melancholic solipsism. He dreams not of power and domination but of popularity. As such, he accepts the disempowerment and depletion of subjective depth. Barsut, Erdosain's object of resentment and in general a sort of scapegoat in the narrative, embodies this negativity, whose positive side (the flexible deployment of political agency through mass-mediatic strategies) lies in the very structure of the novels.

These three characters draw different maps of modernity. Erdosain's imagination, when not invested in revolutionary plans, is prone to escaping into an exotic fantasyland whose bits of mass culture pass for his own deepest desires. The story the Astrologer tailors especially for Erdosain no doubt catches his attention. When in a gloomy mood, the anguished antihero proclaims the total homogenization of global space: "It is the same in every city. It doesn't matter whether they carry beautiful or crude names. If they are on the shores of Australia, in the north of Africa, in the south of India, in the west of California" (346–47), because human misery and ominous labor conditions just reproduce themselves homogenously. So the only possible way out is suicide, he declares and follows through. As in Baudelaire's "Le voyage" in *Les Fleurs du mal*, Erdosain's desire to get away to distant lands is rehearsed as an elegy to the uncharted places that progress drags further and further into the past. Unlike Baudelaire's struggle to live in this paradox, mass culture provides the modernist hero Erdosain with material to fill the gap, and his blindness preserves his naïve belief in authentic experience. The Astrologer's machinations allow Erdosain to draw an alternative mapping of the world that reproduces his own while placing him in control of what he would otherwise have suffered passively.

The Astrologer would agree with Debord's statement (1994, 12) that "the spectacle appears at once as society itself, as part of society and as a means of unification. As a part of society, it is that sector where all attention, all consciousness, converges." But the Astrologer locates his own dominance outside, in the total mastery of every circulation, in the idea that control would be ultimately realized over the population's body, an instrument of labor for the revolution and the consolidation of a new order that demands total subjection to its main exploits: mining and prostitution. This order rearranges the most definitive features of the present. It constitutes, on the one hand, an acknowledgment of the geopolitical assignation to part of the world of the role of supplier of raw material. On the other hand, it represents a reaction to the threat of losing control, to the constant readjustment of the diffuse flows of images needed to preserve the cohesiveness of society. Thus, in the Astrologer's plan power changes hands and it is displaced, while the potentially threatening elements are recognized, co-opted, and suppressed.

In a different vein, Barsut's capacity to survive by staging his own fantasies is comparable only to something that would develop much later in

Argentinean literature and that is now considered one of the early followers of postmodern narrative: the character Molina in Manuel Puig's 1976 *El beso de la mujer araña* (The kiss of the spider woman). Molina is a queer whose capacity to resist authority (in the form of men's politics of any kind) is intimately entangled with his consumption of Nazi melodramas, a practice that saves his psychological integrity despite the ideological analyses of his leftist jail mate. Molina is equally despicable to the leftist militants as he is to the state officials, the contending groups both made up of sacrificial macho ideologists. Barsut appears to be a similar figure for the rest of the "revolutionary cell" and, to an extent, for the narrator. Contrasting Erdosain's naïve reliance on the uniqueness of his fantasy life to the Astrologer's trust in total manipulation, Barsut recognizes how his own imagination carries the ineluctable imprint of the mass-media and performance: "A talking drama would fit me like a glove. It would be entitled 'The Boatman of Venice' [El barquero de Venecia]. I would go in a gondola, rowing in the canal, bare arms and crowned with flowers. A silver moon would cover with orange spangles the black water of the canals" (238).

In the context of the other characters' much more weighty crises of deception, paranoia, and depression, Barsut's position is that of the clown. He redoubles himself by performing his own role in the movie and by being the only survivor who actively participates in the journalistic account of the events, demonstrating a porous border between consumption and production that denies the passivity that the Astrologer, along with some modernist and avant-garde trends, attributed to consumption. Cinema is the mediation (opposed as such to the authenticity of a revelatory moment) whose language allows Barsut to be an actor in the presentation of his own story, rather than the passive object of a kidnapping. It is important to emphasize that the narrator doesn't in any sense redeem Barsut. Actually, it is obvious that the narrator constructs the character as a weak, empty poseur, something of a sissy.[22] But both Barsut and Arlt's literary persona (which is translucent in the prologue to *Los lanzallamas*) share a certain degree of subjective destitution, a reduction of their substantive density in favor of flexibility inside a new system of symbolic exchange. This is a familiarity that Arlt, the writer, wasn't ready to embrace but that the logic of the diptych proposes as an intellectual strategy in the age of world communication.

CHRONOTOPES OF THE PERIPHERY

Argentinean novelist-critic Ricardo Piglia (1986, 21–22) has pointed out that there are two novels that cut across *Los siete locos/Los lanzallamas*, one being the narration of complaints and subjective self-involvement (Erdosain's novel), while the other "feeds on the capacity of fiction to transform reality." These in fact are two trends developed by the vanguard narrative in Latin America and elsewhere: on the one hand, the subjectivist exploration of interior life as a new emancipatory space not yet colonized by the rationalization of daily life, hence the space of free association and flows of desire,[23] and on the other hand the metafictional inquiry into the rules of verisimilitude that made various kinds of avant-garde literature stand in opposition to mimetic assumptions. But both of these trends come together at the kaleidoscopic end of *Los lanzallamas*, with Barsut, the commentator-journalist inside the narration, and the explosion of narratives shifting between film, novel, and journalistic report. The metafictional trend reaches out toward an inquiry of social mediation in the construction of reality, even deep inside the interior life of subjective reveries.

Latin American avant-gardes flirted with mass culture to a certain extent: literary journals were edited in newspaper format, poetry was distributed on billboards, and the borders between low and high were crossed, if somewhat timidly. But the ever-shifting media network that the diptych engages points not to the modernization of literary culture but to the potential impact of means of communication over the uses of culture for the distribution of power, mapping oppressive and subversive possibilities. The groups of white supremacists, or mafia gangs or the projection of spectacular wonders of the Astrologer's vision of total manipulation are transformed (if we are able to muffle his ubiquitous voice and listen to more subtle narrative threads) into the possibility of an intervention from the margins, relying on alliances that are not centrally organized, not aspiring for total control of the state apparatus. In its persistent piercing/crossing of conceptual borders between private and public, subjectivity and culture, national and international politics, center and periphery, spectacle and revolution, the novels suggest that there is actually no privileged arena of political action, and that the field of resonance of this action is always indeterminate.

Arlt perceived as no one else did a shift in the distribution and consumption of cultural production, a shift that implied a radical change in modern subjectivity. This is more telling of Arlt's position in Argentinean culture than the usual adscription of some sort of prophetic vision in anticipating the rise of fascist movements in Europe, Argentina's military coup of 1930, or the formation of the populist, corporatist, and charismatic Peronist movement in the 1940s with its use of mass media in the cultural field. Arlt dispenses with those models of cultural production that the avant-garde challenged but never completely abandoned: the writer as an individual endowed with a unique and superior vision, prophetic or otherwise, the modern artist as a maker of highly personal artifacts, an individual craftsman or genius that mass production was leaving behind. Our novelistic sequel can be read as setting the stage for the fading of that figure from the landscape of culture and the arena of politics. With Jameson (1991, 306), I am inclined to think that "we still admire the great generals (along with their counterparts, the great artists), but the admiration has been displaced from their innate subjectivity to their historical flair, their capacity to assess the 'current situation' and to evaluate its potential permutation system on the spot." This is the basis for a reevaluation of the cultural production of modernism and the avant-gardes, as Jameson argues. A similar intuition is voiced by Erdosain: "Have you ever seen a general in the field of battle? . . . But to explain it more clearly, I'll speak as an inventor: for a long time, you search for the solution to a problem. . . . Then one day, when you least expect it, the plan, the complete vision of the machine, suddenly appears before your eyes, and you are dazzled by its simple perfection. It is a miracle! . . . A plan consists of three main lines, the combination of three straight lines, and nothing more" (1998, 64–65). In the acceleration with which the sequel ends—where newspapers are printed voicing the final events in spectacular captions as the journalist writes the story we are reading, the writer is an intermittent figure whose vantage point doesn't lie outside the system in contemplation of overarching vistas, but exists inside simultaneous overlapping temporalities, within the bricolage of superimposing voices. This doesn't thwart his capacity for action; just the opposite is true. The writer under the mask of the journalist, at the beginning of the narrative, is fully evident at the end of the novel—taking Erdosain's testimony, sheltering him from the police, slowing down his capture and intervening in the seemingly anonymous machinery of the newspaper. This temporality of racing time is the only way to give testimony to the present state of affairs, and not its cancellation through an enlightening instant and utopias of new beginnings.

It has been said of the Frankfurt School that its influential thought emerged partially from the historical conjunction by which its participants witnessed "the two paths that late capitalism has taken to refurbish and resecure itself: European fascism and American mass culture and the consumer society" (Brenckman 1979, 95). Arlt locates himself at this same juncture. Are we to conclude, honoring a diffusionist logic, that his Astrologer is a watered-down protofascist leader, one whose level of grandiose improvisation, whose mix of personal ambition and corruption, is to be found only among Latin American dictators? Is this a farce derivative of European tragedy? Did Hollywood colonize the minds of Arlt's characters, giving them spurious dreams upon which to hang their hand-me-down existence? By reading the novels as an announcement of twentieth-century totalitarianism and submitting the problem of the mass media only to their manipulative use by these regimes (falling prey, by the way, to the Astrologer's mapping of a radical division between consumers and producers), criticism of Arlt has missed all these other aspects that I am trying to highlight, aspects that explain the novels' continuing appeal. The insertion of the mass media is not an addition to the field of culture, but a radical transformation, opening up a new landscape from which to understand culture vis-à-vis political action. The novels are testament to that and they amplify the insight by proposing (albeit somewhat reluctantly) a decentering of stagnant notions of producers and consumers along a geographic divide.

But where do these novels locate a site of resistance? There is no existing site of redemption or autonomy along the spatial axis: authentic places of recovered innocence, or places of adventure, are all revealed as sites of culture. The open land of the Argentinean South (where a colony is planned by the Astrologer as one of the cornerstones of the revolutionary society, where the Gold Prospector stages his tales of encounter, and where Erdosain sometimes envisages himself finally liberated from his constraints) also fails in every case to deliver its promises.[24] If escape fantasies are doomed to failure, only moral pain remains in their place. Buenos Aires, the city whose identity was simultaneously being woven by avant-garde and popular culture alike, is not in Arlt's work the bearer of any sense of place or "local structure of feelings" (Agnew 1993, 263). Devoid of the local characters and the archetypal landscape imagined at the same time by Jorge Luis Borges,[25] the city for Arlt, despite the realistic use of actual street and train station names, is "a space shaped by the poverty of immigrants, the lower strata and technology . . . with materials that have sprung out of the quasi-futuristic landscape of the modern city" (Sarlo 1988, 58–59). The nation, another possible space of recovered avant-garde *criollismo*, is nowhere to be found: Not only are its borders crossed without a hint of recognition by the Gold Prospector, but, more importantly, the group's plans reach well beyond the national frame.

The temporal axis of progress likewise offers no hope, while the extraordinary event—revolution, revelation, crime, or escape from reality—reveals itself as total fiasco. The narrative of progress is revalidated, but with a twist and a final stage of completion, one that is always on the horizon of any teleological ideal. The Astrologer's revolution is an explosion that pushes the logic of modernity to one of its consequences in the manner pointed out by Lyotard (1991, 25): "modern temporality comprises in itself an impulsion to exceed itself into a state other than itself. And not only to exceed itself in that way, but to resolve itself into a sort of ultimate stability, such for example as is aimed at by the utopian project." With space completely colonized, the Astrologer's plan is proposed as a final solution: instead of flux and indetermination, a closed order where the endowed and the dispossessed stand as two separate castes "with a gap between them . . . or rather, an intellectual void of some thirty centuries between the two" (1998, 124).

The imagined prospect of gas and bacteriological attacks is, of course, unsettling. It is presented with a certain feeling of post-Romantic or demonic spirit, a game of studious moral perversion. But the geopolitical implications are indeed more interesting. I suggested that the map holds a special hypnotic power, inasmuch as it does justice to a sense of the unrepresentable. In this sense, the importance of chemical weapons in the narrative, either in the form of lethal gases (a technology developed and broadly used during World War I) or in the form of bacteriological attacks, can be read as an allegory for the invisible, insidious, silent forces whose power is all the more lethal because it is impossible to apprehend.

In dialogue with an anarchist cell (whose underground activities are focused on the printing of pamphlets and the counterfeiting of currency—that is, on resources that are doomed to remain local and national in their reach), Erdosain defends the advantages of those weapons against traditional explosives. The inventor Erdosain is so invested in them that one of his final actions before committing suicide is to deliver the plans for the chemical plant (the sketch reproduced in the *Los lanzallamas* on page 374), along with a report explaining its advantages (e.g. "Chemical warfare is characterized by the production of the most horrible effects in the most extended spaces," 372) and mode of operation. The weapon of choice redoubles the perception of the existence of invisible, incisive, increasingly spreading flows whose presence can be established only when there is no escape from their multiple effects.

Progress, in its purely technological sense, is also a goal here. According to Erdosain, "Bombs were all right in 1850 . . . today we must march in step with progress" (296). His is a notion of progress that is inevitably comparative because it is unidirectional: "The problem is that we are living in a country of brutish, underdeveloped people. Notice that in the U.S., the security guards of the armored vehicles transporting treasures are equipped against gases" (296). But every strategy entails a different geopolitical imagination, and parallel to this narrative of development and underdevelopment there is another mapping that, instead of catching up, is advanced as a way of inverting the logic of development. According to Erdosain, in order to build up a serious capability with explosives (that is, to advance beyond a noisy, spectacular display), the industrial serialization of the production line is needed. Not only is that achievement technically unlikely on the periphery of the industrialized world, even scientific publications are out of reach. A chemical plant, instead, can be comfortably set up in a kitchen: "a domestic plant in order to produce one thousand kilograms a day" (296). Beatriz Sarlo points out that the "knowledge of the poor" is woven into Arlt's narrative: a technical expertise (not an accumulation of culture) acquired from popular magazines and the patchy archives of neighborhood libraries. But Arlt's novel transcends the high-versus-low antagonism inside the national cultural space to engage in a reflection on the simultaneous temporalities of modernity and the ways of presenting resistance to its world-spanning rationality.

Ergueta, one of the members of the prospective revolution, falls into a delirious state at the end of the narrative, perhaps a deformed mirroring of all these geopolitical projections and the group's declared intentions of driving them astray. His world is the imperial mapping of the British Empire, and his own personal political agenda entails saving the civilizing mission from the growing anti-colonial rage, all of which he sees already encoded in the Bible. Moreover, he shares the Astrologer's tragic conception of explosive time, because their subjectivities are equally built around the idea of a visionary chasm, toward either revolution or revelation. Both posit themselves as master interpreters.

Ergueta's world is the world of the train track, built in Argentina on a British loan, an instrument of the kind of agricultural mechanization that gave the Argentinean economy its place in the global order until the early twentieth century—an order in which the alliance of the local oligarchy of landowners with British manufacturing interests played no minor role.[26] The inception of another order is in the air as well. Its most tangible neocolonial dangers, represented by U.S. foreign policy, are constantly discussed by the Astrologer, while some other signs are only question marks in the act of mapping. They are suggested by the map with its movable flags as the representation of the unrepresentable (of which the revolutionary secret society aspires to become the agent in order to use them for equally mimetic and instrumental aims). That is the construction of a global hegemony in which the Astrologer, Barsut, the figures of narrator (the journalist, the commentator), and Erdosain strive to locate themselves. What is to come is not only another neocolonial arrangement, because the actual constitution of this hegemony is altogether different. It is not a modernity represented by the train anymore, or for that matter by a transatlantic liner (both means of transportation of iconic value, even if of different prestige), but spread instead by the radio and the movies. That a writer living in a remote part of the world would be attuned to measuring its world-spanning effects is not surprising if it is considered that "having lived under the shadow of the Monroe Doctrine for nearly a century, South America was the earliest proving ground of the American Century" (Smith 2003, 54).[27]

It is a world that the Argentinean literary culture of the 1920s and 1930s was far from acknowledging in its overreaching consequences. But Arlt's seemingly uncanny perception of elements of competing futures is not anchored in the authority of his individual power and his prophetic vision but in his vision's capacity for connectedness. Resistance is imagined not as impossible acts of catching-up, the creation of local culture, or the revelation of sweeping truths, but as actions taken from the surface of global flows.[28] The utopian result is that a bunch of anonymous inhabitants of the periphery of the periphery can think of their insertion in global streams not as passive consumers or even as fashionably productive consumers (as Latin American avant-gardes are characteristically depicted), but as a force that unsettles the geopolitics of media production and consumption, turning flows into places of struggle.[29]

■ **Chapter 4**

Macunaíma in the Mouth of the Cannibal

Allegories are, in the realm of thoughts, what ruins are in the realm of things . . . [for] in the process of decay, and in it alone, the events of history shrivel up and become absorbed in the setting.

Walter Benjamin, *The Origins of the German Tragic Drama*

The former, though worthy of love and affection, could not rise to the state of individuals; the latter pre-existed somewhat more.

Jorge Luis Borges, "The Circular Ruins"

SINCE ITS publication in 1928, *Macunaíma, The Hero with No Character* has played a fundamental role in discussions of Brazilian literary modernity. Despite the author's wishes, the novel was considered an exemplary incarnation of the *modernista* aesthetic program, that is, an embodiment of its ideas concerning *antropofagia*, which persisted as a fundamental topic throughout the century in the Brazilian cultural debate.[1] In examining the novel I will turn to *antropofagia* not in order to conflate it with the novel (as has often been often done), but to highlight different discursive strategies that the avant-garde made available in Latin America and to analyze their geopolitical implications.

A true collage of the narrative archive of the nation, *Macunaíma* brings together in carnivalesque conviviality a number of ethnographic accounts, colonial chronicles, European and Brazilian travel narratives, folkloric research, and the tumult of São Paulo as paradigmatic of modern urban life.[2] Prime among its bibliographical sources is Theodor Koch-Grünberg's ethnographic travel narrative about the border area between Brazil and

Venezuela. Mário's novel playfully incorporates native legends from Koch-Grünberg and even borrows the central character from the German ethnographer's account. An air of mythical, symbolic thickness is paramount in the novel, but it is always punctuated by a whimsical tone. Not only thematically, but in its very makeup—its incorporative technique and bricolage mode of composition—the novel has always been considered an exemplary anthropophagic work.

ANTHROPOPHAGY

Anthropophagic theory was in the making when Mário was planning *Macunaíma*.[3] In 1924, Oswald de Andrade had published a manifesto entitled *Pau Brasil*. In it Brazilian culture was defined, in a provocative, nonorganic fashion, by its aggressive self-marketing in the arena of international ideas. The manifesto embraced the fact that "brasil" is the name of the first commodity extracted from the territory, Brazilwood, and used extraction as a model for appropriating cultural value from and for the marketplace. In this way, Brazil was portrayed as an agent of its own (colonial) destiny, no longer simply as subordinate and collateral. In 1928, Oswald de Andrade issued a second manifesto, *Antropofágico*. With extra doses of humor and mysterious gravity, the *Antropofágico* manifesto pushed this set of ideas a little further and traced an active Brazilian role in its colonial status, back to the first encounter in 1500. From there, an innocent but savvy savage would swallow and digest for his own benefit whatever is or stands for Western or modern, which would nevertheless come from elsewhere, although the act of incorporation would purge it of its foreignness. In a radical challenge to the metaphysics of origins, the foreignness of the consumed good seemed to no longer be the point. Anthropophagy came to stand retrospectively for the gravitational pull of the whole movement that had been officially launched at the 1922 multiple-arts festival in São Paulo.[4]

The artistic enthronement of anthropophagy might be presented as just another reason to demonstrate the validity of its own postulates, since it is historically clear that dadaism and surrealism (just to mention only the nearly contemporaneous movements) were already fond of the cannibal as (pre)cultural icon.[5] Seen as exemplary of a strategy that is imagined as overarching different cultural practices of the Brazilian people, Brazilian art and literature might then be said to be cannibalizing the European once again, to digest its content and productively incorporate the results in a local milieu. In this formulation, the manifesto would effect a theoretical reversal that would provide Brazilians with a heightened appreciation of and reflection on their foundational practice.

Although mostly favored by artists and critics alike as an epistemological way out of the deadlock of colonial subordination, *antropofagia* has endured criticism from the cultural Left. According to Neil Larsen (1990), the "productive consumption" strategy of *antropofagia* doesn't offer any ground to support the outcome of an autonomous cultural agent. If dependency, as Larsen says, implies "a consumption that is severed from production," *antropofagia* ultimately comes down to "little more than the effort to outsmart rhetorically the dialectic of dependency" (81). At least since Kant, culture and the aesthetic realm that stands for its purified form have been the models of autonomy. What Larsen's critique neglects, in its uncompromised support for the modern quest for autonomy, is that it is exactly the idea of autonomy (cultural, economic, etc.) that is at stake in the manifesto—for which Brazil comes into being only as a way to process its own (inter)dependency. But some of the most fervent defenders of the anthropophagic theory of Brazilian culture, such as Haroldo de Campos (who engaged in a reconsideration of the theory since the 1950s as part of the concrete poetry movement), have emphasized the emblematic character of the cannibal for an understanding of the Brazilian cultural constitution. For this influential poet and critic, the Baroque initiates in Brazil a mode of operation characterized by polemic selection and incorporation from within the universal archive. *Modernismo* was the moment of self-consciousness and his own *concretista* poetic movement the continuation of this development.[6] Despite the subversive intention of this strategy, it ends up confirming the universality of the archive it attempts to contest, which tends to be centered in the European literary tradition.[7]

Ultimately, any critical gesture of measuring the extent of European influence, asserting or denying *antropofagia*'s originality, or affirming the prevalence of its difference reveals a paradoxical case of the anxiety of influence for a theory that started by festively embracing influence. The Latin Americanist desire for difference and originality seems to stand in the way of the most interesting consequences of *antropofagia* theory. The stance enacted by *antropofagia* attempts to destabilize the cultural hierarchies of both universality and originality that condemn the former colonies to a residual cultural existence. The fundamental difference between the Brazilian and European avant-gardes' cannibalistic longings cannot be measured in terms of influence or originality. Rather than the primitivist faith of surrealism in unveiling the unconscious to undermine the Cartesian subject, the most radical point of the anthropophagic theory is that it identifies the cannibal as a particular stance in a global symbolic economy that keeps reproducing a colonial dynamic of modernity in which copying and originality, as well as universality, are factors in the first place.

What is still interesting about *antropofagia*, and what justifies its many reenactments throughout the twentieth century, is that it challenges us to imagine culture outside of the modern regime of metropolitan origins and subsequent peripheral mimicking aftereffects.[8] In fact, the most appealing quality of anthropophagy is that it engages consumption and production on a global scale, and not autonomy, as inescapable factors for cultural definition. This shift is not, of course, without its problems, but reducing them to a preconceived idea of national agency as the only and necessary factor of resistance to the hegemony of transnational capitalism misses the point. In fact, *Macunaíma* transcends at many levels what Mário de Andrade called "the stupidity of borders," not only because the main character crosses them absentmindedly (potentially becoming a Latin American or, perhaps, Native American antihero, not simply a Brazilian one), but also because the novel might be read as an exploration of the conditions of possibility of modern constructions of local autonomy in a Latin American context. *Macunaíma* and *antropofagia* share the *modernista* mistrust for an ontological search for originality and autonomy. That is the extent of their commonality, but *Macunaíma* reads *antropofagia* against the grain, exploring its impasse in relation to the colonial legacy of the modern nation—a legacy that anthropophagic theory was established to contain.

I will thus explore Mário de Andrade's novel as a critique, not only of anthropophagy, but also of projects of national culture that under the name of transculturation and hybridity were imagined and implemented in the Latin American twentieth century. Anthropophagy, transculturation, and hybridity are far from being identical constructs under different names. Nor can it be argued that these latter two phenomena were in any straightforward fashion avant-garde creations.[9] But certainly they participate in a cultural climate that witnessed the demise of the nineteenth-century notion of the nation under the European models of civilization and culture building, and they are the most visible conceptual articulations of a moment of cultural production (including the *negrista* poetry of Nicolás Guillén, the Mexican muralist movement, and Miguel Angel Asturias's *Leyendas de Guatemala,* to name prominent examples) when national identities were being conceived as nonorganic mixes of various sorts, a fluid collage composed of diverse sources that the nation would embrace and supersede, negotiating and overwriting a history of colonial power by which the different parts of the collage came to be components in the first place.

Macunaíma belongs to this intellectual milieu. It mirrors parodically the narratives of both progressive civilization and organic cultural growth. This is typical of Latin American avant-gardes, as was discussed in chapter 2. However, *Macunaíma* doesn't stop at just proposing a cultural mix of its own. It explores the blind spots of these newly hegemonic transcultural narratives. It subjects to scrutiny the strategies of *antropofagia,* transculturation, and hybridity by referring them to the recurring history of colonial domination that they attempt to nationalize and turn around. In this fashion, the novel examines the two sides of a still contemporary debate: the postcolonial/postmodern position that upholds a carnavalesque hybridity against monolithic conceptions of culture and historical formations and the postcolonial/critical position that denounces hybridity for authenticating past and present forms of imperial domination.

I will give an account here of the bare bones of the plot, keeping in mind that any summary of *Macunaíma*'s argument, highly populated by fanciful beings and featuring multiple corporeal transmigrations and metamorphoses, is necessarily limited. Since the novel is also imbued with the air of a mythical tale, childish playfulness, and sheer farce, events that might appear to be dramatic are actually devoid of much pathos and represent instead archetypes or symbols of allegorical value that seem to cry out for a hermeneutic approach.

Macunaíma, the hero without any character, extracted from Koch-Grünberg's travelogue, is born "In the depths of the virgin forest"—thus the opening line of the novel. Very soon the child proves to be precocious in his sexual attraction to women, particularly to his sister-in-law, who falls for him when he temporarily becomes a beautiful prince. His first utterance, one that will come up again and again throughout the narration, is "I feel so lazy." He disregards any kinship rule and communal bond, lying at every occasion and avoiding any obligation, particularly work. After killing his mother, whom he mistakes for a deer, the protagonist and his two brothers, Maanape and Jiguê, decide to set out to explore the world. Soon they encounter a tribe of women, whose chief Macunaíma rapes, with the help of his brothers. Thus he becomes the Emperor of the Virgin Forest and has a child with the Empress Ci. The son soon dies, followed by Ci herself. Macunaíma receives from his dying spouse a magical stone, the *muraquitã*. In the midst of an adventure with another being of the forest (a talking waterfall that used to be a beautiful Indian woman, now enchanted by an elf who later would become the moon), Macunaíma accidentally loses the *muraquitã* when chased by the incarnation of the elf-moon. The magical stone, the hero is later informed, ends up being sold to a rich giant of the city of São Paulo, the Peruvian-Italian Venceslau Pietro Pietra—who also bears the name of Piaimã, corresponding to a giant of an Amazonian tale.

Driven by a single-minded mission to recover the stone, Macunaíma and his brothers travel to the big city, facing multiple adventures as expected. Confrontation with these new environs proves to be an introduction to modern life: the importance of machines, the value of currency, and the lax sexual customs, all of which Macunaíma ponders and absorbs. His heroically charged quest is sometimes diverted, since Macunaíma doesn't really change his slack ways, particularly in his sexual fascination for women of European descent.[10] The hero and his brothers make multiple attempts to recover the stone. In one instance Macunaíma is nearly eaten, but the giant ends up defeated, eaten himself—by his own wife—in the form of an Italian dish.

The *muraquitã* now recovered, they head back to their native lands, only to find that everything has changed. Jiguê, Macunaíma's brother, tired of being betrayed and cast aside by the hero, becomes a leprous shadow who spreads the sickness to the hero. And Macunaíma, tempted now by the charms of a Portuguese lady, loses the opportunity to marry a daughter of Vei, a feminine native incarnation of the sun. The offended mother creates a seductive mirage that makes Macunaíma jump into a lake, where the hero expects to encounter a Uiara (a sort of Amazonian mermaid), but instead he is attacked by piranhas and loses the *muraquitã* for the last time. Sick and hopeless, the hero decides that it is time for him to ascend to the sky and become a constellation (the Big Bear). A parrot, who preserves the lost language of the tribe and the story of the hero's adventures, flies off to Portugal, but not before conveying the tale to the writer-narrator.

Incorporating and conflating elements of various origins in an idiosyncratic mixture—certainly with little regard for any hierarchical organization of its components—the novel seems a perfect enactment of the anthropophagic ethos. But despite all its whimsical humor, *Macunaíma* transmits an inescapable air of sadness. The triumphal overtones characteristic of an anthropophagic rhetoric that assumes the digestive, transgressive capacity of the national culture as always already present since the moment of the colonial encounter (e.g., "We have never been catechized. What we made was a carnival," according to the manifesto) is nowhere to be found. Instead, the eulogy for things lost sets the tone for the narrative's conclusion. Although this longing is finally sublimated into an abstract presence (the inscription in the sky, and the novel itself standing for what is declared irrecoverable), they seem to point to a melancholic core, to an absence haunting the construction of a hybrid Brazilian identity. The fact that *modernista* production was, from its inception, particularly sensitive to the problem of coloniality (and *antropofagia* would foreground the problem, if only to attempt its reversal) undoubtedly prepared the ground for the novel. *Macunaíma* calls attention to the deadlock of *antropofagia* as a model for organizing an alternative modernity for the nation—a model that was about to become prevalent after the 1930s with the inauguration of the authoritarian and populist nation-state as the principal actor of the administration of culture.[11]

NATION AND INTERPRETATION

In an intent to clarify its mystery, often equated to the enigma of nationhood, Brazilian literary criticism didn't fail to produce a number of interpretative approaches to *Macunaíma* in which symbols are tracked down with philological zeal or with structural precision. These readings are often accompanied by a tendency to pair the novel with genres that are either nonmodern or popular—such as the epic or folktale—as if looking for a lost ontological ground.[12] No doubt any reading benefits from the findings of an exploration of the sources of the novel. Indeed, *Macunaíma* is a novel that offers itself to interpretation. But this hermeneutic drive is engaged in the explanation of a symbolic quality. It intends to make the novel stand for the sum of Brazilian nationality, or at least for the reconstitution of its fragmented nature, whose foundation would be thus encoded in the novel. These interpretations might be divided in two groups: the pessimistic, eulogistic, melancholic ones and the optimistic, anthropophagic ones. Take the lack of character of the main hero as the example of the polysemic element in question. It points to his immaturity, his amorality, lack of determination, indecisiveness (to embrace a tropical civilization by marrying the sun's daughter, for example), and his laziness, as well as to his openness, flexibility, receptive creativity, and capacity for enjoyment. Both lines of interpretation take the symbolic quality of the novel as a given and proceed from there.

It complicates matters in an interesting way to look at how Mário de Andrade characterized his own novel, as both a symbol and a symptom of Brazilian nationality. "Now, I don't want you to imagine I intended to make this book an expression of our national culture. God forbid. It is now, after it is done that I seem to discover in it a symptom of our culture," Mário wrote (Lopez 1974, 91). If the expression of national culture entails a self-revelatory conception, the symptomatic quality of the book must point for Mário, the reader of Freud, to obscure points that have to be uncovered, to hidden and scattered truths left for the interpreter to reconnect retrospectively.[13] Literary criticism has certainly taken the enterprise seriously, constantly drawing the contours of a new hermeneutic circle. But the metonymic aspect of the narrative—in which everything is in a constant transformation—works against the closure sought by symbolic interpretations. Indeed, if one thing is clear in the multiple readings of its symbolic values, it is that the novel's symbols have no resolution. *Macunaíma* exists as a model for the essential mystery of Brazilian identity, a modernist compound of unresolved elements, always open to new readings.

Instead of adding to this collection and with no intention to remedy this indeterminacy, I propose to allow the negativity implied by the symptom to speak for what remains unbound by symbolic sutures, eschewing the temptation to make them take part of new symbolic formulas. Whereas Macunaíma, the character without character, who is many times dubbed tongue in cheek the "hero of our people," stands for an array of contending symbolic possibilities, the novel is also full of fragmentary elements that point to an allegoric fabric that also eschews symbolic closure. *Macunaíma*'s thrust vis-à-vis *antropofagia* rests on this reluctance to be projected as a narrative of self-accomplishment or the symbolic base that would grant an autonomous existence.

By recasting the tension between optimistic, anthropophagic interpretations and pessimistic, eulogistic, melancholic interpretations along the symbol-allegory axis, I am not only revisiting a recently revitalized literary tradition.[14] A tension between the allegorical and the symbolic divides many of the novel's contentious readings, precisely because this tension is integral to its construction. The reenactment of an insurmountable gap lodged in the narrative signals the failure of the national form to resolve under its framework the continuing emergence of its colonial origins. In fact, *Macunaíma*'s symbolic order is always undermined, in various ways, to the point that what the novel finally enacts is the impossibility of every symbolic closure it circumstantially assumes, the collapse of the different fables of identity—from autochthony, to transculturation, to cosmopolitanism—that parade through its narrative.

There is no need to dig deeply in *Macunaíma* to find symbolic presence. The novel is seemingly organized as a circular narrative: from the depth of the virgin forest to São Paulo to the hero finally returning to his origins. Mario de Andrade's reading of Sir James George Frazer's *The Golden Bough*, the first edition of which was published in 1890, surely might have had something to do with the appearance, once the hero gets to his native land but before his death, of the *bumba-meu-boi* ritual that suggests a redemption of the hero.[15] In chapter 16, we attend the birth of this dramatic dance, considered by some, Mário de Andrade among them, to be an artistic and popular national unifier. It was Mário's belief that the dance, enacted in different regions at different times of the year but referring to the cycle of vegetation, constitutes a spontaneous artistic response to the problem of Brazilian nationality.[16]

In the fictional world of the novel, Macunaíma is at the inception of what is still an actual practice celebrated throughout Brazil. The persistence of the typically romantic circular temporality both in the main narrative's trajectory of departure and return and in the inclusion of the dramatic dance points to a symbolic renewal that defies both the forward acceleration of modern São Paulo (in relation to which the hero is an anachronism) and the irredeemable temporal flow in which Macunaíma is born and dies—the tribe becomes extinct, and its language is forgotten. If read under the lens of this circular temporality, the novel would be akin to a conservative modernism also influenced by Frazer (for example, T. S. Eliot's *The Waste Land*), whose intellectual strategy entailed this opposition to the inauthenticity of linear time by recourse to allegedly more primal ways of organizing temporality that are attached to a sense of belonging and a natural religion. But no reading of *Macunaíma* can stop there.

This circularity is always a unifying factor for a set of heterogeneous traits. In Frazer's masterwork, circularity was immanent in the object, an all-encompassing narrative of regeneration and vegetation underpinning a number of multifarious (but necessarily inter-translatable) myths and practices of non-European peoples. The comparative hermeneutic power of the armchair anthropologist is necessary to give coherence to unrelated phenomena and thus to arrive at a universal theme. For the Brazilian *modernista*, the circular novel mirrors the ritual because its very existence performs the knotting together of the sheer enormity of Brazil's diversity, and not because it illuminates a common denominator. The intellectual gesture is akin to what, for Mário and later critics, represented one of the major achievements of his novel, the act of "degeographization," that is, the intended juxtaposition and convivial proximity of components of different sections of Brazil (animals, plants, places, Amerindian expressions and artifacts, etc.) brought together in the novel with no particular concern for taxonomic order or regional origins. As much as this strategy can be related to what James Clifford (1988) has called "ethnographic surrealism"—a destabilizing shock effect produced by the fortuitous encounter of the primitive and the modern—shock in *Macunaíma* is a medium to destabilize and bypass long-held (racial, regional, political) divisions and make national unity possible under the sign of convivial diversity. The symbolic circularity is at every point deceptive, inasmuch as it is predicated upon ironic self-reflection or the split of every component of Brazilian nationality between itself and its degeographized, transcultural duplication.

In order to complete this circular trajectory, Macunaíma must not only leave his native land in order finally to make it back, he has to recover the magical stone, defeating the giant collector Pietro Pietra. It is clear that the *muiraquitã* stands symbolically for the unity of the virgin forest, for lost love, for an alternative tropical civilization, whereas the giant, an urban collector of stones, represents the alienation of those values. In other words, whereas Pietro Pietra represents the interchangeability of values, the separation of means and ends, the *muiraquitã* in the hands of Macunaíma stands for the real thing, the kernel of identity. Even when symbols are obviously not stable (Pietro Pietra, for example, is also the mythical Amazonian Piamá, and his wife doubles as the mythical Caapora of Tupi mythology), the opposition between Brazilian and foreign remains strong, arguably even stronger than it would be if their locations were fixed, because it plays out as constant moral pressure endured by the hero to ponder alternative, contending choices.

For the symbolic reading of the novel to come to terms with this instability, it has to make instability the main symbolic quality. Thus, recognizing that the symbol is actually empty, the proverbial lack of character of the hero might not only be read as symbolic, but actually constitutive of the key to the novel's symbolic order. In other words, the lack of character is the master symbol of transculturation. Criticism has typically applauded this "lack of character [which] ultimately proves to be an ability to function as an instance of mediation between contradictory elements, to conjugate different qualities of the racial, social and cultural Brazilian universe" (Finazzi-Agrò, 322). It would correspond to the compositional process of the novel, which by borrowing profusely from various sources, as Brazilian folk singers do, radically revised the hierarchy of original (full) and copy (empty). Therefore, a lack of character is what allows the primary strategy of mediation and incorporation, a strategy that is already at the origin (the popular singers would prove it; the *modernista* vision confirms it). But inasmuch as lack becomes itself the symbol and, moreover, the key element of the symbolic order, nothing sustains the searched-for final unity. However, this empty signifier supports a discourse of conciliation, incorporation, and possibility that would have enormous weight in Latin American understandings of its modernity. Alberto Moreiras (1994, 212) calls this "the hegemonic position within the Latin American tradition." It can be related to narratives of transculturation and hybridity, but also to more idiosyncratic constructs on national character, such as Sérgio Buarque de Holanda's influential theory of the cordial man [*homem cordial*] as the icon of Brazil's flexible receptivity or to José Lezama Lima's Latin America conceived as "Gnostic space" that allows the "reception of generative corpuscles" of the Western spirit (1969, 121). In the case of *antropofagia*, there is always the reference to a spontaneous deployment of its logic of incorporation, which the *modernistas* would recreate in a programmatic, forward-looking fashion.

But criticism has failed to explain why, despite the flexibility allowed by the incorporative strategy, the ruins of symbolic unity are everywhere. In other words, there is an allegorical quality to the narrative—which was already suggested in the instability of the symbols. The circular time of regeneration is proposed only to be debunked, starting from the fact that the whole circle of departure and return that forms the skeleton of the narrative is never quite a circle: Nothing is the same when the hero returns, the magic stone is lost forever, and any sense of kinship is dissolved. However, the novel doesn't remain in this nihilistic position of lamenting the failure of cultural unity, producing another modernist eulogy for the search for cultural redemption. What is ultimately the point (and explains this fluctuation between symbol and allegory) is that the novel borrows from the prestige of the symbols of mythical origins to speak for a present topography of relations that can't be accounted for under any fable of national identity.

The novel alludes to another circle of completion, with a cultural authority of a different kind: the European tour as a narrative of personal accomplishment, a particular version of cosmopolitan privileges that was famously practiced by the Latin American artistic elite. The benefits did not stop with the acquisition of artistic prestige and expertise, they typically produced an extra gain in cultural capital. Indeed, its most cherished outcome was that it unexpectedly facilitated the recognition of cultural value in the artist's native land and prompted a symbolic recuperation and/or a real return. Therefore, in order to rescue the *muriquitã,* Macunaíma and his brothers plan to travel to Europe (where Pietro Pietra has gone for leisure and to recover from his illness) under the auspices of an artistic grant from the Brazilian government. Macunaíma is discouraged by the large number of applicants for governmental support, and the discourse of Americanism, mockingly recuperative without even having to set foot abroad, furnishes a symbolic consolation: "Patience, brothers! I am not going to Europe. I am American, and my place is America. European civilization would surely devastate the integrity of our character!" (115). This outspoken, compensatory integrity cannot but ultimately precipitate an iterative failure of its Americanist faith. Only a few pages later, Macunaíma is again tempted by what seems to be a mirage of a transatlantic liner. The hallucination includes a number of inviting "refined Argentineans" on board and, of course, a handful of cheering beautiful ladies that make the adventure even more palatable (120). The hero obviously ends up on board, saluting his brothers in another phantasmagoric departure to Europe. When the mirage suddenly dissolves, all that is left are representations of decay (the refined passengers are sick, the smokestack exhales insects, etc.).

This consciously baroque game of illusion and delusion is typically allegorical and points to an impossible closure that Mário, who never left Brazil, knew well. He is mocking the pursuits of intellectuals and artists who place themselves, in conceptualizing Latin American and Brazilian culture, as the critical factor in a controlled, transatlantic mediation. Mário's suspiciousness is directed toward the Eurocentric peripheral intellectual who returns from the metropolis as a completion of a *Bildung* to rediscover faith in the native land (Lloyd 1996, 264–65). Mário, a reader of Argentineans with avant-garde ties—such as the young Borges, Oliverio Girondo, Ricardo Güiraldes, and González Lanuza[17]—as well as his fellow Brazilian *modernista* and later rival Oswald de Andrade, caricatures their intellectual strategy.[18] *Macunaíma* underscores the melancholic, repentant quality that this embracing recuperation of the native land and of its half-concealed elitist preferences entails. Leading Brazilian critic Antônio Cândido (1970, 53–56) pointed out that traveling to Europe as an instrument of cultural mediation constitutes a continuity in the practices of the Brazilian intelligentsia from the nineteenth century on and that the writings of Oswald de Andrade are to be placed in this tradition, as is the whole idea of *antropofagia*. Mário shows this tradition as already symptomatic, not as a way to transcend the national symptom, hence the parody and illustrative allegory found in the novel. However, other allegorical aspects of the novel are not so clear cut, inasmuch as they enact the author's own intellectual project of articulation of divergent popular practices.

But even though the hero remains in Brazil, the native land—the virgin forest—appears irrecoverable for him and his brothers. Macunaíma's life lacks purpose and unity until his coupling with Ci, who provides him with a quest (symbolized by the *muiraquitã*) even after her death. When in multiple moments of his trajectory Macunaíma escapes from the perils he faces in his ordeal, his search as well as his flight becomes symbolic, occasions for bird's-eye vistas of the Brazilian territory. Personal and territorial unity are symbolically woven together, but this unity is achieved only momentarily, as an aftereffect of loss, and always on the verge of dissolution. Not only is the way back home plagued with sickness and famine, the first abode in the virgin land has its own particular way of being displaced, its own degeographized aspect that is not recuperated in a final unity. Indeed, upon his return, the hero's own hut is occupied by a colonizer, João Ramalho, who disrupts Macunaíma's short moment of serenity with the question: "Who are you, noble foreigner?" The novel draws from colonial chronicles in which Ramalho figures as a sixteenth-century Portuguese who went native and married an Amerindian, provoking the scorn of the Jesuits (Proença 1987, 220).

The fact that this transcultured character takes over Macunaíma's primal abode is no doubt significant. It points to the displacement of the ideal of native originality by the ideal of the transcultural, of symbolic unity by allegorical combinatory multiplicity. The narrative sequence makes clear that this achievement of the national narrative depends on its subordination to the consequences of colonial expansion—which is lodged now in the heart of the nation, where it keeps reproducing itself. After this encounter, the Portuguese departs with his numerous hybrid offspring in search of "new lands with no inhabitants" (148), spreading hybrid seeds as only colonizers can. But the old, bearded Portuguese appears very tired, as much as the feeble Macunaíma, perhaps because both native and colonizer stand for a fading symbolic purity that should be overcome by the transcultural moment.

Macunaíma is the only survivor of his clan, and his last hopeless actions already have an unmistakable tone of elegy. Crippled, followed by a voracious shadow representing his revengeful brother and the threat of leprosy, among other things, and rejected by various mythological forest entities, he tries to find a dwelling in the house of a substitute father, the Pai do Mutum (Father of Mutum). The mutum is a bird that is believed to sing when the Southern Cross is at its apogee, and the Pai du Mutum, who also stands for the Southern Cross, thus has powerful symbolic resonance as an emblem signaling a differential location in the southern hemisphere.[19] Although he recognizes the hero as a living symbol, a survivor from the beginning of time, the Pai do Mutum apologizes for not offering help by saying that Macunaíma is arriving too late. Tardiness is equated with origins, suggesting that origins are irrecoverable, by definition always too late. These temporalities do not find any dialectical resolution with the present, and Macunaíma finally ascends to the heavens to suture the gap symbolically, confirming Paul de Man's affirmation regarding the symbol, that "it is impossible to state unity except in terms of not-being . . . in terms of death" (1993, 154).

The inscription in the sky attempts a recuperation of symbolic order. It represents a final transition from transcultural irony (which accepts the death of native origins and authenticity) to an ontopoiesis that institutes under this regime a new foundational fiction, which mourns the dead and moves on. But a final, iterative trajectory renders this sublimation in a celestial order unstable. The flight of the parrot (the purveyor of the lost native tongue) to Portugal, perhaps in a final impulse to inscribe a lost originality within the European archive, acknowledges the desire for an impossible recognition.

TEMPORALITIES FOR AN ALTERNATIVE MODERNITY

The persistence of a symbolic thickness that nevertheless shows its impossible closure is sustained by this "unity . . . in terms of not-being"—by Macunaíma's lack of character, which keeps the hero, an open signifier, in going through successive metamorphoses. But Macunaíma is nevertheless a modernist hero and as such announces a renewal in the understanding of race and culture that promises to reset the time of Brazilian modernity and take it along a singular path. Alternative paths, characteristic ways to be modern that are culture-specific, are indeed enacted in the novel, but they ultimately confront an unsolvable dilemma.

The idea of alternative modernity, a weapon of choice of good willing liberal theories, tends to obscure power dynamics by congratulating the oppressed for its "creative adaptations." If we understand, with the editor of the volume *Alternative Modernities* (Gaonkar 2001, 18), that creative adaptations are "the site where a people 'make' themselves modern, as opposed to being 'made' modern by alien and impersonal forces," the formula avoids positing the main question of how modernity was inscribed in the very construction of 'the people' right when it tries to multiply the paradigm of modernity by making 'the people' an agent in their own colorful condition.

In another formulation akin to this one (based this time on Charles Taylor's separation of cultural and acultural theories of modernity), the cultural theories favored by theories of alternative modernities sustain that "different starting points for the transition to modernity lead to different outcomes" (Gaonkar 2001, 17). The openness celebrated in the gesture of diversifying modernity only obfuscates the fact that there was no 'people' eager to articulate its relationship to modernity before the 'starting points' were decided. The model of alternative modernities continues a basic denial of the peripheries in the definition of what is modernity and as the basic operation for that definition. Theories of alternative modernity reinstall the separation of inside-outside that reproduces the basic imbalance, which they attempt to counterpoint with a subsequent, but always too late, gesture of recognition of their "alternative" circumstance.

In fact, using Charles Taylor's division (2001), it can be stated that *Macunaíma* presents acultural theories of modernity (those that suppose a final homogeneity which is either celebrated or abhorred), and their shift toward cultural theories of modernity (within which *antropofagia* and transculturation are to be included) that imagine different paths permeated by cultural features. The discourses of race, which I will discuss, are cases at point. But more radical than staging and welcoming the transitions, the novel problematizes the projects of modernity as always reproducing colonial power structures, to which the idea of cultural adaptation is destined to remain subordinate.

As is the case in most Latin American countries, positivist racism masked as evolutionism shaped the discussion about race in nineteenth-century Brazil. But unique to Brazil is the imbrication of a diagnostic pessimism (for other than white races) with a liberal optimism that, through education and miscegenation, expected to reverse the biological imbalance. The idea that an increasingly racially mixed population would lead to the prevalence of white traits (*embranquecimento*, "whitening," came to be the name of the theory) is no doubt one of the most peculiar recombinations of diverging positivist trends, that is, its faith in progress and its biological determinism. Well after the demise of positivist biologism, whitening persisted as an ideal embraced by many Brazilian intellectuals with sociological and anthropological interests.[20]

This ideological background is presented in *Macunaíma* when the hero, right before entering the city of São Paulo, takes a bath and, magically and very conveniently, whitens. The metamorphosis here is a parodic performance and resolution of the racial discourse and its internal tensions, adequately combined with the hygienist recommendation of healthy bathing. On the other hand, the whole scene is also an exposure of the contextual, social determination of racial assignation, since contact with the urban center might turn out to have whitening effects, so to speak. Moreover, the metamorphosis is admired (by the animals and "forest beings" around), and envied (by Macunaíma's brother), pointing to the spectacular value of race as a way to organize a regime of the gaze. This is also inscribed in the hero's own subjectivity, as his sexual desire peaks when he is in the presence of white women in São Paulo.

The exhibition of racial features was for the positivist science an instrument of population study and control and later became a tool of the populist state for the promotion of its embrace of Brazil's spectacular diversity.[21] In this condensed scene, *Macunaíma* unveils the ideology underlying positivist racism and facilitates a plurality of determinants for racial categories. The narrative doesn't support the idea of an already achieved racial democracy, since it unmistakably hints at a pervasive racist imagination that would make modern Brazil (represented by São Paulo) more white when more modern.[22] But the fluidity of the racial features does align with the kaleidoscopic displacements that the novel constantly puts on stage and is part of undoing the hierarchical arrangement of the components of the Brazilian sense of nationhood. In this sense, the novel dramatizes and promotes a transition from a set of evolutionist notions (biological, social, cultural) to notions of convivial relativism.

We can now locate *Macunaíma*'s efforts within the relativist idea of a cultural mosaic; that is, the response of metropolitan humanism to the turn-of-the-century crisis of the model of linear, universal history. Cultural difference appears in its relativity, its value no longer assigned by a unifying scale. The anthropologist emerges within this paradigm as the figure who crosses the borders inside the mosaic and makes cultural translation possible. The importance of the discourse of anthropology, not only for Brazilian *modernismo* but also for other trends of the Latin American avant-gardes, is explained by the new value that this discourse gave to differential cultures, imbuing Latin American literature of the early twentieth century with a new sense of authority.[23] Mário de Andrade's distrust for the figure of the cosmopolitan doesn't transfer to an equal distrust for the position of the anthropologist, although they arguably share some commonalities, since cosmopolitans and anthropologists "pass themselves off as masters of otherness . . . [in] a world of discrete cultures, the classical mosaic of relativism" (Friedman 1995, 79). Moreover, it can be argued that the 1924 trip at the beginning of the *modernista* movement, in which a handful of urban artists and intellectuals got together under the auspices of an acclaimed European poet (the Swiss Blaise Cendrars) to "rediscover" Brazil, merged these cosmopolitan and anthropological trends, showing their common ground.[24] The first was more consistently pursued by Oswald de Andrade and the latter by Mário de Andrade.

Advancing a critique of European civilizing reason, avant-garde primitivism critically mobilizes the "denial of coevalness" (Fabian 1983) that characterized the operation of anthropology. But the cultural relativism on which primitivism is based, which imagines a mosaic of cultures, doesn't represent so radical a departure from the linear development of universal history when we consider that the mosaic froze the category of culture in a state of unrelated historical immobility. European primitivism was based on the momentary stalling of an evolutionary ladder in order to search for what was overcome but that outlived itself presumably in a state of suspended time. The different primitivisms fluctuate between a notion of primitive culture as a reservoir of human values sorrowfully left behind in the advance of modernization and a gardenlike cultivation of the other's difference for its shock effect in a critique of the bourgeois notion of civilization. Whether mythic, static, circular, or just repetitive, the other's temporality is rooted out, and historical change is rendered irrelevant inside the mosaic's picturesque pieces.

A child of cultural relativism, transculturation might be defended as the response of the Latin American intelligentsia to this state of intellectual affairs. The idea that different cultures come together through all kinds of historical and geographical flows (slavery, colonization and conquest, trade, migration, intermarriage, etc.) to produce an original mix renders much more fluid the dynamic of cultures that were, under the model of the mosaic, allocated to their particular locale. Moreover, transculturation grants Latin America for the first time a privileged place in the construction of modernity. *Macunaíma* acknowledges the transition from primitivism to transculturation, in this sense debating the practices of European avant-gardes and their solidarity with colonial structures.

The fact that Macunaíma is born in the ahistorical world of the rain forest, inhabited by an isolated tribal family, is no doubt a parody of the timeless quality of the primitive, unspoiled other. But a virgin land that is portrayed as plagued by all sorts of diseases and threatening creatures, emptied of material and cultural riches, and lacking any sense of community is not a desirable destination for any conqueror or rescuer of cultural values. The only riches of the rain forest, material or cultural, are found in the female tribe of the Icamiabas—which of course is not primitive at all, being no less than the Amazons of the European colonial imagination that gave the region its name, here nationalized under a native name.[25] It is when Macunaíma leaves this primal site behind, when he and his brothers set off to explore, to conquer, and to distance themselves from a state of scarcity, that the landscape starts to be filled with material and cultural riches of symbolic value (the magic stone, Macunaíma's kingdom, his marriage, etc.). It doesn't suffice to name Mário a precursor, in his negotiation of his intellectual practice through the figure of the anthropologist at the convergence of Brazilian cultures, of transcultural positions that would acquire literary relevance with such figures as José María Arguedas, Juan Rulfo, and Guimarães Rosa (as Angel Rama famously did in his *Transculturación narrativa*). Mário is indeed working on transcultural, not primitivist soil, but many situations in the novel expose transculturation as an open wound.

That is why the idea of the virgin land becomes valuable only retrospectively, that is, when this first abode is left behind. It is remarkable that in many of the most compelling interpretations of *Macunaíma*, the encounter with the feminine entities of the forest (Ci and, after her death, the possible union with Vei's daughter) represents a promise of unity, a hopeful national romance between culture and nature that is nevertheless spoiled by Macunaíma's indecision. In fact, for many critics, these episodes stand for a moral recommendation for taking the path of a tropical civilization as a way out of Eurocentric values. Mário's attachment to this "tropical" oppositional identity has been traced back by some critics to the author's reading of Oswald Spengler and Hermann Keyserling, but the explicit mention of a tropical civilization can also be found in José Vasconcelos's 1926 book *La raza cósmica*. The idea of a tropical civilization, not mentioned as such in the novel, has been nevertheless read into it as a teleology of possible realization, an open path into futurity whose abandonment the novel, in a certain reading of it, would lament. While attempting to challenge the unilinearity of universal history, the "civilizational" theory recasts its argument by diversifying the number of self-enclosed 'civilizations' that might rise up to dominate the global field of forces.

It is remarkable that these readings do not take into consideration that the virgin land is a retrospective fantasy or that Ci the virgin is gang raped by Macunaíma and his brothers—a metaphor, I want to suggest, for the primal scene of transculturation, presented here not as an alternative path toward modernity but as a metaphor for the conquest. The virgin land is not only far from Arcadia, the propitious soil for cultural redemption; it is not only a retrospective fantasy of a national transculturation, it is always already a violation, a remorseful fantasy of recuperation that disguises its own violence. The fact that Ci first opposes any contact and later bears the child of Macunaíma is a further confirmation of the effectiveness of the transcultural operation, which sublates an act of violence into a token of identity. It is also a narrative decoy for any reader who would look at the novel as a celebratory example of that operation and its magisterial symbolic realization. Instead, the novel not only unpacks, in anthropophagic and transcultural mode, the assumption of an original racial or cultural purity that might be recuperated. It also denounces as complicit with violence the model of festive transculturation, consummated or projected into the future, with which Latin Americanist discourse from the avant-gardes attempted its own challenge to the assumption of purity and contributed to the culturalist, postcivilizational climate of the aftermath of World War I.[26]

The *muriquitã* (the magic stone that is the trace of this first mythic union with the Amazon) might stand as a token of an extinguished organic union connecting the land, the couple, and their people, but only inasmuch as this Arcadia is a retrospective fantasy that hides and sublimates that previous violence. Furthermore, it is the Amazon's appropriated fortune that enables the hero to travel to São Paulo and make this treasure valuable. Chapter 9 of the novel, the "Letter to the Icamiabas," is the transcription of a letter by Macunaíma to his conquered subjects. The letter is written in a pompous and semi-educated rendition of formal Portuguese that the chapter parodies, disguising the real intention of the missive: a mundane appeal for money and a rhetorical smokescreen to cover up Macunaíma's own personal misdeeds.

This letter has been read mainly in consonance with the hero's lack of character, as a parodic portrait of Brazilians in their inclination toward luxury, pleasure, and bodily appetites, combined with their provincial or colonial admiration for the respectability of continental Portuguese and their mimicking of everything European. But at this point in the narrative and in relation to the Icamiabas, Macunaíma the hero with no character, the empty signifier through which transculturation is made possible, comes to symbolize the colonizer and actually takes over that position. Read in the context of this shift, Macunaíma's cupidity doesn't stand symbolically for an inherent national flaw or lack of determination, but for the divorce between, on the one hand, the discourses of colonization and nationalization—which Macunaíma comes to embody—and, on the other, the actual cannibalization that is their material base. We should come back to this appetite for the Amazon's land, body, and wealth, in relation to *antropofagia*.

"A distracting presence of another temporality that disturbs the contemporaneity of the national presence"—Homi Bhabha's definition of hybridity (1994, 143)—is everywhere in *Macunaíma*. Indeed, the novel makes a case for the fanciful overlapping of the time of myth and the time of history, the time of tradition and the time of modernity, to destabilize these oppositions. Moreover, it can be affirmed that this strategy is the trademark of *modernismo*, the blow inflicted to the positivist discourse of homogenous modernity. But is it as disturbing as Bhabha suggests? Brazilian cultural discussion fairly quickly came to terms with its own modern geography of uneven temporalities. Indeed, the irreverence with which *modernismo* in general confronted the clash between different temporalities and heterogeneous codes is what radically makes its texts impossible to integrate under the normalizing master code that would grant the subsistence of the mimetic premise in the realist novel. Granted, not long before the launching of the program of cultural anthropophagy and the appearance on the national scene of the polemics that it triggered, the combination of temporalities had proved to be profoundly disturbing. The presence of an extraneous temporality in the body of the nation had been remedied with the force of the army in the northeastern village of Canudos, and the disturbance is the drama of *Os sertões* (1902), Euclides da Cunha's troubled chronicle of the reconquest. Only twenty years later, however, the national intelligentsia was ready to embrace the disjointed temporality of the nation as a defining feature of a particular Brazilian character, and da Cunha's tragedy was converted into a comedy. The critique of Eurocentrism that affected the cultural climate of the early twentieth century and inspired the relativist anthropology of the mosaic of cultures is fertile ground for the happy juxtaposition of the cultural mixes.

In fact, one of the main features of *modernismo* was to bring to light and celebrate those heterogeneous niches of divergent temporalities thriving at the very center of the urban order, not only on a national scale. Accordingly, *Macunaíma* highlights practices deeply ingrained in city life that are anything but a model for understanding modernity in terms of order and progress (as the positivist motto inscribed in the Brazilian flag goes). The narrative follows Macunaíma as a transcultural hero from forest to city in his effort at translating modernity, adapting it to a different use, coping with its customs and mores, converting cacao beans into the national currency, as any migrant is forced to do. In fact, Macunaíma is himself an agent of transcultural mixing in actions that might be called less ironically "heroic," inasmuch as they represent a struggle to impose his own worldview in the midst of uncongenial modern city dwellers. Tokens of his transcultural pursuits are the incongruous items (a Smith and Wesson rifle, a couple of foreign-breed chickens, a Patek watch) that he carries from the city to his primary dwelling on his way back, where he plans to implement "some improvements that would facilitate our existence" (79).

The Afro-Brazilian *macumba* ritual in which Macunaíma participates (chapter 7) to gain power against Pietro Pietra, or Piamá, seems to demonstrate the feasibility of an actual degeographized practice, to use Mário's own category. Incorporated into the novel as living proof of the *modernistas'* cultural theories, the Afro-Brazilian religion was already a transcultural practice—brought to America by African slaves who in their encounter with Catholic beliefs created an energetic border zone, later transplanted and thriving in an urban setting. Here, anthropophagy and transculturation transcend the question of origins through a teleology of mixed ends, and the allure of the concepts resides precisely in this modern openness and flexibility. Therefore, the *macumba* enacts this anthropophagic opening to new components: Modern artists as much as Amazonian natives might find their place in it. At the end of the chapter, when the ritual is ending at sunset and the participants dance *samba* together, it is revealed that the *macumba* aficionados are artists affiliated which the *modernista* group (Raul Bopp, Manuel Bandeira, the Swiss Blaise Cendrars, and others). They are not named until the chapter reaches its end, surely to emphasize that the *modernistas* have blended in, that they are completely at ease being part of the syncretic world. But less promising is the fact that the *modernistas* and Macunaíma fail to recognize each other. Yes, there are different temporalities, and *modernismo* celebrates them as an asset. But the *macumba* that for the *modernistas* was a party, was for Macunaíma the protagonist a matter of life or death. What is apparent, if we pay attention to the lack of recognition, is that the pieces aren't the components of a transcendental unity; despite the fact that the scene mixes Afro-Brazilian, Amerindian, and European descendants, the narrative doesn't support the "fable of the three races," as anthropologist Roberto DaMatta put it.[27] It is only from some overarching gaze that there is a potential conviviality, although this gaze is nowhere to be found, and the plot silently points out a mutual blindness between the native hero and modernist intelligentsia, and between the races involved.[28]

Mixed temporality, mixed geographies, mixed cultures, mixed aesthetics, mixed sources: The questioning and reversal of hierarchies that *modernismo* is able to perform has been criticized from the Left as a celebration of the "aspects of Brazil that were the result of our position as a banana republic," that is, as a celebration of uneven development (Schwarz 1992, 33). This criticism is fair but somewhat caught in modernity's own self-understanding as a necessarily homogenizing affair. *Modernismo*'s contribution to Brazilian culture seems to reside precisely in imagining and making it possible that the "other temporalities" mentioned by Bhabha were indeed incorporated. This patchwork of uneven temporalities in continuum displacement, clashing, reaccommodation, are held together by a generous celebration, rather than by a single line of development, ultimately confirming national unity.

Still troubling the national form is not the temporality of the various non-Western others or their stories (the stuff of the popular subject), or the temporality of the transcultured ritual, or that of the forest, or even the clash between urban modernity and whatever stands in its way. It is the haunting presence of the colonial that imposes in Macunaíma a belatedness that can't be solved inside the narratives of the nation. The novel represents this kind of disarray of synchronicity by presenting certain narrative elements stuck in their geographical locale, eschewing every impulse of degeographization, not yet cannibalized, not integrated into a transcultural choir.

Consider the panoramic fugues of the hero, in which degeographizing narrative techniques join the speed and individual freedom of modernity to shake up the character's proverbial laziness and facilitate his survival, making him traverse lands and cross geographical as well as physical barriers with ease. But every time Macunaíma runs away to save his life, what he encounters are pieces of history—more precisely, disjointed colonial history. In comparing José de Alencar's Romantic 1865 novel *Iracema*, the prominent literary critic and researcher on the sources of *Macunaíma* Manuel Cavalcanti Proença (1987, 34) wrote, "in Alencar, the colonial chronicle writers speak; in Mário, the ethnographers do." But colonial sources are indeed present in the novel's makeup, although the core of it is more properly ethnographical. That Proença's philological reading plays down colonial sources is telling. What is at stake is the ghostly presence of the colonial, not as a discursive source, a bibliographical ragbag from which to sew the national patchwork, or a volume in the archive of the national patrimony.

The barely surviving colonial characters have no place in the present, but they are nevertheless stuck somewhere in Brazilian territory. The temporality of the rain forest might be distracting or enchanting for city dwellers in São Paulo, but the temporality of the colonial is haunting even for the overarching transcultural spirit. It distracts not only from the track of progressive rationalization that seeks to encompass the whole nation under the same temporality, because the whole *modernista* project is in fact an alternative to that idea of modernization. A gravitational and expelling force for the narrative, the traces of the colonial attract and reject at the same time, constituting a vortex that renders the idea of an alternative modernity and its creative cultural adaptations unviable, calling it back to its position in a modern world constantly redefined by its coloniality. While an array of "other" temporalities were celebrated by *modernismo*, what *Macunaíma* insists on stubbornly is not the presence of the various others but the ghostly apparition of the same, the tie of its modernity to a reproduction of subordination.

The main character's flights to save his life depend on an empty geography that permits a reallocation of its components in a disparity that is meant to transcend distances and divisions. Therefore the character flies across frontiers, to Guyana and to Venezuela, without noticing. But in this hopeful conviviality, made possible by the dislocation of everything, Macunaíma finds archaic traces stuck in their immobility. Treasures from colonial times, we discover, might be still waiting to be dug up. The territory is haunted by, for example, "the enchanted little silver chain that indicates for the chosen one the presence of a Dutch treasure" (66). "Before the city of Espírito Santo [Macunaíma] almost crashed his head against a stone with a bunch of incomprehensible paintings. No doubt it was buried money" (53; see also 115). In the fast pace of his flight, the hero also comes across archeological marks that are just waiting to be deciphered by the informed eye: "Passing through Ceará he deciphered the indigenous signs of Aratanha; in Rio Grande do Norte . . . he deciphered another. In Paraíba . . . so much inscription amounts to a novel. He didn't read it because he was in a hurry" (107). These treasures, yet to be monumentalized or digested, are waiting to be incorporated by the national patrimony.

Every artifact can potentially be resignified within the national frame and incorporated in its history, which stays open to both native and colonial remnants, equated under the frame of cultural patrimony. If only there were time to stop and ponder. But Macunaíma is not taking a meditative stroll among ruins. Neither elegiac nor celebratory, neither too late nor at the beginning, he is escaping from being eaten, propelled in a vertiginous present in which the ruins of history don't stand as a soothing reminiscence capable of restoring the present unrest. Toward the end of the novel, being again chased by a somber spirit, Macunaíma's flight crosses paths with characters taken from both colonial and ethnographic sources: a priest from colonial times dwelling apart from the flow of history in a cave, a naturalist and photographer who speaks French and takes notes on the songs of birds (143). In both cases, the hero fails to mediate because he is in such a hurry that he just passes by, not able to listen or perhaps even to make sense of their untimely speech for long.

Historical traces thus inhabit the national theatre in a state of suspended time, stuck and obsessively repeating themselves, unable to make sense of their story, with no one who can pay attention to reinscribe them in the present, no one to dig up and turn them into cultural capital. In returning to the virgin forest, Macunaíma sees a fort built by the Portuguese against Spanish colonizers, its anachronistic soldiers permanently fighting against omnivorous forest ants (147)—a construction that doesn't belong anywhere, not recuperable, not degeographized or cannibalized, although not yet completely dissolved. Whereas contemporary regionalist novels dramatize the tension between the forces of nature and national civilization for a program of domestication of the wild components of nationality, the battle is continuously reenacted in *Macunaíma* as a colonial logic that shaped the nation and stages there its after-life, a circular scene from which there is no escape. Indeed, the transcultural geography of the novel, magically rearranged by the speed of modernity, and the unspoken, indigestible history that is stuck in its topography have a heterogeneous logic and don't mix.

Guided by the quest for identity, a symbolic reading of the novel would do marvels by tracing back to Lévy-Bruhl's anthropology the final figure of the parrot who speaks the lost language and recounts the tale to the narrator. For the French anthropologist, the relation between totemic Bororo tribesmen of the Brazilian rainforest and their parrots is one of participation, or complete identification.[29] *Macunaíma* would recuperate for this identitarian reading the totemic figure of the parrot transculturally as a national signifier. But the parrot's final flight to Portugal, with which the book ends, represents something that (at the very point when the overarching modernist spirit is supposed to encompass differences and redeem for all that was displaced and lost) escapes closure and keeps speaking in tongues. In this sense, *Macunaíma* undermines, from a postcolonial place of utterance, what most critics have either read in it or mourned through it: the very possibility of Hegelian historicity—"a movement from original unity through disunity and alienation to a recovered unity characterized by self-knowledge" (as Bender and Wellbery [1991, 10] have characterized it).

"*Macunaíma* . . . long since enshrined as veritable Ur-text of modern *cultura brasileira*—owes its popular as well as critical canonization to what may be described as a literal, if ironic, adherence to the principles of *antropofagia*," points out Neil Larsen (1990, 84) in his critique. Needless to say, any adherence to these principles is always already ironic, since it necessarily stays distant from any exclusive attachment to the native or foreign sections of the divide, strategically identifying with both. But what exists in the novel is not an adherence to the possibility of a savvy incorporation of different cultural traits but a profound problematization of that possibility. In that sense, *Macunaíma* operates under two different logics, one at the level of the composition and one at the level of the argument. At the first level, the principle of anthropophagy works well and presents itself as an example of a good mix of native and foreign. By the end, the story is framed within a historicist narrative of national literature that transcends, by incorporating it, the dead spoken native language, and *modernista* literature resituates it in a national teleology. But this operation has a cost, transparent at the second level. The cost is shown by Macunaíma's resistance to being eaten, absorbed, and incorporated into a body that remains foreign to him—despite the hero being the empty signifier of all adaptations of transculturations, the vanishing mediator that assures the transition from theories of backwardness and evolutionary racism to alternative passages to modernity. Contrary to the festive consumption and digestion proposed by anthropophagy, Macunaíma is always on the verge of becoming the object of consumption and objectification in the giant's collection. Pietro Pietra/Piamá is already a transcultural subject, as Mário de Andrade insists on pointing out in order to prevent the novel from being read as a facile opposition between foreign and native. But he is, strictly speaking, the only cannibal in the novel, since the other flesh-eating entities are not human. The Italian-Peruvian merchant and collector's cannibalistic drive only confirms that, for *Macunaíma*, anthropophagy is the new name for an incorporation that, like more obvious narratives of modernization and progress, has been assumed at the national level and continues a dynamic first imposed by a colonial apparatus. Every trace of native sense of community might be subsumed and perpetually consumed by a transcultural national or continental narrative. These narratives cannot account for the colonial structures that are their absent cause, and the novel displays traces of colonial institutions, discourses, treasures, and so on, unbounded within its transcultural bricolage.

Therefore, *Macunaíma* exposes the basic fault of the incorporative model of happy consumption. In order for the transcultural to be national, it must retain a native, pretranscultural trait that, projected onto the past, will be continuously pursued only to be discarded with the guilty awareness that the purpose of the unending quest is to consume and subsume this object of desire. From the vantage point of the hero of the people, the hero with no character, his own strategy to escape incorporation ends up speeding up the process it was meant to prevent.

If Macunaíma is the vanishing mediator in the transition from biological evolutionism and the narrative of civilization to transculturation and the creative adaptability of cultures, in sum, from homogeneous to alternative modernity, the novel reveals, on the other hand, ruins of the past perennially surviving, agents of colonial history mysteriously frozen *in situ*. A hiatus opens between the forward temporality of the hopeful narratives of transitions toward modernity, of which transculturation and *antropofagia* are versions, and the weighty presence of the colonial past in the geography of the nation, a hiatus that threatens the passage to modernity with stagnation. Transculturation and *antropofagia* are symbolic mechanisms of particularization, of swallowing up the universal order of modernity to process it into a particular outcome, but *Macunaíma*'s critique of modernity is more radical than these models for a new cultural hegemony. The hero runs away to avoid being cannibalized by universal history. The novel points to an uncanny dynamic by which the more the hero of all transculturations runs in order not to be cannibalized, the more the geography of his escape is a haunted scenario that pulls him back to a colonial history that he was meant to overcome.

This temporal paradox is expressed in the novel through a disjointed national geography. This is the other side of the antihierarchical, celebratory degeogaphizing that rearranges the national under the spell of conviviality and that propels the hero to easy border crossings. The presence of stubborn survivors of what postcolonial history had purportedly left behind speaks to impossible incorporations, much more indigestible than that of divergent popular traditions. It speaks to the incapacity of the national signifier to give what it names a place that is not already subordinate to universal history, to the incorporation of the peripheral nation into this universality under the sign of belatedness and the paradoxical effort to supersede this condition.

If the truth of Macunaíma, the symbol, lies in its symptoms, these are not those of a lack of maturation in the Brazilian character but of the immobility of the colonial order that remains entrenched in the national body as an impossible incorporation.[30] Whereas there is continuity from the native subject Macunaíma (dead, but sublimated in a symbolic inscription in the sky and in the novel) and a transculturated national history ready to take its alternative place within modernity, the traces of the conquest remain in the territory as a traumatic event that, repeating itself, resists being placed in a historical continuity. Thus the air of sadness and eulogy of the narrative is due not to the extinction of the native subject, whose celebratory burial is a necessary condition of every transcultural modernity, but to the narrative performance of the rise and fall of the paths toward alternative modernity through creative, incorporative adaptations. Macunaíma, as Walter Benjamin's angel of history, is propelled by a blowing storm we call progress—which has adopted different names in the peripheries, such as development, *antropofagia*, and transculturation. But unlike the angel of history, Macunaíma is also propelled by his own will to survive, amid and perhaps through this progress, engulfed by an anthropophagic current. Where national history saw a chain of events always transitioning to a greater whole, from colonial subjugation to emancipation, Macunaíma, like the angel, sees only debris, "one single catastrophe which keeps piling wreckage upon wreckage and hurls it in front of his feet" (Benjamin 1969, 257), amid which he can make out the glint of his own reflection.

■ **Chapter 5**

Leaving Home
Cosmopolitanism and Travel

"Theory" is a product of displacement, comparison, a certain distance. To theorize, one leaves home.

James Clifford, "Notes on Travel and Theory"

FROM THE period of nation building on, Latin American traveling artists and intellectuals performed the roles of cultural mediator (between tradition and modernity, country and city, native and foreign, etc.) and agents of cultural development, complicated in the late nineteenth century by the ethos of individual artistic freedom. The division between explorers (of the interiors) and cultural travelers (abroad), between ethnology and cosmopolitanism, between local particularities and spatial universalities, presupposes a set of hierarchies and a sense of historical direction that was losing ground at the time of the avant-gardes. The strategies deployed by travelers linked to the avant-gardes went from a compensatory reversal of the hierarchies to an active investigation, within the surroundings and within the self, of the assumptions that sustained them.

Travel writing always involves a conceptualization of the unstable ground upon which it finds its justification. A sense of an increasingly dynamic historical reality and ongoing cultural change on a worldwide scale was the pervasive thrust that the avant-gardes welcomed, ushered in and repudiated. During this period, the attachments and detachments that travel writing is forced to negotiate, the viewpoint that it must constantly rearrange, the distance that it charts actively engages the instability of a larger cultural or philosophical order.

"I said to myself: This ship is navigating with literature. That annoyed me because I wanted this trip to be very anti-Brazilian, very far from literature," Mário de Andrade (1983, 210) wrote in his travel journal. Indeed, the discursive horizon of "Brazilian literature" that accompanies Mário is formed by versions of the inclusion of the nation in Western discourses. Mário's annoyance with these incisive discursive strongholds, from which traveling was meant to free the traveler, show the persistence of the tradition of travel writing in shaping Latin American culture and in dealing with this inclusion. The fabric of the continent's lettered culture, it has been widely argued, is permeated by traces of the writing by conquerors, church officials, naturalists, missionaries, ethnologists, traveling artists, and experts of various kinds. For those attuned to postmodern themes, however, there is a certain seductive tendency to find in this grounds for a new metaphysics, where contentious discourses and epochs are reconciled under the ontological umbrella of displacement, deterritorialization, dissemination, and the like. But contrary to this transhistorical poetics, travel writing in the era of the avant-gardes reveals itself as a multilayered construct in which, as I have been arguing, the sedimentations of previous epochs—the narratives by which Latin American cultures imagined their stance in the West, narratives that have tended to reproduce subordination—exert historical pressure and still survive in latent form. Charting individual trajectories unleashes a discursive thickness loaded with historical significance.

The homogeneous time-space projection that supports modernity's self-understanding and direction—that is, historicism—was typically challenged by the avant-gardes through different aesthetic strategies. The presentation of tradition and modernity as pieces of a fragmentary collage, or the display of a worldwide urban simultaneity that compresses time into a total present, might be articulated for this purpose. Assuming in their fictional and poetic texts the mobility of the traveler's eye—as Vicente Huidobro, Pablo Neruda, Magda Portal, Maples Arce, Oliverio Girondo, Raúl Bopp, and Oswald de Andrade, to name just a few prominent examples, often do—is no doubt a way of foregrounding the variables of space and time to shake loose the detached standing of realism and the fixed viewpoint of the symbolist-Parnassian poetic travails that preceded the avant-garde generation.

But of interest in reading travel writing is that the construction of a vantage point on unstable terrain is also implied in a confrontation with other contemporaneous spatial and travel practices that posit a living historical challenge to the artistic viewpoint. In writing down their travel experiences—Mário de Andrade as an idiosyncratic ethnologist, Roberto Arlt as a journalist—these writers found themselves confronted with situations where mapping the practices that constituted a shifting notion of culture was a condition for articulating their own thoughts. These texts perform a history of a present replete with past discourses, overshadowed practices, expelled subjects, contending spaces, and outmoded artifacts, all of which fail to add up to a narrative of territorial integration, historical overcoming, or a promising future. Instead of the language of survival (of traditions) and evolution (toward modernity), these texts exhibit an effort to conceptualize a present that escapes the main narratives of modernity, a present that is suddenly out of joint. Through these cracks, minor stories and voices can unexpectedly be heard.[1]

THE APPRENTICE TOURIST

Mário de Andrade's 1927 and 1928–29 travels were meant to continue the spirit of his 1924 trip through the colonial towns of Minas Gerais, which had helped the *modernistas* in the revalorization of their national heritage for the construction of their avant-garde aesthetics. The inaugural trip included the main *modernista* figures (Oswald de Andrade, Mário de Andrade, and the essayist and financial supporter of the modernists Paulo Prado) and one avant-gardist of international renown (Blaise Cendrars), and according to the leading Brazilian critic Aracy Amaral, it "reenacted the road taken by conquerors when arriving in a new land" in order to dig up "traces of its former inhabitants" (117–18). Thus, the trip partook of a certain ethnological spirit, in the sense that it attempted to "describe the culture as it was before Western intervention" (Pratt 1986, 42). But what is evident in the name a "voyage of discovery of Brazil," with which the enterprise entered into Brazilian literary historiography, and what is even more evident in Amaral's comment, is that the effort to describe the culture as it was before Western intervention travels along the same road established by the conquerors. This figure of the conqueror was indeed the privileged but also unlikely witness of the preceding state of affairs (unlikely inasmuch as he didn't bear the perspective of modern nostalgia) that his very witnessing, the inaugural act of Western intervention, terminated. The state of Minas Gerais, "general mines," a center of economic and cultural activity in colonial times, provided a propitious arena for this highly ironic exploration of historical traces from precolonial and colonial times. The intellectual strategy at work requires a detached multiperspectivism through which the cultural riches of the past are rediscovered and redeemed from colonial history by a reenactment of history that relocates them in a colorful present.

The fact that these inaugural *modernistas* were all São Paulo natives or denizens points to another underlying narrative of national significance: that of the history of exploration of and expansion through the hinterlands by the *bandeirantes* (the pioneer carriers of the flag) in a national appropriation of the logic of conquest. During the nineteenth century, the presence of a frontier in the very heart of the nation, an interior exteriority, as it were, represented a challenge for the new nation's conquest of its own future, a national destiny encoded in its territorial self-achievement.[2] Undoubtedly, the voyage of discovery was an operation of reconstitution of a new sense of nationality under a *modernista* flag, an operation that recuperated unevenness as a mark of a simultaneous diversity.

The Amazonian region and the *sertão* (the rugged backlands on the Brazilian Northeast), the areas traveled by Mário de Andrade, are far from being easily integrated into a homogeneous national territory and have a problematic place in the constructs of the Brazilian intelligentsia. In addition, the Amazon's power over the Western imagination in the 1920s was very much alive as a site of miscellaneous appropriations.[3] "Everyone poses as well versed in things from this pompous Amazon, from which they extract a fantastic, improbable vanity, 'land of the future' and so on. . . . But the only ones who know something are the ignorant people of the third class. Rarely had I ever experienced . . . the learned disorientation of these travelers, generally English-speaking" (99), writes Mário in his diary. The Amazon represented both an exteriority and a surplus of the body of the nation that the writer intended to consolidate. Although more a Brazilian affair, one that was far from carrying an equal weight in the metropolitan imagination, the northeastern *sertão* region explored during his second trip occupied a comparable position of interior exteriority in relation to the national body: an untamable remnant that had stood as a hindrance to modernity (most dramatically evoked in Euclides da Cunha's seminal *Os sertões*). However, it could set the tone for a never-ending conquest (of the irrational conjunction of its social backwardness, its endemic poverty, and its extreme and exuberant religiosity) and thus be recuperated in its very powerful mystery as another key to national identity.

Three years before the trip to the Amazon, the presence of Blaise Cendrars had furnished the "voyage of discovery" with a token of European intellectual support, which guaranteed a vantage point to sustain the ironic position of multiple, cheerfully nonconflictive identifications. On this new voyage, however, Mário developed different strategies of conceptualization. The travelogues are indeed an effort to distance himself from the *modernista* project as much as from the ethos of the metropolitan traveler, and the writer explores the limits of available narrative strategies to articulate nation, culture, and territory. But the practices that he encountered, from labor to artistic expressions, among which he reconsidered how his own project (as a writer, a researcher, a traveler) and that of the Brazilian intelligentsia played an active role in challenging the writer to develop alternative ways to map out the shifting dynamic of cultural production. The result is a text that can hardly account for what it presents.

His travel journals, only partially published during his lifetime but prepared for publication in their totality, bear the general title *O turista aprendiz* (The apprentice tourist).[4] The title makes transparent from the start the tentative, unstable negotiation with different travel practices. As if to emphasize the complexity, the folder corresponding to his second trip carries the subtitle *Viagem etnográfica* (Ethnographic travel), thus juxtaposing ethnography and tourism and presenting his as a playful, flexible position, following a common modernist practice. It can be argued, however, that in opting for the less intellectually charged category of tourism (a practice related to mass consumption and usually dismissed by modernists, who were more given to imagine themselves involved in a quest or a mission of historical consequences), and doing so from a position of apprenticeship, points to a desire to create an experimental space of writing that does not constitute a discipline, a space outside "literature" from which his travel writing would strive to unpack some of the prevalent layers that composed the Brazilian literary archive. This tension between dislocating earlier places of authority and the creation of a new space for thought is present throughout the journals.

However, although ethnography had a prominent place with the Latin American avant-gardes in general and in the *modernista* movement in particular, it was Mário's intellectual project that engaged with this discipline more fully. The fictions of ethnographic reports included in *O turista aprendiz* provide a terrain in which to explore different anthropological standpoints, that is, different uses of "culture" as a refuge from Western expansion. We find, for example, the writer as fictional explorer, back from a short Amazonian excursion in Peru, voicing an Americanist reinterpretation of the civilizing mission practiced at that time by ideologues of a redemptive *indigenismo*, when he narrates a dialogue in which he half-seriously accuses an Amazonian Indian of being in a state of decay, of never having achieved the civilizational level of the Incas (116). But on another page, Mário tries out a version of primitivism and attempts a tongue-in-cheek eulogy of the ancestral ties between an Amazonian tribe (that he invents) and the mythical *preguiça*, or sloth, race—"laziness" being the value subsumed by the Western mastering of time under a productive grid (161–62). Literary authorship is constructed for these occasions under the guise of a parody of prevalent discourses with ethnographic underpinnings, and as a conscious mockery of his own identification with the figure of the ethnographer.

During the trip to the Amazon, Mário attempts in different sections of his journal to fictionalize his traveling gaze by assuming the vantage point of an ethnographer of two separate tribes: the fictional Do-Mi-Sol and the Pacaás Novos. The latter carries the name of a real river where some tribes dwelled in relative isolation until the rubber boom in the second half of the nineteenth century.[5] Everything is set up to make of these "observations" a deforming mirror of ethnographic assumptions: tribal-centered organization, cultural and territorial isolation, non-Western rules of kinship, the central role of religion (which includes necessary doses of ritual cannibalism), and a set of curious myths and legends of origins. Ethnography seems to carry the seed of comparison: Recall the European tradition of ethnographic self-critique, mobilized as an instrument of satire or ironic reflection of European society (e.g., Jonathan Swift's *Gulliver's Travels*, Diderot's *Supplément au voyage de Bougainville,* etc.), long antedating the Victorian universalism of Frazer and the surrealist upsetting of cultural orders through juxtaposing incongruous ethnographic findings. Mário's fictional tribes are indeed a comment, by reversal, on the particularity of Western modernity (the Do-Mi-Sol are a communist matriarchy, for example). In addition, they effect a critique, by the sheer humor of the ethnographic display, of ethnographic reason and its main assumption of cultural difference as available for the observer to single out and reflect upon.

Despite the presence of these narrative experiments, no performative exploration of ethnographic discourses seems to satisfy the author, who, two days after writing the myth of the lazy tribe in his diary, declares his intentions of giving up the idea of continuing the project of ethnographic parody (1983, 168). The irreverent combination of critical humor directed at ethnographic discourse and the critical use of ethnographic examples to enrich the composition of Brazilian modernity, which already were signature *modernista* strategies, had ceased to provide this travel writer a position from which to relate to the actual life of the people he encountered—who were the traditional object of ethnography in the first place. To free these subjects from the anthropological gaze might have been the reason he invented a tribe from scratch in his second parodic attempt (the Do-Mi-Sol), instead of insisting on a comical version of the existent Pacaás Novos. An entry for this same day (July 24, 1927) is an example of the kind of encounter that undermined the modernists' system of multiple viewpoints, which was in its turn meant to destabilize the archive of discursive authority. A boy of Indian descent,[6] whose labor involves loading the vessel that transports Mário, asks the apprentice-tourist-turned-fictional-ethnologist to be taken to the city of Belém, capital of the Amazonian economy:

> The request is full of desire and anguish. Now I smile and have nothing to reply. I come down from the ship. The work was already done, so I approach the guy and start to chat. I consider leaving him some pennies, as consolation. "Do you know how to read?"
>
> "I dunno!"
>
> "And would you like to learn?"
>
> "Sure . . . but with what money? . . ."

I didn't have the courage to give him those pennies.

I went on board with my heart rent. Only after the vessel departed did I realize I should have given him the pennies. They were meant as a consolation! (168)

Mário's paralysis reveals a fissure in the symbolic resources with which he is prepared to articulate his experiences. Encounters like this one find the writer off guard, not because of the sheer misery of the hinterlands but because all his ethnographic assumptions, which at least could enrich this misery with a distinctive culture, their flexible multiperspectivism notwithstanding, are undermined in a single stroke. In relation to this impoverished, illiterate Amerindian who fosters dreams of migration to the city, the definition of culture can't be attached to an anthropological reliance on self-enclosed specificities ready to be appropriated and unrelated to the problem of citizenship. Already involved in the transportation network that irrigates the Brazilian economy (and from a region, the Amazonian, very early internationalized by rubber production),[7] Mário's interlocutor hollows out all the different positions assigned to him by the ethnographic enterprise. Mario's flexible system of shifting perspectives comes to a halt in confrontation with the boy's life constraints. The boy's transient identity, a factor of the conditions of his existence, pushes the ethnographic frame into a crisis, and this is when the (parodic) ethnographer turns into (reluctant) folklorist of what he will later call "mobile traditions"—those that change to respond to the problems of the present.[8]

Mario's opposition between mobile and immobile traditions underscores "tradition" not as the site of permanent values but as the object of constant reappropriation, as the arena of power struggles, as the field of a permanent resignification. It is worth mentioning that folklore is ancillary to salvage ethnography in its approach to identifying and recording cultural practices—the folklorist being the intellectual who mainly strives to reestablish national continuity by rescuing practices threatened by urban culture with fragmentation and disappearance. Although he was an expert on music and versification, a reader of different folklorists (whom he criticized for their purely intellectual or linguistic approach), and a traveler who reported on his findings, Mário nevertheless was unwilling to be identified as a folklorist. This might be explained by his desire to distance himself from the discipline's penchant for salvaging and preserving what otherwise might be lost, an enterprise that would seem to be in opposition to the constant mobility of traditions, whose reaccommodations Mário deems important to understand.[9]

This suggests how far Mário stands from the Latin American ethnological avant-garde, the *modernistas* among them, who fostered the cultural turn in which, according to Roberto González Echevarría (1990, 154), "the institutions founded by the various governments and the avant-garde artist sought the discovery or creation of a national culture, a discourse, as it were, bespeaking the uniqueness of Latin America and of each individual subculture within it." When crossing the border into Peru, Mário finds very odd indeed the redemptive embracing of Inca pride and makes a humorous remark about Brazilians who, following that trend, "wanted to launch a Marajoara style" (115). Marajó, an island at the mouth of the Amazon in the state of Pará, would certainly fulfill the ethnographic ideal of isolation and, by virtue of a commonly practiced synecdoche elaborated by virtuoso intellectuals, come to represent the whole. But the capricious choice of Marajó over every other possibility speaks for itself. It is not only that Brazil does not "contain" a culture from the past available for incorporative sublimation and that can be singled out and appreciated in terms of European parameters of high civilization, which privilege urban organization and sedentary settlement. It is the very system of assignation of value that appears problematic.

Only a few days later (August 1), already toward the end of the Amazonian journey, the street market of Belém offers Amerindian products that Mário finds unappealing (although the apprentice tourist buys some). Still, they trigger the following reflection:

> The Brazilian lack of organization is such that all that the Indians sell is legitimate. It is quite ugly, worthless, used. No one has yet pointed out that it is by counterfeiting that these things acquire value, not only making them prettier and better than what the Indians are producing, but also by valorizing their wares by making them legitimate and more rare. The value is not in truth but in legitimacy, don't you think? I don't know if I think so, but I have already written it, so I'll keep it. I attribute it to Brazilian disorganization. (183)

The observation resonates with a postmodernist approach to cultural production that emerges from a critique of authenticity and that moves away from the salvage or preservationist enterprise and from the patronizing assumption that indigenous practices would be unable to adapt and to flourish under the historical pressure of contact with the West. James Clifford (1988) has introduced the analysis of "systems of authenticity" to question the assumption of spontaneity and lack of self-awareness of indigenous cultural production that is posited as an inversion of Western self-reflective modernity. Nestor García Canclini (1989) is also part of this realignment of the disciplines when he emphasizes "prosperous traditions," that is, the ones continuously recreated as a value of the present and not a remnant of the past to be preserved in its (always already defunct) originality. We can certainly locate Mário in this constellation and praise his remarkable intellectual vision as a precursor of an anti-ontological trend of anthropological thought in which tradition is in a permanent state of reinvention and resignification.

But the problem arises as soon as the "ugly, worthless, used" traits of certain cultural expressions resist being converted into cultural value, thus pointing to the limit of the happy finale of the "prosperous tradition." Moreover, I will argue that this is how we can interpret the performative contradictions and hesitations of a commentary that leaves the objects in question floating between a constructed legitimacy and a valuable counterfeiting. At the same time that he promotes fostering prosperous traditions through a system of authenticity (to put it in the terms of Clifford or García Canclini), the legitimacy of the nation's authority to valorize these objects is put into doubt, and the possibility of other systems of value is suggested only to be denied. It is not only that these objects appear abject even though potentially valuable. Subaltern practices are revealed in this moment of disarray in which the objects resist alignment with the national system of authentication of the popular or with any other system that regards cultural practices in terms of accumulated capital in a cultural patrimony.

Mário's ethnomusicological accounts illustrate this resistance, the resistance of what is "worthless"—what falls in between the systems of assignation of cultural value. While in the Amazon region, Mário attends some dramatic dances (*bumba-meu-boi* on May 24; the *ciranda* on June 12) and publishes an article in *Diário Nacional* that narrates how he and his fellow travelers happened to witness the *ciranda* in the coastal village where they end up. The distance between observers and their subjects of observation is apparent, but distressing only to the former: "They didn't feel threatened by us, despite the extravagant commotion that we caused among those extremely poor people, we dressed as explorers, with 'pullovers,' gloves, colonial hats" (335). Mário partially advances the *modernista* agenda when he points to the dancers wearing "hats inspired by indigenous artifacts [*cocares*]" and to "the same crude colors with which [modernista painter] Tarsila [do Amaral] so wisely Brazilianized her own paintings" (335), thus highlighting an idea of autochthony as an always already hybrid product and the *modernistas* as the felicitous continuation of an already existing tendency of the permanent reconfiguration of traditions. But Mário's conclusions after attending the dance are not yet another instance of a self-reflective critique of metropolitan positions and a dutiful practical application of the *modernista* agenda. Despite his good disposition, the writer becomes disappointed with the *ciranda,* comparing it with "the dramatic legitimacy of *Boi Bumba.*" In his terms:

> In the end, this dramatic confusion doesn't go beyond a children's game for which some adults, though primitive people, furnished a more interested role . . . aping love, religion, hunting, and taboo animals. Even the dance lacks value, being monotonous, unoriginal, primitive, very close to those indigenous dances that Martius and Lery described. What is worthy is the music . . . that by an uncanny coincidence strongly recalls some Scandinavian popular songs. . . . If the similarity of our melodies with those of the Russians is an already established fact and doesn't surprise anyone, I confess that this likeness between our natives and Swedish music haunts me. Because the original melodic elements are true ethnic syntheses, and it seems unconceivable that the people of this village had conceived of some musical movements that are the national norm among the northern Europeans. (336)

Mário's aesthetic judgment unties, again, the system of assignation of cultural value. The accidental folklorist is doubly haunted—on the one hand, by the unrecognizable: the presence of the unfamiliar, when a certain characteristic can't be reduced to a particular ingredient in the Brazilian mix, Portuguese, Amerindian, or African; on the other hand, by the irrecoverable: the ghostly return of a too-familiar literature, the ethnographic observations of von Martius (*Reise in Brasilien*, 1823–31) and Jean de Lery (*Historie d'un voyage fait en la terre du Brésil*, 1578) that signal two moments of Brazil's incorporation into the West.[10] Mário's anxiety over being discovered in colonial attire is reflected in reverse in a performance that seems to mimic European travel chronicles resurfacing in this colonial theater, where the ghosts of history come back scandalously unsynthesized. There is something monstrous in this untimely echoing of metropolitan texts and Nordic tunes that fail to constitute a voice, something that, through the interstices of this dance, visits the whole project of national reconstitution.

Mário is taken by surprise by the cosmopolitan sophistication of these people, whom he describes as "absolutely untraveled *[desviajada]* and isolated in the dessert of Solimões" (336) and nevertheless at home under the scrutiny of the extravagant metropolitan travelers.[11] How this mix came about among these untraveled subjects is a pressing question, inasmuch as traveling appears here to be related only to the elite practice that he is performing. Perhaps the neologism *desviajada* accounts for a conception of attachment to a particular place as already a negation, secondary to traveling. What is clear is that there is an insurmountable gap between the immobility of these primitive and infantile dancers and their sophistication and mobility, a gap that can't be accounted for by the alternative system of authenticity that he is striving to develop. So these practices appear to be meaningful only as they fall back into a colonial system of meaning over which the whole enterprise of postcolonial modernity was meant to prevail. The people appear to be unconsciously fixated on history and repeating it, according to Mario's reading of the dance; although what the entry bears witness to is a mobility that constitutes these actors' response to the reiteration of the theater of colonial encounter, of which the writer himself is a reluctant protagonist. Even though the text mentions the aspect of the performance ('performance' not only in terms of the dance but in the whole scene of ethnological encounter) that actually defies the colonial subalternization of the dancers, this operation is obscured by the system of metropolitan references used to study the object.

But the attempt to find a place outside literature (that was the starting point of the travelogue), outside the master texts of the national archive, also entails the articulation of a viewpoint outside the *modernista* effort to rediscover popular practices for a project of national revalorization. In this sense, Mário distances himself from this new hegemonic alignment inside the nation-states that the avant-garde strategy made possible in Brazil and elsewhere. Mário struggles to depart from that strategy through the articulation of mobile traditions, not as creative adaptations of traditions to the impositions of modernity but rather in terms of cultural production involving a discontinuous geography of present movements encountering, becoming, and clashing with forces (economic, demographic, and institutional) not distinctively included within the realm of "culture." Folklore thus shows its underside as a subaltern practice that is not "cultural" in the sense that the appropriation of "folklore," as a token of authenticity or legitimacy of the people, obscures the capacity of practices embraced by this category to respond to these forces. It appears in a raw state, not entirely transportable, not an objectifiable, finalized product.

On the second trip, to the *sertão*, Mário undertakes more consistent folkloric research into music and dramatic dances, focusing on transformations more than on the preservation of an original nucleus. *Coco* songs might live in a process of incorporative adaptation, for example as when an elated Mário registers a *coco* singer who "celebrates the modern turbines": "Where did I see a modern turbine? . . . / In the Brazilian powerhouse" (272).[12] The celebrated adaptability seems to refer to the openness of this form to the icons of modernity and development in a dynamic that demonstrates the possibility of a convivial, imaginative incorporation, away from a dreaded historical stagnation. Even more interesting than the celebrated openness of the popular songs to the signs of the new is that the folklorist registers a challenge to his own apparatus, thus performing a critique of the modern creation of subalternity. Through the inscription of the itinerant singer Chico Antônio's songs, the travel journal examines its own epistemological limits. The singer addresses Mário with his sung greeting, which the writer obediently transcribes and in which the one who is mobile and bids farewell is not the folklorist-traveler but the subject of his research. The song alludes to the instruments of high, sedentary culture at the moment when the singer is about to depart, moving away from the role of native informant. "Good-bye chamber! Good-bye chair! / Good-bye piano for playing! / Good-bye ink for writing! / Good-bye paper for inscribing!" (279) (*papel de assentá*—which in Portuguese carries the meaning of both inscribing and settling down).

It is not by chance that Mário de Andrade was captivated by Chico Antônio, since the singer both mirrors and undermines the position in which the folklorist sometimes finds himself trapped, opening up other ways to conceptualize the relation between elite and popular practices, mobility and culture.[13] This song erases the na(ra)tion that Mário de Andrade is attempting to write down. It names, in advance of the subject that performs the chronicling, the moment of the overarching inscription and prevents that writing from becoming an abstract totality. Mário seems to be stunned by the unexpected mobility of Chico Antônio, puzzled by the heterogeneity of his mapping, when just before departing, the singer tells him that "when I arrive in my homeland I will miss him; but when I come back to these lands I should make someone call him and he would be back" (279). Mário silences his own pressure to achieve synthesis, to read from the expectation of what has or has not been "Brazilianized," and opens the space for this subaltern to speak. Folklore doesn't exhaust its potential for contestation by merely adapting to what is new. Mobile traditions no longer imply a vantage point for observation of a crystallized object in the archive of tradition but a site of interlocution that allows an emergence of these power games.

But Mário's own ambivalence toward the consequences of his own concepts is obvious in the case of another informant, Jimmy, who also fascinates and repulses Mário—the encounter would become the subject of his column "Taxi" in the *Diário Nacional* (April 13, 1929). Even when the writer recognizes in Jimmy a kind of cosmopolitan experience that sets him apart from the majority, he ruthlessly discredits this "black guy as just like any other one in Paraíba" (1976, 86). The history of this "anyone," we find out, is filled with seasons in France, Italy, and England as a servant of a rich Brazilian traveler who chose Jimmy because of his agreeableness—an association that lasted until the aristocratic traveler, in sudden need of cash, sold him as a slave in Bombay. Brazilian authorities, as soon as they find out through Jimmy's mother about the situation of this citizen, order his repatriation.

The matter that arouses so much astonishment in Mário is that this nobody—who at the time of the interview was working as a watchman for the British railroad company Great Western—vigorously eludes the representative function expected from native informants. Despite the interviewer's praise of his vocal virtuosity, Jimmy declines to sing *cocos* and other native rhythms: "No, Sir! I don't sing that thing! I only sing the *Maedelon*"—a song popular with French soldiers during World War I.[14] "Perfect pronunciation," adds de Andrade, astonished (1983, 375). By "perfect pronunciation" he presumably means "French pronunciation."

Jimmy mobilizes his European allegiances to resist the folkloric scene of interlocution proposed by Mário. The dismissal of his assigned role frustrates the writer's epistemological drive and his inscription of this scandalous subalternity of unexpected, illegitimate attachments. Unable to listen to the subject with whom he is confronted, de Andrade treats Jimmy as acculturated, vain, and pedantic. The contentious exchange might illustrate Doris Sommer's important remark (1999, 20) that "to ask if the subaltern can speak, as Gayatri Spivak had asked, misses a related point. The pertinent question is whether the other party can listen." But clearly, listening doesn't depend on good will alone; it also requires the construction of a conceptual framework able to reveal the situation of interlocution outside subject-object polarities. Mário's mobile traditions, despite being predicated as a theory of confluences, articulation, and contestation in permanent historical process, don't seem to create a space to give credit to a strategic cosmopolitanism that challenges in situ the patronizing design of this cultural encounter. It is notable how Mário persists in his deafness, maybe because of a fundamental connection that it is the purpose of this incapacity to deny. That connection is the alliance between the transnational forces in which Jimmy was immersed (those of British colonial rule and of the struggle of World War I), which are irrecoverable for the conformation and nationalization of mobile traditions, and their role closer to home, with Jimmy's labor for the British railroad company, whose very operation permits Mário's own mobility. The searched-for cultural object cannot contain as such these contradictions, despite the mobility attributed to it—but the travel journal performs, by inscribing voices and silences, the impasses of the culturalist pursuit.

Let's go back to a related moment of the Amazonian trip. Mário travels by train from Madeira to Mamoré, a line with a history of promises of national economic expansion and integration, like all the railroads in Latin America. It is in fact impossible to think of the modern nation without what we can call the chronotope of the train, from which the national space was imagined even before the system's actual implementation.[15] This particular railroad, besides standing symbolically for the conquest of the rain forest, projected a future of Latin American unity across borders, between Brazil and Bolivia.[16] The writer shares the coach with an Indian, whom he refers to as a Pacaá Novo, and with a German. The latter seems convinced, in his metropolitan search for authenticity, that the former is the really true Brazilian, a comment that upsets Mário, who goes on to list to the "silly German" other "true Brazilians" of mixed national origins such as "Líbero Badaró, Grandpa Taunay the painter, João VI, Matarazzo, more than me!"[17]

It is a remarkable entry, one in which Mário carefully abstains from any comment, although the situation is very charged with contesting narratives of nationhood. The Indian also contradicts the German's assumption and assures him that his plan is to marry a true Brazilian, by which he implies a racially mixed *mulata*, and to work as a telegrapher. Nothing seems to slow the march of hybridization, but the progress of this train stalls somewhere along the way. De Andrade confesses his reluctance to go back to the ship, for in the many ports he is obliged to engage in the role of national intellectual, his travel facilitated by regional bureaucracies and financially supported by a progressive elite. Instead, he remembers on the train the immigrant labor that made possible the building of the railroad: "Thousands of Chinese, Portuguese, Bolivians, Barbadians, Italians, Arabs, Greeks, coming for pennies" to make it possible that today "the poet travels with his friends . . . on a very clean car, well accommodated in comfortable seats" and eating "roasted turkey made by a master cook [in English in the original] of the first order, who gets on the train in Vitória, hired by the [British] Amazon River [Company] just to season our lives" (151–52). He goes on listing items of his comfortable mobility (including the act of *codaquizar* ["Kodaking"] the landscape). But beneath his *savoir vivant* of modernist cosmopolitanism that he now regards with disdain and the primitivist metropolitan reason of the German lie other practices that resurge spectrally:

> What did I come to do here! . . . What is the reason for all the international dead that are reborn in the noise of the locomotive and come with their small eyes of weak light to peep at me through the car's little windows? . . . And in Guajará Mirim, around 9 p.m., a reception. Fatigue. There isn't accommodation for everyone. I feed an explosive state of mind. I scarcely speak, making an effort to be unpleasant; I reject things. I refuse to sleep in a private home, I will sleep in the train car! There is no water for a shower. I shower with *cachaça*. And I sleep in the car, heroically, with no fear of malaria or of the dead, with a rabid taste of fraternity on my hands. (152)

A moment of awakening is figured in this reluctance to sleep, in this desire not to fit in with the living, in this dwelling in an impossible site, inside the stories underplayed by the train of history. With his refusal to acquiesce to the official reception and accept comfortable lodging, the writer redoubles the absent history of the international migrant workers who never made it into any redemptive narrative of historical direction. "And I shake myself, monotonous, in what is one of the most horrific railroads in the world" (151). The world appears here with a different face, giving testimony to the fact that the mobility of traditions is intertwined with the movements of capital, commodities, and population.

All sorts of middle passages that this train doesn't take on, of travels that don't fit into the construction of national identity, of trajectories left out of the narrative of the forward-moving train of history, make themselves present through their tangible absence. A train that acquires significance in its immobility gains distance from the nineteenth-century train of historical progress, understood as part of the universal *grand voyage*. But neither is it the early twentieth-century slow train of the lazy tropical civilization nor that of progressive national unity through hybridization. By glancing into a set of alternative cosmopolitan practices that these master narratives silenced, Mário de Andrade constantly questions the assumptions of his own intellectual project and opens his writing to other, undocumented voices.

Another encounter narrated by Andrade will give closure to my reading of the *Turista*. We went from mocking anthropologies to mobile traditions to the instances in which these traditions articulated dissent and on to cosmopolitan practices that reveal a history disjointed from the narratives of progressive hybridization. The Amazon and the *sertão*, the conflictive areas of these travels, are not just incorporated into the cultural map of a diverse nation representing future possibilities and past perils. The mobility of their inhabitants is both geographical and a moving away from the intellectual frames with which they have been granted a subaltern place in modern narratives. In this confrontational dialogue, the map emerging from the journals is not one dotted with signs of the past and the future but rather one marked by present power struggles—as in the story of the Amazonian family who was chosen to represent the Brazilian people for the Ford initiatives in the region.

The family to be photographed was chosen by some executives when Ford was planning to start its own rubber exploitation in the region and hoped to showcase subjects for promoting the healthy living conditions of the area. The father was a man who, despite his malaria, had very handsome offspring. When the family is photographed, the father, ashamed not so much of his sickness but of the chance that his condition might be the sole factor that would deprive the whole region of its promising future, wraps himself in his hammock so as not to be seen. Nevertheless, the chance that the power of the camera may actually reveal what he tried to hide drives this poor man to a permanent state of anxiety. Despite the half-humorous tone of the account—the fascination of the intellectual with this seemingly atavistic, primitive belief—the entry gives testimony not only to a perceived omniscience of transnational corporations as a sort of optical unconscious of the modern world, but also to this man's acute perception of the objectification of his existence, an objectification that no project of national development and prosperous integration could possibly alleviate.

ETCHINGS OF URBAN LIFE

From 1918 until his death in 1942, Roberto Arlt wrote for the newspaper *El Mundo* to produce what constitutes one of the most impressive bodies of journalistic writing of his time. For many years, his signed columns that appeared almost daily and bore the general title "Aguafuerte" (Etching), sometimes also qualified by the location: "porteña" (from Buenos Aires), "patagónica" (from Patagonia, in Argentina), "fluvial" (for his travels along the rivers of the Argentinean littoral), "madrileña" (when in the Spanish capital), and so on. Until very recently, the writer's most celebrated journalistic production were his "Aguafuertes porteñas," where Arlt wrote on characters and places of the city, fascinated by both the typical and the bizarre, molding his artistic persona as a chronicler of daily life.[18] Sometimes picturesque, sometimes denunciatory, the chronicle allowed Arlt to map out different trajectories while establishing his own literary path with his characterizations of multiple corners of the city. The pleasures of recognition and self-recognition are prevalent in his earliest production, especially the Buenos Aires period. Traces of *costumbrismo*, a Hispanic realism focused on sketches of customs and manners, are still present, often showing the impact of positivist sociology and criminology. Marginal subjects (petty thieves, beggars, prostitutes, etc.) are often presented in the chronicles only as colorful component of a rich urban life, satisfying the curiosity of the reader of the column with the respectable distance of a spectacle.

We can locate Arlt's *porteño* period within a context of the cultural sedimentation of a city that grew immensely during the decades before and after the turn of the century, largely because of an influx of European migrants.[19] Urban problems received increasing attention in the press during the 1920s (Gorelik 1998, 309–15), while avant-garde artists fixed their attention on Buenos Aires's particular set of myths and icons. The young Jorge Luis Borges's reconsideration of the city's characters and liminal places in the 1920s evoked this milieu, and his fascination with borders and outlaws was to persist in his work. It might be productive to juxtapose Arlt's *aguafuertes* with the Argentinean critic Beatriz Sarlo's reading (1993) of Borges's poetics of the *orilla*, the edge of the city, a critical-epistemological position standing for the periphery of the West. The archetypes of a universality woven from tango legends and marginal neighborhoods might, by virtue of its unexpected location, challenge European exclusivist claims to universality. But as the critic also makes clear, this investment in the archetypical (and the whole *criollista* strategy of the *Martín Fierro* magazine in which Borges participated) is also devised as a nostalgic countermovement against the growing presence of unrecognizable subjects in the urban landscape.

Arlt's journalistic production weaves particularity and universality differently, since locality stands not as a barrier against global flows, but as the only site where they display their effect and might be contested. While supporting the self-absorption of the city's effort to consolidate its identity, Arlt simultaneously countered this tendency with his permanent attention to what in the social space disrupted a sense of a well-rounded locality. Depictions of odd professions inhabit Arlt's column, but so do the unemployed and underemployed urban denizens, undermining the solidification of identity, upsetting the assigned "occupations" in the literal sense of the assignation of place and function in the labor market. "The crowd of the apparently curious who form a line near the metal curtain" that attracts the attention of the passerby is actually standing in line for a job (Arlt 1981, 173–75). They are not there to satisfy a curiosity but to respond to a necessity, and Arlt's chronicle performs a self-reflective critique of the curious gaze of the walker and the newspaper reader.

Arlt's preference for criminal practices, such as blackmailing and counterfeiting, echoes a romantic, picturesque treatment of marginality favored by some other avant-gardists of the Left (e.g., Raúl González Tuñón), but it also represents an insinuation that every performed identity (including his own as journalist and writer) is already built upon consecrated mechanisms of bad faith and forgery.[20] Immigration fosters these same internal tensions, since the foreigner might appear as an exotic feature in the landscape of the metropolis or might stand for a history of impossible settlements, of worldwide geopolitical displacements that fail to reach a happy ending in the promising South American capital.[21] Moreover, the reader's attention is drawn toward elements of the city that stand in a state of unreadiness, ruins of buildings that were never completed, remnants of projects unfulfilled.

A reference to flânerie seems to be an obligatory critical cliché when dealing with Arlt's criticism in his "Aguafuertes," but I intend to go beyond granting his work a vicarious theoretical prestige. If we are to take the Benjaminian connection to its critical consequences, it doesn't suffice to highlight Arlt's urban roaming, we must attempt to unpack Arlt's particular strategy with respect to the national and urban projects of modernization when he illuminates them in petrified form. Arlt's wanderings drive him to appreciate the indefinitely unfinished quality of some buildings, which stand still "as if the construction had been all of a sudden interrupted by a cosmic strike, something beyond human forces" and ended up being a provisional shelter for the disenfranchised ("Unfinished Houses," 1981, 88).

"During the war," remembers Arlt, "the abominable blacklist left many German families in the streets. And in this ruin, cornered by poverty, a family of my acquaintance found dwelling. But since they were not the owners of the catastrophic house, some Russians also came to live inside, and then the two families had to make an alliance to prevent all the vagrants from [the neighborhood of] Villa Crespo[22] from taking up residence in the infernal house" (1988, 89).

It is difficult to separate, in the image of the house, local catastrophes from global ones. Two different dialectics of modernity conflate in their failure: ruins of European history that, when spreading its debris to the peripheries, encounter the forever pending modernity that has already become ruin. There is no vantage point for understanding this conundrum, which, Arlt seems to suggest, is of cosmic proportions, beyond human comprehension. It performs, again, the paradox of simultaneity. But Arlt's writing of place is engaged in this project of mapping ungraspable cosmic catastrophes.

Whereas in the 1930s the state devoted its efforts at urban modernity to the reconstruction of the historic city-center district in order to counteract a disorganized urban sprawl regarded as devoid of character (Gorelik 1998, 317–37), during this same decade, Arlt moved more and more out of the center to explore the city's edges. But he was not searching like Borges for that mythical marginality of the *orilleros* as an enclave against an increasingly unrecognizable city. In "Abandoned Cranes on Maciel Island" (June 5, 1933), the truth encoded in the landscape of this obscure and outlying part of Buenos Aires—an industrial area that is part of the structure of the city's port and therefore a pivotal point of larger economic circuits—doesn't rest on its cultural distinctiveness. "In certain directions, at eleven in the morning on the island, it seems to be three in the afternoon. You can't tell if you're on the edge of Africa or on the outskirts of a new city in Alaska. But it is apparent that the ferments of a growing civilization are being forged amid the sound of strange languages and the overalls of workers who slowly cross roads paralleling train tracks that lead who knows where" (1981, 64).

Echoing ready-made narratives (exoticism and civilization's grandeur are brought to the scene for the reader to savor and admire), the vision attempts nevertheless to name the radical difference that blasts established dichotomies between urban and rural, center and periphery, tradition and modernity, and that leads ultimately to a messianic tone, the announcement of something new to come. The organic "growth" within the barren decay of this vision points to something beyond progress and decline, beyond an already attempted novelty (of the new technology, of a powerful economy), the gigantic presence of a pending dream.

As if a different, more radical newness could only be figured through the archaic, Arlt keeps describing the landscape: "the most noteworthy spectacle upon entering the island . . . is a guard made of twenty steel giants, dead and menacing in the sky. . . . They are twenty cranes that until a few years ago were working in front of the coast of the capital. One day it happened that the [British meat-processing] company built new cold-storage plants that made them obsolete, and since that day they have not moved an inch" (1981, 64). The spectacle of journalism, the phantasmagoric quality of its production of novelty, is defied here by the presentation of a stagnant remnant of the past, of artifacts left behind by the production line that no longer feed the direction of the present.[23] Arlt incorporates hints of the desire for urban spectacle that he is called to fulfill in the iterable and consumable presentation of his column, but by the same token, he delivers what can be rightly called a dialectical image in the Benjaminian sense.[24] In the place where the construction of past utopias persists in their ruined state, among abandoned and collapsing leftovers, the train tracks retain a shadow of unidirectional progress. This concrete space thwarts its own commodification, not by virtue of its localized isolation, but rather because in its presence as the persistence of an already eradicated past, it has retained traces of an imagined future.[25] Again, it is as if a cosmic force had struck—"one day it happened that the company built new plants"—and the anonymous mobility of the British capital that managed the meat industry leaves behind the fossilized print of its presence. This border can be called a "contact zone," if we are to follow the postcolonial theoretical emphasis on sites of cultural negotiations, but only to point out that this is not a zone of successful mixes but rather a ruinous, phantasmagoric realm, an effect of the expansion of capital that is always ready to relocate.[26] In this, this zone might not be the exception. The "skeletons of dromedaries in the desert," the wheels that "seem to petrify on their axles" (1981, 65) mark the return of what exists against the background of time once the glimmer and charm of the hopeful present is lost.

It is not just about ruins as a baroque moment of disillusion with an order (and here the order is historically specific: Argentina as an exporter of meat and other staple goods). Unlike the perspective of unused commodities that awakes the metropolitan flâneur from the hypnotic phantasmagoria of displayed commodities (window shops, advertisements), Arlt's vision is awaked by abandoned means of production in the peripheries (of the bourgeois city, and of the world). And a preoccupation with the means of production might be found throughout Arlt's work (as we saw in chapter 3), as well as in his more civic emphasis on the economic development in many of his chronicles.[27] Arlt's noteworthy taste for frenetic activity—which ranges from business, shows, and nightlife all the way to crime as a mark of a vital impulse—has no place here, since the image of the outmoded cranes freezes in time their former dynamism.

"The metaphysics of the railway is the metaphysics of linear history," proposes Agnes Heller (1993, 222), pointing to the iconic value of this fascination with a naturalized force of the locomotive that seems not to be subjected to anyone's agency. Arlt's images of the tracks and the crane thus have a profound resonance in the iconography of modernity. The vacant tracks of uncertain destination, the overwhelming absence dominating this landscape, seem to freeze for an instant both the forward movement toward industrial development and technological mastery and the backward movement to the mythological pampas or the peripheral barrios. Like a flash passing through the steel structures of modernity, the writer illuminates for a brief instant not a site of fulfillment but a site of abjection. In this forgotten place, where the means of production are a rusty waste, consumption itself has become abject: "A cook from a barge wakes up a vagrant, while shouting at him to offer him leftovers" (1981, 65).

The Marxian concept of commodity fetishism implies an operation of obscuring the sites of production in the moment of consumption. Benjamin develops the consequences of this mechanism in order to highlight the intervention of the logic of representation, since commodity fetishism points not only to the replacement of use value by exchange value, but also, more radically, to the submission of both to symbolic value, evident in the exhibition of commodities.[28] Arlt maps these obscured moments from a geographically specific site of writing: Walking around the edges of a peripheral city that has failed to achieve its dreamed place in the world circulation of commodities, he finds what wasn't meant for exhibition but is now brutally present—the site of production in its demise, circulation left vacant, and consumption as a repulsive spectacle. Nothing is veiled or fetishized in this obscene presentation. On the contrary, everything seems to be present here, like an open wound after a blast that disrupted and disarranged the organic functions.

This site of writing is also part of a correlated symbolic economy. The representation of the countryside as a seat of inexpugnable autochthony—a traditional trope for the Argentine intellectual bourgeoisie and one that acquired new force in the 1930s—also experiences a setback. The international circulation of commodities is the hidden face of the labors presented as archaic ritualistic remains, paradigms of authenticity looked upon as a national spectacle in the instantly canonized novel by Ricardo Güirales *Don Segundo Sombra* (1926): the taming of horses, the cattle drives, and so on. By his analytic portrait of the site where production (the meat industry), consumption (of leftovers), and circulation converge, presented as the unassembled fragments of a broken machine, Arlt charts a constellation of roles in an economy that can't be melded together through the cultural turn of a peripheral *orilla* or contact zone.

Tempted by strolling around the port of Buenos Aires, Arlt embarks on a freighter that calls at different Argentinean ports, and on board he continues to write what he now dubs "aguafuertes fluviales."[29] Negotiating his new position, he mocks the tourist's obligation to endure a "bothersome social life" and prefers instead to travel with workers, as his travel is also work-related.[30] Three years earlier, in 1930, the writer had made a brief, disappointing foreign incursion into Uruguay and Brazil. Neither a wealthy, properly dressed Argentinean nor a prestigious European, he had reached the conclusion soon after the ship departed that "my psychology is of a third-class passenger," but he was already booked in first class (chronicle of February 21, 1930). In a chronicle called "Argentinos en Europa" (1981, 232), he had taken issue with the peripheral subject, dazzled with "indigenous admiration" for Roman ruins and Parisian cafés without noticing "the millions of people that live exercising thousands of different occupations." No doubt, Arlt's provocative accusation of the Argentinean bourgeoisie as "indigenous" itself perpetuates the white man's notion of the Amerindian as reduced to a position of mimicking awe. But more interesting than accusing Arlt, I believe, is noting the way in which the recurrence of the realm of production as an epistemological standpoint disarrays social hierarchies existing between him and whoever is the subject of his inquiry, whether high-cultured Europeans, Argentinean sailors, or Amerindians.

Nevertheless, the expectations of a certain distance and epistemological superiority when he is sent to depict life in the backward provinces for a Buenos Aires newspaper can't be so easily ignored by Arlt. And toward the end of the 1933 trip, allegedly as a result of letters from readers complaining about the superficial representation of the cultures he encountered, he assumes the position of a tourist in relation to an economy of gazing. Arlt defends his vision as a "cinematographic" one.[31] The motivation to initiate this trip "was born after I began to walk around the port and observe, in the most superficial way possible, the kind of life that seemed to take up those on board the barges and pontoons" (*El Mundo*, August 10, 1933). In Resistencia (the capital of Chaco province, with a strong Amerindian presence), he complains about the postcards portraying the population in their condition as aboriginals, since the only natives he has seen were more easily identified as working class. Against the accusation of being superficial, he defends his position by taking up the accusation and recasting it as a way to distance himself from the roles of cultural traveler and ethnographic inquisitor that he is expected to embody.[32]

It could be said that if he did not see aboriginal peoples, it was because he failed to enter more deeply into the indigenous cultures of the coast, and one could accuse Arlt, just as some of his supposed readers did, of lightness. But one has to listen to Arlt's call for a uniform modernity, with neither uneven development nor local temporality and differential cultural gardens, in order to understand the implications of his rejection of the depth of culture and its replacement with the machinery of production. He distances himself from the educated reader who desires some degree of empathy with the Indians and expects the reporter to perform the translational work of producing a national identity as a colorful mosaic. For that reason, in the final note on his travels to the coast, in addition to presenting his vision as superficial once again and as not penetrating and cultural, he makes clear that what he saw and observed was the unmitigated fact that on the coast, there existed great economic misery, high unemployment, and a lack of cargo to transport.

In the ubiquity of production, the homogeneity that Arlt presents permits him to escape the subordinated "indigenous" or cultural position: something like: "Here, just as there, there is production, and not culture—which is what downtrodden people are allowed to make." Moreover, it is what prevents the exercise of epistemological superiority—the superiority of the cosmopolitan avant-garde, of the cultural traveler—as he places himself and his writing within the friction of the machinery of production as it operates for the great majority.

When Roberto Arlt ceased to call his column "Aguafuertes," upon returning to Buenos Aires from a yearlong trip through Spain, he began to write another column called "Tiempos presentes" (Present times) during the early months of 1937, and around October it began to be called "Al margen del cable" (On the margins of the newswire). The differential handling of distances made possible by his positioning within the communication networks was the condition of Arlt's writing once he returned to Argentina from his travels through Spain, where he had witnessed the advent of the civil war.[33]

The switch from the title emphasizing presence (Tiempos presentes) to a title that highlights a movable, relative perspective is symptomatic of a preoccupation with what I have been calling positionality. Arlt strives to render proximal events occurring far away. In a strategy that could be called telescopic, Arlt's handling of distance departs from the perception of the numbing, spectacular dimension of newscasting. Aware that even the rise of fascism and the beginning of World War II have little effect on the anesthetized sensibility of readers, he focuses instead on what goes on within homes and on the psychology of families who live under the threat of deadly gasses and aerial strikes. When Arlt travels, he insists on the superficiality of his examination, and he identifies with the camera. When he works at the newspaper, he presents his writing as a means of mediating between the coldness of telegraphic reports and direct experience. He takes disengaged news reporting and examines it as if through a magnifying lens, defamiliarizing it by bringing to life and bringing near the depersonalized events of the newswire.

But it is also clear that by means of his strategic position in the information networks, the events of the world seem to him increasingly interrelated. In the newsroom, he tries to capture a logic that for him is worldly.

It is the place where he is no longer concerned with whether he is in the south or in the north, in a sleepy town or at the center of a metropolis, since now he is dealing with the roar of a unified world. Certainly, Arlt laments the fact that he is no longer bearing the direct witness that characterized his journalistic persona. But nowhere will eyewitness experience be more complete than in the mediated "no place" of the newsroom. Arlt anticipates a position that is not the one of the newspaper reader but that falls closer to our own contemporary relation to streams of information, assembling pieces and magnifying bits to solve the puzzle of a worldwide dynamic and to engage his reader in the narrative. The purported neutrality of these streams hide their character as sites of discursive struggle, and it is as such that Arlt engages with them.

News that an explorer, a Soviet aviator, had reached the North Pole provided Arlt with an occasion to exercise this combination of critical approach and distance (June 5, 1937). "It might occur to someone to go to the North Pole by submarine. To someone else, to set a new record for height in outer space. . . . A piece of news. Three lines. A photograph. A name. And on to something else." Notice the switch from the means of transportation to the means of communication. The modernist anxiety about the ending of the era of the voyage, the flight to distant places with the tragic awareness that their mystery is fading from the earth, is reconfigured here as a factor of communication technology that brings distant things near.[34] It is indeed from the perspective of the reader of the newspaper that this conquest and the advance of technology that speeded up the process in the first place is no longer a source of astonishment and admiration. It doesn't even arouse much interest, because "we are far today from those times of Peary and Cook, whose simultaneous discovery of the North Pole provoked debates in the newspapers more vicious than what most contemporary events provoked."

Arlt's journalistic camera does not focus on the goings on of this new expedition in order to inject it with an emotional element lacking in the "three lines" of a wire story, but instead focuses on the relationship between space and history, a relationship aptly exemplified, it would seem, by this trip to the North Pole. The illusion created by speeding up communication is that of coordinated simultaneity, of a world unified by the availability of information. The newspaper, far from being a site for reflection, has come to hamper thinking by bringing the news in a fleeting instant before going on to the next novelty. That is, simultaneity not as mapping but as spectacle. Arlt presents this phantasmagoric homogenization pessimistically, for if, as the title announces and the last line of the column iterates, "the North Pole is no longer in the North Pole," is there any alternative, desirable direction for modernity, that is, any space whose conquest we can expect hopefully? The network of communication that covers the planet has undone distances, and there are no longer any utopically empty spaces where human imagination can project the achievement of a universal history and colonize the future.

It is remarkable that during the same decade, the North Pole was also a metaphor for historical inquiry in Walter Benjamin's *Arcades Project*: "Comparison of other people's attempts to the undertaking of a sea voyage in which the ships are drawn off course by the magnetic North Pole. Discover this North Pole. What for others are deviations are, for me, the data which determine my course. On the differentials of time (which, for others, disturb the main lines of inquiry), I base my reckoning" (2003, 456). Roberto Arlt, too, was attracted by unpredictable directions, not in order to dwell on the margins (of the news cable and of the metropolis), but to render glimpses of a totality from there.

The shadow of fascism is no doubt on the horizon of Arlt's claim that humankind has become more insensitive, while "the horror of the present civilization has quintupled in just a few years." The ambiguous anxiety present at the end of the article ("Is it perhaps that other North Poles, more glacial and flashy, are hypnotizing the eyes of humanity with their new auroras?") negotiates the line between utopia and dystopia, as if to show the universality of a floating, aspirational, yearning mode whose goals remain nevertheless unclear, whose fulfillment is as desirable as it is dreadful.

Trying to think, like Benjamin, through the "differentials of time," Arlt linked them to the differentials of geographical location. Arlt's disdain for the local—his insistence that production encompasses all and his interest in the flat photographic perspective—is a critique of the idea of cultural autonomy as the site of contestation, but this critique is complemented by a logic of geographical location as the only available vantage point. The problem becomes apparent in many articles—for example, in "El pesador de monedas" (The weigher of coins) of March 13, 1937, where Arlt rescues and amplifies an unremarkable newswire item and describes what can be read as an inverted mirroring of the writer's strategy during the 1930s. The column reflects on a studious collector of antique medals and coins, Percy Webb, who, strategically placed far from the action of the world, the better to study what falls out of circulation and separate fakes from genuine artifacts, dies in London "with the same indifference that made monotonous his life of half a century, distant from all the anxieties of humanity." During World War I,

> men fell by the thousands in the battlegrounds. Airplanes and zeppelins flew over London, and deadly gasses were invented, the stealthy submarine reached gigantic proportions, and electrical waves crossed the planet right and left. His Majesty the Czar of Russia was shot and His Majesty the Emperor of Germany left for Holland to dedicate himself to growing fruit. Communism and fascism appeared on the planet . . . and Mr. Percy H. Webb continued as Secretary of the Royal Numismatic Society, looking down his nose at coins of dubious origin.

In this differential positioning—Webb's and that implied by the reporter—I see two kinds of universalism. Instead of being a collector and assessor of those things that are out of circulation, Arlt places himself where circulation is constant. Instead of withdrawing from the world in search of a secure site to ponder, Arlt can be seen during these years as an echo chamber for all the sound and fury of the world. Like Webb, he is fascinated by fakes and falsifications, although without the intention of separating the false from the real: On the contrary, Arlt emphasizes the possibilities of circulating what is false and explores the mechanisms of authentication.[35] Webb and Arlt share the same world, but from different epistemic positions, two different ways of handling critical distance. The first, resting upon the edifice of a fading imperial power, builds his vantage point from the world-ranging institutional practices that sustain this power (Webb is even decorated as a member of the Order of the British Empire) and acts from a world where the debris of history accumulates slowly, in an orderly fashion, unidirectionally. The Latin American writer, from a marginal position with no authorization for all-encompassing outlooks, does not offer a calm analysis, but collects a series of snapshots taken at varied distances from the object. Master narratives and institutionalized grand perspectives do not secure his intermittent but consistent mapping, his exercise of reading a world dynamic from the interstitial places he managed to carve out.

■ **Chapter 6**

Cosmopolitanism and Repentance
The Homecoming of the Avant-Garde Poet

Our first declaration of war must be against the philosophies of return.

José Carlos Mariátegui, *Mundial*, Lima, March 29, 1930

AVANT-GARDES in Latin America purposely and sometimes defiantly eschewed nativist narratives and every construction of inexpugnable cultural origins, favoring instead a sensitivity toward the global dynamic of cultural production that informed their sense of place. In the 1940s, however, many of the avant-gardists who are more easily identified as cosmopolitan, who formerly resented or simply avoided any narrow sense of local attachment, found themselves longing for places of identification to call home. Moreover, this reaction against their own former cosmopolitan, ironic regard toward native values was typically charged with a remorseful affect, as if a manic sense of free access to the house of the modern was to be followed by a melancholic reparation of things broken at home. Or to put it differently, it is as if the investment in certain promises of modernity (associated with an open-ended history, possibility, movement, vitality, novelty, individual freedom, etc.), when combined with a sense of local attachment, led inevitably to a dismissal of the emancipatory aspirations that the former modernist faith announced.

It is in fact a common understanding of Latin American literary historiography that the 1940s represent a decade tinged by the idea of return and of searches for origins. As expressed by González Echevarría, "the Latin America [of the 1940's] was, for intellectuals and artists who . . . had experienced the European avant-garde, a place for rebirth and reimmersion." No doubt, historical sea changes in Europe partially triggered this cultural shift. The rise of fascism, the defeat of a Hispanic version of socialism in Spain, and the beginnings of World War II are factors in an historical conjunction that paved the way for "one of the most significant [phenomena] in modern Latin American cultural history" (González Echevarría 1993, 98–99). Its significance for the literary culture of the continent partially rests upon the role that this "rebirth" played in the conceptualization of *lo real maravilloso* (1949) by Alejo Carpentier[1]—an aesthetic introduced by this author as the authentic New World alternative to the exhausted magic of European surrealism—and the consequent emergence of magic realism and the Latin American "boom" in the 1960s.

The significance of this aesthetic doesn't rest upon the return itself but upon making of homecoming the key to a broader mapping that transcends the rhetoric of an organic homeland. *Lo real maravilloso* is always entangled in the historical, aesthetic, and epistemological consequences of the colonial encounter. The continuing reenactment of this clash is what keeps returning. Despite the fact that *lo real maravilloso* was proposed as a break with surrealism, we can trace a continuity, albeit a contentious one, between the avant-garde texts that I have analyzed and the aesthetic politics of *lo real maravilloso*, a continuity that doesn't depend on the development of European modernisms or on decontextualized stylistic features.

This development shaped the way Latin American literature—and by extension, a notion of the region's culture as a whole—would be packaged for international literary markets. As a result, there was a pervasive tendency to read this trajectory within the general scheme of a dialectical process in which the final point constitutes the achievement of a synthetic balance between modernity and tradition, cosmopolitanism and nativism, universalism and particularism. But this tendency had an antecedent in the dismissal of cosmopolitanism by Peruvian cultural critic José Carlos Mariátegui, who, in the seminal 1928 essay "The Process of Literature," which set the key in which to write literary historiography of Latin America, referred to cosmopolitanism as a provisional stage in a teleology of self-achievement. The term names for Mariátegui a period that, following one of mostly innocuous imitation of metropolitan Spanish literary culture (save for a few figures such as Inca Garcilaso), is characterized by the incorporation of modern literary influences from Europe. This process represents a necessary step toward a real national literature characterized by a certain present-oriented *indigenismo*—not pursuing a return to an indigenous ideal, but engaging in the vindication of a cause. A maturation of the national literary character would succeed the stages of mimicry and incorporation. The essay concludes: "Through universal, ecumenical paths . . . we are approaching ourselves more and more" (Mariátegui 1969, 325). The path from cosmopolitanism to a new nativism, in some narratives of integration and achievement, was mediated in the 1930s by a trend toward social engagement and revolutionary or internationalist politics—often depicted as a return to more humanistic concerns—from which an embrace of the local would naturally follow.[2] This dialectical transition toward self-achievement is often elaborated through a particular notion of transculturation, a transculturation that Angel Rama's elaborations in the 1970s, dividing the cultural field between *los transculturadores* and *los cosmopolitas*, only helped to make explicit. In this process, the artist or the intellectual is seen as the privileged agent of translation between the appropriation of the foreign and the native.

My reading intends to unsettle all these narratives of transition. I will attempt in this chapter to use the critical tools introduced by the avant-gardes in Latin America in order to pose an alternative to the fluctuating opposition of home and abroad, attachment and detachment, organic wholes and decadent fragmentation, identity and alienation—the site of cultural mediation to which literature has been destined. The long-standing critique of the privileges of detachment enjoyed by the intellectual elite—a critique that these avant-gardists themselves pursued in one or other of their populist (re)turns—has already changed the face of Latin American cultural criticism, and now it is time to move on. I have been showing the complexities of artistic projects that can't be reduced either to the construction of a new creole national hegemony that expropriates the popular or to an abstract identification with metropolitan tendencies. Instead of commemorating the reconstitution of a nativist spirit in the

1930s and 1940s as an achievement in the grand narrative of identity construction, dismissing cosmopolitan preoccupations as akin to sheer alienation or mimicry, or celebrating mimicry as the postcolonial strategy par excellence, I will investigate in this chapter the possibility of a sense of place informed by the geopolitical insights of the 1920s.

This is where the concept of cosmopolitanism plays a key role, and it is time to expand its reach beyond a celebration of a free-floating individualism. I have been purposely using the concept to characterize different practices and artistic projects, not in order to conflate their positions but to show their interconnectedness and ultimately to highlight some radical differences. If, on the one hand, cosmopolitanism accentuates individuality, on the other, it points to an embodied universalism that is always under construction. Although much of what passed for cosmopolitanism certainly can be equated with a simple, unidirectional admiration for European culture, the concept is also relevant to the effort to imagine strategies of postcolonial contestation, because they are necessarily based on a self-reflective, nonorganic understanding of belonging that opens the capacity for cultural actors to adopt different viewpoints and go beyond their local alliances to converse across borders. If it is true that avant-garde cosmopolitanism navigated between these two poles, it is also the case that the intellectual project recently identified with postcolonialism—questioning the reproduction of epistemological subordination worldwide—has a strong antecedent in the contributions of the avant-gardes.

Let us start by conceptualizing this era of cosmopolitan enthusiasm, coming back later to what is implied in its dismissal. Avant-garde cosmopolitanism in the 1920s, as the critic Jorge Schwartz has observed in his study on the phenomenon, *Vanguardia y cosmopolitismo en la década del veinte* (Avant-garde and cosmopolitanism in the 1920s, 1993), is predicated on an emphatic affirmation of an urban lifestyle. Whereas the whole enterprise of the regionalist novel during the same decade was based on a negative understanding of the city as either a purely Weberian space of achieved secular homogeneity or a site of fragmentation and decadence, thus denying the space of the city any differential value to which some sense of identity could be tied, the avant-garde cityscape clung to the a notion of universal spatial diversity.

True, it is easy to observe in many poems of the avant-garde that the space of the city is ordered in an imaginary, world-embracing web that, as an allegory of the modern lifestyle, is suggested by the chaotic enumeration of significant toponyms that render visible the promised universality of the modern era.[3] These poems achieve a sense of unity via the transformation of asynchrony into simultaneity, of fragmentation into vivid collage, of difference into spectacular diversity.[4] This is one of the modes of cosmopolitanism that Schwartz studies, primarily in the work of Oliverio Girondo and Oswald de Andrade, but variants of it are also present in the work of some of the most influential artists of the era (poets Vicente Huidobro, Manuel Maples Arce, Alberto Hidalgo, Nicolás Guillén, Luis Cardoza y Aragón, and painters Tarsila do Amaral, Xul Solar, Joaquín Torres García, Diego Rivera, etc.). Embracing the cityscape allows the artist something like a free flight to witness the varied surface of the world, a perspective that doesn't invite in-depth analyses but that rather privileges snapshots of convivial fragmentary perspectives. This circulation is warranted, more than by the often praised new means of transportation or communication, by the position of the (predominantly male) writer who grants himself the chance (in the words of Schwartz [1993, 17]), "to adopt any fatherland . . . to speak in various languages" while keeping his integrity intact—the writer who, in order to match his cosmopolitan ideal, must safeguard his equally distant viewpoint.[5]

The urban location is, no doubt, a symbolic overcoming of native boundaries whose particularity is inscribed into a collage of universality constructed by parts and held together in a studied distance from the wanderer's eye. The strategy is also at work when the poet focuses on a particular city, since the city of his or her affection comes to symbolize any city as the space of convergence of different spaces and times. In "Santiago, ciudad" by female Chilean poet Winétt de Rokha, the Chilean capital is apostrophized:

> Se produce vida en ti, como en Constantinopla,
> en París, en Londres, en Ginebra, en Nueva York, en Roma;
> te visitan los acontecimientos y las estrellas,
> y acaso una canción sin nombre
> o el nombre milenario de una canción.

> Life is produced in you, as in Constantinople,
> in Paris, in London, in Geneva, in New York, in Rome;
> you are visited by events and by stars
> and perhaps by a song without a name
> or the ancient name of a song. (Grünfeld 1995, 254)[6]

This literary strategy is especially relevant when we consider that it constitutes a giant step away from the kind of cosmopolitanism exercised by Hispanic American turn-of-the-century *modernistas*, who preserved a cultural geopolitical hierarchy that placed Europe at the top. Even when they favored an idiosyncratic appropriation of French artistic trends in order to challenge the cultural status quo internally (since they rebelled against the cultural hegemony of the Christian Hispanism and conservative nationalism of the patrician elites), their critique remained attached to Europe's cultural hegemony. In that respect, avant-garde cosmopolitanism unfolded a potential emancipatory drive vis-à-vis the same elites, but also cleared the epistemological ground to enable a critical stance toward inherited cultural hierarchies at a global level. Cosmopolitans started with the certainty of a radical simultaneity, as the "Actual Number 1" manifesto (posted in the streets of Puebla, Mexico, in 1921) suggests when it declares, "Let's cosmopolitanize ourselves.... We have already arrived.... Everything comes closer and farther in the affected moment. The environment is transformed and its influence modifies everything" (Schneider, 45).

There is a tendency to imagine cosmopolitan viewpoints as fervently opposed to nationalist ones. I will discuss this perspective by taking issue with the aforementioned book by Jorge Schwartz, both because it is the most thorough study of cosmopolitanism in Latin American avant-gardes and because it falls into a common deadlock. The critic defines cosmopolitanism in a purely negative way: that is, what is not anchored in the search for or mere assumption of native values as an aesthetic program. He posits cosmopolitanism as a reaction against the nationalist ideologies of the eighteenth century in the European context. But to regard cosmopolitanism, as Schwartz does, as a kind of universal "opening of cultural frontiers" that tries to overcome a "violent nationalist ideology" (17) overlooks many important issues in Latin American cultural history. The kind of vindication of avant-garde cosmopolitanism advanced by Schwartz tends to share a cosmopolitan enthusiasm that runs the risk of neglecting the historical fact that, needless to mention, violent ideologies are at work in the opening of cultural frontiers, as well.

Even if we forget for a moment the history of the violent opening of territorial and cultural frontiers, the process of building national ideologies is always engaged in operations translating constitutive heterogeneities into an overarching, dominant language through which differences are imaginarily overcome. On the other hand (to start where Schwartz does, skipping for the sake of practicality the discussion of ancient cosmopolitanisms), the eighteenth century in Europe was certainly the time of the "cosmopolitan purpose" posited by Immanuel Kant in his two seminal articles, "Idea of a Universal History with a Cosmopolitan Purpose" (1991a) and "Perpetual Peace: A Philosophical Sketch" (1991b).[7]

In Kant's view, cosmopolitanism is an ideal within a general conception of teleological historicism, a progressive march of humanity toward rational government drawn upon the Northern European model. Furthermore, cosmopolitanism and nationalism are not contradictory terms in Kant's philosophy, and he develops his anthropology of the empirical subject accordingly, as well as his critiques of the transcendental subject of rationality.[8] At the historical conjuncture of the worldwide inception of the national form, cosmopolitanism and nationalism were thus logically linked. They epitomized ways to imagine the universal language of politics via a model of representation in an articulation of differences that is founded on an eventual superseding of all such differences through progressive rationality; or, complementarily, via the assumption of the convivial translatability of these differences, opening the door to thinking cultural diversity.[9] Nationalism and nativism might be grounded as much as cosmopolitanism upon the same predicament of translation of cultural differences from a transcendental (or ironic) distance, but cosmopolitanism makes evident these negotiations, while the former two are predicated upon their dismissal.

An unacknowledged cosmopolitanism—if we hold a partial but operative definition of the concept as a process of translation and self-reflective distancing from primary attachments—was also at work in a new inception of the Latin Americanist ideal at the time of the avant-gardes—no longer presented as a transhistorical spirit (Latin American, Hispanic, native, or otherwise), but identified with a moveable perspective. Mexican poet Carlos Pellicer provides a good example when calling for the same instruments of detachment of which cosmopolitan futurism was so fond. His post as private secretary to Mexico's minister of education, José Vasconcelos, a promoter of a new "cosmic" racial hybridity, offered the poet many chances for cultural mediation. Moved by the repeated experience of landing in Brazil, for example, Pellicer is prone to imagine the continent from an airplane. "Mas desde el aeroplano se medita en la gloria / de unir banderas y cantar canciones./ Se ve hasta el polo Sur [But from the airplane one ponders the glory / of uniting flags and singing songs./ One can see all the way to the South Pole]"—a vision that is finally revealed as a "síntesis del Continente amado [synthesis of the beloved continent]." From the heights, the poet summarizes, "la patria es continentalizable [the fatherland is continentalizable]" (88–90). As we see, the technology that sustains the traveling cosmopolitan is also a pillar of this bird's-eye perspective, posited as a privileged mechanism of translatability and transparency for the ideal of Latin Americanism, which becomes identified with the native fatherland by means of a strategic detachment.

It might seem that the subject who promotes this aerial vision could have perfectly well endorsed a globalized one, but the affective charge of his "fatherland" keeps him grounded in this sudden continentalism achieved at a distance. However, this distance, in order to ensure a glorification of the spiritual dimension of Latin Americanism, negates itself. His is a practical example of how cosmopolitanism and nativism (whether regional, national, or Latin American) can be different but ultimately continuous ways to open frontiers, and no charge of violence can be automatically ascribed to any form of detachment. It follows that in order to differentiate this cosmopolitanism from nativism of different kinds, it is necessary to open up the definition sketched above and add that cosmopolitanism—besides being aware of the self-reflective distance that every sense of belonging implies and of the process of translation that this awareness brings about—tends to diversify places of identification to include distant and removed, natural and unnatural ones. This practice, in order to remain cosmopolitan, cannot aim at the conflation of difference, but should leave a gap open, an acknowledgment of a certain untranslatability. In Pellicer's case, if this process stops within Latin American horizons, it is no doubt in order to subsume all differences into a purported, celebrated unity. Significantly, these overcome differences are all imagined as already "nationalized" ones, inscribed by the symbol of the united flags.

The cultural shift of the 1940s, to which I will return soon, had an important antecedent in the 1900s, when the Uruguayan critic José Enrique Rodó hinted that the acclaimed Nicaraguan poet Rubén Darío was not a true Latin American poet.[10] Poet and cultural critic confront each other here as different social roles and subjective positions in a struggle to define the location of Latin American culture. The charge made by Rodó, the self-proclaimed ambassador of a new Latin Americanism, generated a partial revision of the poet's aesthetic program, at least momentarily bracketing the quest for ideal beauty and supreme freedom in the aesthetic realm and bringing forth the both self-accusatory and self-defensive "Yo soy aquel que ayer nomás decía [I am the one who just yesterday used to say]," the line that opens his *Cantos de vida y esperanza* (Songs of Life and Hope, 1905).

The poet had to reposition himself regarding where to locate a Latin American poetics, and more and more Hispanic and indigenous cultural references would be aligned in his poetry with classical European ones. He thus incorporated the position of the critic—who is allegedly more rooted in and attuned to the business of identity—via a subjective division, producing a new synthesis through retrospective self-reflection. This tense coupling is sustained by a new ethic of literary production now more concerned with the idea of authenticity, elaborated as a return to local, particular, identitarian, originary quests, a disavowal of past pleasures and vanities in favor of a rhetoric of honesty and depth, all of which is crowned by a gesture of remorse and repentance, as if something had been irrecoverably wasted in previous poetic quests. The importance of the dynamic I am tracing becomes apparent if one considers the regular insistence of these arguments in the debates about Latin American modernity. In particular, the trajectory sketched here was rehearsed again in the late avant-garde poetics of the 1940s, when the poets become suspicious of their own cosmopolitan betrayal. Arguably, the ever-changing dichotomies that were played out in the defense of the local against absorption or subordination by foreign forces reproduce the same blind spot, since this defense necessarily predicates a local alignment (national or Latin American) that denies the power of forces operating within that locality. I will sketch these dichotomies in several avant-garde intellectual projects to arrive at a notion of cosmopolitanism that eschews them.[11]

Although the narrative of return alludes to that of Ulysses striving to recover his native abode and overcome the threat of becoming someone else, a stranger even to himself (and the actual reference to *The Odyssey* appears often in the corpus I am focusing on, as will be seen), the unnamed story that seems to be underpinning the poetic quest is that of the prodigal son, with its moral chastising of the indulgence of dangerous desires, the abandonment of the primary communitarian bond, and the consequent reinforcement of obedience to paternal law.[12] A critical drive is of course central to post-Romantic poetics, but in 1940s Latin America this critique was advanced toward the poet's former aesthetic choices and intellectual allegiances. That self-critique is not in the mode of poetic self-reflection or of ironic self-consciousness, but appears as a punitive consciousness identified with the communal bond, a consciousness that looks back particularly toward its former cosmopolitan production and reads it as deviant, egotistic, wrong-headed. Or, to put it in the words of the ex-avant-gardist Jorge Carrera Andrade (2000, 187) (who had portrayed his poetic persona of the 1920s as a "Man from Ecuador under the Eiffel Tower"), "En los más diversos idiomas / Sólo aprendí la soledad / Me gradué de doctor en sueños / Vine a América a despertar [In the most diverse languages / I learned only solitude / And I graduated as doctor in dreams. / I came to America to wake up]."

In this poem, written during the 1940s and named, significantly, "Viaje de retorno" (Return voyage), the dream of a monolithic Latin America transcends, through its territorial unity and purported simplicity, the biblical condemnation of language divisions and redirects the poetic first person toward a forgotten, shamefully abandoned unity. As we can see, the narrative of return restores unity through a performative negation of cosmopolitan irony, sophistication, individualism, and detachment, and it constitutes the end of a teleological movement that inscribes the identitarian, nativist quest into the poet's concerns.[13] A remorseful consciousness, although in each case referring to a former abandonment of the tangible reality of the native land, might instead be the result of the repression of critical insight with regard to identitarian attachments (as always strategic, never fixed) gained from the cosmopolitan position of "diverse languages." Or, to put it differently, the retrospective critique of former intellectual projects spares the present recuperated nativism from any exercise of critical vision, and thus the gained unity is predicated upon a mechanism of scapegoating.

I will examine how this dynamic plays out in other major Latin American vanguard poets, mapping out their local and cosmopolitan attachments to unfold their implications. The cosmopolitanism-nationalism polarity seems to be widespread in Brazilian literary historiography of the modernist movement. Already in the 1920s, cosmopolitanism and universalism, in the mouths of regionalists and right-wing nationalists (later to develop into the Verde-Amarelo protofascist vanguard), had become accusations intended to disqualify the whole *modernista* enterprise. In the core São Paulo *modernista* group of the 1920s, Oswald de Andrade constructed a kind of nationalism that was processed through his self-assigned role as globetrotter cosmopolitan (whereas Mário de Andrade never left Brazilian territory, as mentioned earlier), and in the 1930s, he switched to a left-wing internationalist position.

It was within the tradition of the Latin American intellectual voyager that Oswald constructed his literary persona. His poetic prose of this decade is partially a carnavalization of the Latin American lettered cosmopolitan tradition. Both *Memórias sentimentais de João Miramar* (The sentimental memories of João Miramar, 1923) and *Serafim Ponte Grande* (Serafim Grosse Point, written in 1929, published in 1933) are centered on parodic poetic alter egos whose longing for traversing geographical distance is inscribed in their names.[14] Both characters are nineteenth-century aristocrats, well-traveled and embarked on international journeys. Each work is sarcastically framed as a failed, fragmentary, parodic Bildungsroman, as if to close the age of languishing European longings and promising the arrival of new cultural actors and new circuits of cultural exchange. But since Oswald himself was problematically related to the decadent character he mocks (he was himself an international traveler with aristocratic affiliations and lectured at the Sorbonne about Brazilian culture), his conversion to left-wing internationalism was a way to preserve his cosmopolitan spirit while overcoming ideologically his own indebtedness to an old regime (it occurred immediately after the 1930 skirmish that gave birth to the Estado Novo, the new state that promised to bring to an end the era of political hegemony of regional oligarchies).[15]

In 1933, in the preface to *Serafim Ponte Grande*, Oswald announces that he is ready to move on and turns his back on the book he is introducing. The condemnatory look is directed at all his literary production of the 1920s, and the *modernista* movement in which he was a major actor. *Serafim* is declared a dead letter, "a document" of times past: "Necrology of the bourgeoisie. Epitaph of the person I was." The clear-cut departure from his former incarnation as the "clown of the bourgeoisie" who tries out "transatlantic nudity" as a historical solution (1971, 132–33) and his current social and socially engaged reincarnation paradoxically seem to save Oswald from any real subjective involvement, despite this theatrical self-accusatory gesture. The ideological break between the book and its preface mirrors the split between the former decadent self and the present one, and Blaise Cendrars is mentioned as *le pirat du Lac Leman* (in French in the original), emblematically blamed for having promoted a new avant-garde abstract universalism and thus inducing the mirage of an equal footing for European and Latin American cultural production (as well as hinting at his Brazilian period as an illegitimate appropriation). Oswald performs the split in the division between preface and book, but finally offers himself as the new hero of his own repentance, redoubling his modernist faith, but now under the banner of the "proletarian revolution" that marches to the pace of "History," so this whole conversion is framed in a narrative of progressive overcoming and doesn't leave any potentially suspicious subjective remnant: "My watch always goes forward. So does History," concludes the prologue (133). His militant writing of the 1940s, the most uninteresting chapter of his literary production, is the overly convinced gesture of a repentant.[16]

Chilean Vicente Huidobro perhaps represents, within the avant-gardes of Latin America, the epitome of the cosmopolitan writer. His poetry articulates equally in French or Spanish the experience of a universal subject of modernity, an open space of free flights between angst and acceleration that is characteristic of post–World War I Europe but that a South American might have exhibited as cultural capital:

Una corona me haría
de todas las ciudades recorridas
Londres   Madrid   Paris
Roma   Nápoles   Zurich

I would make myself a crown
of all the cities I traveled
London   Madrid   Paris
Rome   Naples   Zurich
("Exprés," in *Poemas articos*, 1918)

This universal exhibition as personal triumph does not prevent Huidobro's poetry (in his long poem *Ecuatorial* of 1918, for example) from registering the colonial adventures of the era, the world united by telegraphs and ominous airplanes, the explorations and migrations, the European territory opened wide with trenches. On the one hand, the poetic voice assumes a disembodied bird's-eye view through which a world in chaotic fragmentation finds a momentary point of convergence, while on the other, as seen in the title, the major frontier/trench is the equatorial line itself, in a phantasmagoric figuration of the whole world as a battleground where he, a poet from the South, has to build his strategic loci of enunciation. For a master of disembodiment, his perspective is quite positioned. His major work, *Altazor o un viaje en paracaídas* (Altazor, or a voyage by parachute, written at the end of the 1920s and published in 1931) is already a transitional model: It sings of the lyric ego's disembodied abstraction through which distances are easily traversed and heights conquered, although at the same time it constitutes a farewell to the detachment of the speaking subject, advocating a return to some humanist ideal of reconciliation with the plain word, a centered subject, a world united—a project that is spelled out in the "Total" manifesto of 1932: "Basta ya de cortar el hombre y la tierra y el mar y el cielo [Stop cutting up men, earth, sea, sky]" (1963, 699).

As with the work of many other avant-gardists, Huidobro's writing in the 1930s is colored by the poet's engagement with the discourse of social change and revolution. Part of his literary production projects a future and celebrates its advent, another condemns societal ills. When, in order to embrace poetry's engagement in social conflicts, Huidobro turns away from total creative autonomy that he had championed as the major achievement of the avant-garde, the abandonment of former ways of conceiving of the poet's role doesn't necessarily bring about any gesture of repentance or remorse. Internationalism is in fact another understanding of cosmopolitanism and represented for some an updated version of the aspiration to a universal ideal. It was sharply at odds with the quest for native or local values. Thus, internationalism was not regarded as a return, but only as a necessary progression in accord with the times.

This future-oriented outlook cracked in the 1940s, when the poet went back to Chile after a long European sojourn. Huidobro appears to have been torn apart by his own retrospective judgment, which found himself guilty. To what extent his heirs (his daughter in particular) edited his posthumous volume *Ultimos poemas* (Last poems, 1948) is impossible to determine, but I can't help reading through the volume's opening line all the way back to Darío's famous poetry of repentance (by which he also initiates his book). Huidobro's poem "El paso del retorno" (Return passage) opens with the line "Yo soy ese que salió hace un año de su tierra [I am the one who departed from his land a year ago]" (11). It can't be ascertained if Darío was on Huidobro's or his daughter's mind, but if there is a use for the slippery category of unconscious citation, this should be presented as a case.

The poem, written in the Europe of World War II, where the poet was a foreign correspondent, continues with a retrospective look to the perplexing pilgrimage that the return announced in the title. If the departure had started under the sign of detachment, "Buscando lejanías de vida y muerte / . . . / Guiado por mi estrella / con el pecho vacío / Y los ojos clavados en la altura [Looking for remoteness of life and death / . . . / Guided by my star / with my chest empty / and my eyes riveted on the heights]," the return of this "viajero sin fin [traveler without end]" is consummated with his entrance into his definitive abode as a narrative of completion: "Heme aquí de regreso de donde no se vuelve [Here I am, back from where there is no returning]" (13), a place for a subject that has achieved a lethal unity as a recuperation and restoration. This traveler, who describes his past self—"Andaba por la Historia del brazo con la muerte [Walking through History arm and arm with death]" (15)—exudes the air of a recent, although melancholic, convert, having recovered his earthly dwelling in the return to the native land.

The radical modernist of the 1920s and the social revolutionary of the 1930s, in both cases a believer in the advance of history (in relation to which he placed himself at the forefront), now meets his new poetic self only by rejecting both history and his earlier poetic project. The place of return, a place "from where there is no returning," is stubbornly territorial, that is to say, it is static, equal only to itself, firmly grounded as a place outside historical contingencies. The time spent elsewhere can be regarded reprovingly as sheer loss of touch with his (new) real self: "Cuánto tiempo perdido. Este es el hombre de las lejanías [What a waste of time. This is the man of remoteness]" (13). And this reattachment, this new religion, seems to stop time altogether, as if to make certain that it will no longer be wasted on poetic flights. Thus, the incriminatory gaze is turned toward the self, toward place and past, as the only shelters from the failure of the critical perspective of broader horizons opened to the sound and the fury of the world, the present, and the future.

The trajectory of the Argentinean Oliverio Girondo intertwines with Huidobro's. In the 1920s, Girondo was the ultimate incarnation of the poet as cosmopolitan traveler, tasting the richness of different urban spaces (his prismatic poems are dated from different locations: Buenos Aires, Paris, Venice, Rio de Janeiro) and welcoming the advent of modernity and its possibilities of mobility. In contrast to Huidobro and others in the 1930s, Girondo didn't embrace the internationalist political cause. Nevertheless, he produced a rather more disquieting work—his 1932 volume *Espantapájaros: Al alcance de todos*—that seems to explore a dark corner where modernity is no longer presented as a colorful multiplicity but rather as a deceiving subjective experience full of fractures and entrapments.

Girondo's poetic project moves from free flights to free falls, from parodic fragmentation to the violence of dismemberment, from a playful depersonalization to alienation and sheer loss—in sum, from the promises of modernity to its dystopian possibilities.[17] But this exploration stopped in the 1940s, when Girondo consummated his modest return to a reconciled, hopeful spirit. *Campo nuestro* (Our land, 1946) is posited as the cure for the wounds that modernity, and clearly Girondo's own cosmopolitan roaming, had opened. The compensatory quality of this recuperation is prefigured in Girondo's short story *Interlunio* (1937), when the narrator declares himself to be amused by the protagonist's "contrast between his usual skepticism and his hyperbolic enthusiasm for the country" (*Obras*, 250). In the 1946 book-length poem, the writer recreates the "Pampean" religion of the Argentinean landowner elite (to which he belonged and now returns), and kneeling in front of this altar, begs forgiveness while turning his gaze toward his past poetic production. This apostrophe unmistakably paraphrases the Christian prayers echoed in the title, and from this vantage point, his earlier poetic self is retrospectively blamed for having been superficial, self-involved, vagabond.

Prayer and land are the means for rediscovery of a new and humble true self that reconstitutes itself in firm opposition to spatial movement. The land is invoked as the primary addressee: "Una tarde, en el mar, tú me llamaste / pero en vez de tu escueta reciedumbre / pasaba ante la borda un campo equívoco / de andares voluptuosos y evasivos [An afternoon, on the sea, you called me / but instead of your unadorned severity / a mischievous land was moving past the gunwale / with voluptuous and evasive steps]" (380). As Robert Eric Livingston (2001, 148) rightly points out, place "is commonly the bearer of moral order, [thus] erosion of place subverts ethical understanding as well." We can appreciate in these few verses the contrast between what in the 1940s came to be read as the superficial, sensual pleasure of deviant travel through foreign territory and the final return to the homeland as a reencounter with depth and perennial values. Peruvian poet Magda Portal seems to point directly to her fellow avant-gardists and their masculine, heroic narrative enacted in their transatlantic crossing when she writes: "mentira sus sirenas de encanto— / los hombres no aman el mar / sino los caminos del mar— [a lie their sirens of enchantment— /men don't love the sea but only the sea's routes—]" (Grünfeld 1995, 484).

Girondo's identification with Ulysses can be read along the lines of Adorno and Horkheimer's suggestion in *Dialectic of Enlightenment* (1998, excursus 1) that the Homeric epic is one of modernity's founding myths, inasmuch as it accounts for the renunciation of worldly sensuality required by the dominant, self-controlled, self-reflexive subjectivity. The tired Girondo elaborates on the same myth not only to articulate a temptation and the consequent heroic renunciation, but also in order finally to make self-reflexivity into a punishing tool for a critique of cosmopolitan modernity that secures his "return to his homeland and fixed estate" (Adorno and Horkheimer, 47).

In light of these readings, it is time to formulate a conceptual concern: If both cosmopolitanism and post-Romantic poetry are anchored in the ironic distance that allows self-reflexivity, how are we to interpret poetry that claims to have cancelled that distance in order to return to the comforts of transparent mimesis, monolingualism, and native identity? One way to approach the problem is to follow Paul de Man's suggestion (1988, 222) when he regarded a "regression in critical insight found in the transition from an allegorical to a symbolic theory of poetry [that] would find its historical equivalent in the regression from the eighteenth-century ironic novel . . . to nineteenth-century realism." I am not so interested in de Man's language of the progression and regression of critical consciousness, but I nevertheless believe that critical consciousness is being obscured in the poetic trajectories I am analyzing and that the shift can be explained more in terms of the repression of critical viewpoints in the face of the need to yield to sociohistorical pressures. But while the formation of new nationalisms in many places of Latin America in the 1930s and 1940s is discussed as a straightforward historical fact in any account of the era, the cultural phenomena I am analyzing would be comfortably explained away by appealing to the artist's new commitment and political alliances in this process.[18] I am not advocating a new ahistoricism, but a historical reading of a larger breath that does not limit its scope to the immediate (national) context. If, as we have already discussed, one of the acknowledged achievements of the Latin American avant-garde was the elaboration of a view of identity that adopts a critical distance in regard to any form of nativism, a stance that involves a moveable viewpoint from which to assess the Latin American position in the discourses of the West, what kind of critical move must the authors of these movements make in order to turn away from and against their own critical achievements?

The answer, once again, involves the relation between allegory and symbol. The multiple layers of the cosmopolitan poem are allegorical inasmuch as the text posits the question of the conditions of its production, that is, how to make sense in a particular language (Spanish or Portuguese), at a particular historical time, out of a modernity that primarily speaks other languages and considers these Latin American speakers out of place. Finding this task increasingly uncertain, without prospects, these poets resorted to symbolic wholeness once again, to a place outside time and contingency.

Oliverio Girondo might be paradigmatic of the anxiety of this time in his use of the heroic image of the modern self in a sea of temptations to symbolize the "planetary expansiveness of subject matter" with which Bruce Robbins (1993, 181) has characterized cosmopolitanism, as opposed to the territorial contraction of location.

Self-reflexivity and self-consciousness, when paradoxically put to work to attain a symbolic whole, ultimately negate themselves and at the same time deny this denial. A guilty consciousness, inasmuch as it is a witness of what it intends to negate, consequentially appears as an affective charge. If cosmopolitanism has to establish a critical distance from the search for native values in order to present them as a subject of translation, we see in the poetic corpus just examined that, in order to go back to native attachments, this critique has to turn against itself, thus making an ironic turn that denies the possibility of irony. Following again the insightful articulation of Paul de Man (1988, 214): "ironic language splits the subject into an empirical self that exists in a state of inauthenticity and a self that exists only in the form of a language that asserts the knowledge of this inauthenticity. This does not, however, make it into an authentic language, for to know inauthenticity is not the same as to be authentic."

The acknowledgment and further negation of this ironic standpoint is perhaps the moral base for the persistent, nostalgic remorse that resurfaced over and over again among the repentant avant-gardists. Whereas cosmopolitanism constitutes a willed distance from the authentic, symbolic word, this regionalism, or nationalism, or nativist Latin Americanism is usually grounded in the denial of the embedded mechanisms of translation that would signal the possibility of inauthenticity. In fact, it can be argued, as Carlos Alonso (1990) has, that this internal anxiety is the destiny of every nativism. But the remorseful affect with which this is processed in the cases I am studying is due to the temporal split by which the recuperation of the native has to be claimed as a reflective reaction against previous mistakes.

César Vallejo's poetry provides an end (a very open one indeed) not only to this chapter, but to the narrative I have been constructing throughout this book. The poet constantly questions the place of his own enunciation and gives his poetry a cosmopolitan breath without ever renouncing a place of belonging, without closing off access to the enigma of community by engaging in the free flight of cosmopolitan detachment. Moreover, Vallejo overcomes some of the articulations of culture centered on the identitarian quest (either national or continental, native or transcultural) to which some avant-gardists ended up returning. He doesn't embark on criticism of his own enunciation in a further, secondary, and backward-looking stage, because his critical insight anticipates the kind of problems that other poets would realize only by going back and forth between detachment and nostalgia, irony and ontological quest. That is why at no point in his career is it possible to pin down Vallejo's preoccupations as cosmopolitan, or nativist, or transcultural in-between. Vallejo names the problems pointed out throughout this chapter and transcends their deadlock without having to resort to sweeping gestures of self-erasure.

Vallejo's position in this discussion is key, since he is primarily interested in the epistemic situation of the production of Latin American art and literatures, and it is with this concern with positionality that he approaches issues of cultural belonging. Although he mistrusted profoundly the cosmopolitan detachment of the figure of the world citizen, he lived in Paris (with temporary stays in other European capitals) until his death, and he never completed the circle by fulfilling the expectation that he would return to his native Peru. But he also never resorted to the fetish of the modern urban space as a synecdoche for what is universal or to the sort of repentant nativism of some of his contemporaries. He was, however, among the avant-gardists most attuned to the entrapments wrought by a peripheral location in the West. The poet's concern with the locus of enunciation available to Latin American intellectuals is clear in his articles and chronicles from Europe. In a 1928 article ("La juventud de América en Europa" [American youth in Europe]) Vallejo examines the canonical, colonial-minded trip to and from the metropolis. Writers and artists "who play the role of intellectual leaders of [Latin] America," are usually "sick of continental optimism" (1987, 324), showing a tendency to interpret their transatlantic allegiances in terms of cultural gains for the constitution of their native culture. The metropolitan prestige of the cultural traveler, is of course, at the center of the *Bildungsroman* of many Latin American intellectual biographies.

Instead, his poetry bears witness to a radical division that is not occluded by fast-forwarding the promises of modernity or by a perennial trust in the auratic past.[19] As much as the idea of coming back to a home left empty recurs throughout his poetry, the poems lack the kind of rhetoric of remorseful homecoming we have seen in other works. This is because, although Vallejo wrote from a place of highly localized affiliations, he explored them in regard to the strangeness that constitutes place and subjectivity.[20] "Homeland is the state of having escaped" for Adorno and Horkheimer (1998, 78), as well as for Vallejo, and never something prior to this primary separation. That primary split may be the reason why his most vocally political poetry of the 1930s (at the height of Vallejo's engagement with the Spanish Republic) never felt like a departure from earlier projects and was sustained not by rejection and negation of previous poetics, but by maintaining a fundamental, primary division: "¡Cuídate, España, de tu propia España! [Beware, Spain, of your own Spain!]" (1979, 212). His poetry doesn't project a celebratory cosmopolitan detachment but envisages a way of belonging that is also a critical distance because it is predicated upon the awareness of a fundamental strangeness within the self that affects both cosmopolitanism and belonging.

Consider one of his posthumous prose poems:

> Algo te identifica con el que se aleja de ti, y es la facultad común de volver: de ahí tu más grande pesadumbre.
> Algo te separa del que se queda contigo, y es la esclavitud común de partir: de ahí tus más nimios regocijos.
> Me dirijo, en esta forma, a las individualidades colectivas, tanto como a las colectividades individuales y a los que, entre unas y otras, yacen marchando al son de las fronteras o, simplemente, marcan el paso inmóvil en el borde del mundo.
>
> Something identifies you with the one who moves away from you, and it is your common power to return: thus your greatest sorrow.
> Something separates you from the one who remains with you, and it is your common slavery to depart: thus your meagerest rejoicing.

> I address myself, in this way, to collective individualities, as well as to individual collectivities and to those who, between them both, lie marching to the sound of the frontiers or, simply, mark time without moving at the edge of the world. (1978, 207)[21]

In contrast to the return of the wanderer Huidobro to a place from which there is no return, for Vallejo there is always return, inevitably, even prior to departure. The problem, posited in the poem in very precise geographic and demographic language touches upon the constitution of an identity that can't be sustained by attachment to or detachment from a particular place: Neither the one who moves away nor the one who stays can be fully the one or the other. By locating a categorical split between both options, the poem signals this movement back and forth between cosmopolitanism and the return to a native autochthony as constitutional of Latin American discourses without a dialectical resolution, without the teleological comfort that narratives of transculturation and hybridity provide.

Written in the 1930s and probably after the outbreak of the Spanish Civil War, the poem partially borrows from the patterns of political speech, and it also elaborates on a subjectivity that can't be resolved by the will of a unified political subject. Something is always unattended to by the desire for closure:

> Algo típicamente neutro, de inexorablemente neutro, interpónese entre el ladrón y su víctima. Esto, así mismo, puede discernirse tratándose del cirujano y del paciente. Horrible medialuna, convexa y solar, cobija a unos y otros. Porque el objeto hurtado tiene también su peso indiferente, y el órgano intervenido, también su grasa triste.

> [Something typically neuter, inexorably neuter, stands between the thief and his victim. This, likewise, can be noticed in the relation between a surgeon and his patient. A horrible half moon, convex and solar, covers all of them. For the stolen object also has its indifferent weight, and the operated-on organ, also its sad fat]" (1978, 206–7).

The secret of these exchanges and extractions lies in what is thrown aside, as we will see.

The problem of identity traverses the poem, and individual collectivities and the collective individualities stand for two interchangeable modes of dealing with it. As if trying to get around the impasse caused by the entrapment in the binary logics (abroad or home, individual or community, etc.), the poem searches for a third space, a borderland, through the constant exploration of paradox and oxymoron (e.g., the separation from the one who stays, the commonality with the one who moves away, the rejoicing in slavery, etc.).

The problem of identity is put forward from the very beginning—"Something identifies you"—perhaps in the hope of further unveiling its mechanics. But later in the poem that "something" keeps moving away, becoming more and more unnamable, a trace fallen out of circulation and beyond possible reappropriation, a "something" that exhausts the specular mechanisms of identity. That is to say, the neutral element presented here can't be reduced to the stability of an archaic trace, the house of the father where identities seeking remorseful homecomings look for a primary or final dwelling space. There are indeed polarities in society, thieves and victims, surgeons and patients, ones and others, and, between them, exchanges are performed, objects stolen, and organs removed. There is, no doubt, a share of violence. But there is also this heterogeneous "something" that is expelled as abject, that doesn't find a proper place in the circulation. As Maurice Blanchot (1981, chapter 9) suggests, the neutral element is neither a transcendent element (it is not the unsubstitutable), nor is it a unity (it is not a whole). The something that identifies us, the something that is the moveable kernel of this poetic discourse, is inexorably neuter because it resists articulation in the auratic trace of remorseful homecoming or in the free-floating cultural exchanges of the cosmopolitan traveler. That is exactly the truth that the authors of optimistic cosmopolitanism and its repentant return eschewed. Seduced first and disappointed later by the augurs of the global order, by the total translatability of the local in a multifaceted modernity traversed by the ironic distance of the poet, they introject as guilt what was left out of the global order and seek the lost aura that they left behind.

As if thematizing the trajectory of the avant-garde poet, the poem concludes: "¡Alejarse! ¡Quedarse! ¡Volver! ¡Partir! Toda la mecánica social cabe en estas palabras (1986, 120). [To move away! To remain! To return! To depart! The whole social mechanism fits in these words (1978, 206–7)]." But as we see, despite the talk of social mechanics, Vallejo announces the elements by which any mechanistic view of society fails. That is, the lyric voice is pointing to matters that go beyond the narrow, mechanistic view of cultural production held by some sectors of the left—to which César Vallejo, who, as a journalist, frequently praised the Soviet state, undoubtedly belonged. At the end of the poem, despite the fact that he seems to be articulating social mechanisms in just four infinitives—to move away, to remain, to return, to depart—the words, divided by exclamation marks, remain disconnected moments that reinforce the failure of the expected semantic parallelism.[22]

No doubt the idea of social mechanics goes back to Vallejo's familiarity with Marxist literature. But as William Rowe (1996, 112–23) has suggested, Vallejo pushes political discourse to a point of exhaustion. The political discourse in question here is related to the modern utopia of the mechanization, control, measurement, and administration of social flows implemented by communist regimes, in which Vallejo saw the possibility of social change. But the enunciation of a progress toward total articulation is not what we encounter here in Vallejo's social mechanics. Instead, Vallejo breaks apart the idea of mechanics as a feasible metaphor to account for social phenomena and their relation to language, disputing, by opening indefinitely the final articulation, the idea of the social mechanism ever "fitting" or taking place in language. With Vallejo, we are in what Alain Badiou (1992) called "the age of the poets": when poetry is able to elaborate on interrogations that are inaccessible to a social theory and a philosophy blinded by scientism and historicism (or by scientific socialism). This elaboration is fundamental in the midst of the Latin Americanism of the avant-garde, for which round-trip journeys are performed as promising sublations and syntheses of new national or cosmopolitan totalities. Vallejo disorients the orientation of this teleological drive.

Origin, for Vallejo, is always an interrogation, and not a site from which the poet flees, only to go back and search for it where it was left. While

Cuban poet José Lezama Lima would conceptualize the radical split of the poetic subject from its origins—"deseoso es el que huye de su madre [wishful is he who flees from his mother]" ("Llamado del deseoso" in *Aventuras sigilosas*, 1945)—Vallejo is more specifically situated. This original place that produces the poetic subject, by pushing this subject outside of itself and of the site of originality, is already divided. "Hay, madre, un sitio en el mundo que se llama París [There is, mother, a place in the world called Paris]" (1987, 6–7), the poetic voice utters in another posthumous poem, as if to furnish a theory of origins in order to explain where children, along with some Latin American poets, come from. If Paris epitomizes, for Vallejo and previous generations of Latin Americans, the cultural metropolis, he recognizes the intimate debt, inscribed in his subjectivity, by remaining intimately attached but not completely identified with different places "in the world." But then he continues, explaining his own return to the place of origin, to the mother: "Mi adios partió de un punto de su ser, más externo que el punto de su ser al que retorno [My farewell set off from a point in her being, more external than the point in her being to which I return]" (6–7). Vallejo exercises in these poems what has been called border thinking, a "dichotomous locus of enunciation" whose epistemological thrust is to thwart the division of the world into dichotomies (Mignolo 2000a, 85).

This is a mistrust of any discourse that is postulated as originary. It is a return with no recuperation of the lost aura because there is no remainder completely outside global articulations, no primitive trace that is left at home, in the unified mother tongue, in the fatherland. To emphasize the importance in Latin America of this critique of origins is a position that doesn't dwell in a deconstructivist affinity but in the persistent use of the argument of origins to justify actual systems of domination. Giorgio Agamben characterizes poetry as a constant oscillation between expropriation and appropriation, identity and nonidentity, exile and motherland. Vallejo doesn't act out this alternation in his life in order to entrust himself to only one of the poles, and ultimately, to negate their interdependence. That is how he escapes the romantic alternatives pointed out by de Man that I related to nativism and cosmopolitanism: the search for the authentic symbol and the ironic distrust in its authenticity. His poetic discourse enacts this constitutive oscillation and imbues it with cultural significance. Vallejo lives in the dichotomy that is his locus of enunciation, and it is from there that he is able to envision a situated knowledge that is other than Western: "¡Rotación de tardes modernas / y finas madrugadas arqueológicas! / ¡Indio después del hombre y antes de él! [Rotation of modern afternoons / and refined archeological sunrises! / Indian after man and before him!]" (1978, 86–88). His poetry establishes the ground for a cultural critique that is not based on ironic distance and subordination of the particular and thus envisages the construction of an inclusive, positioned universalism that has different names and that I described as cosmopolitan.

■ **Chapter 7**

Epilogue

Sited over the parallel
Let us contemplate our time

Vicente Huidobro, "Equatorial"

IN THIS book, the assignation of "avant-garde" was not predicated on matters of style, on the understanding that "avant-garde" is tantamount to "artistic experimentation"—whatever that may stand for—or on declared affiliations. Even when the Latin American avant-garde artists did renew the formal aspects of their craft, opening the door to all sorts of innovations, the most relevant aspect of this change was the interrogation of the conditions of possibility for and consequences of declaring something to be innovative and modern. The embrace of novelty fueled the most interesting production of this particular historical time, causing the avant-gardists to examine their positions in the "streams of cultural capital" (Palumbo-Liu 1997), that is, in terms of how cultural value circulates—and changes everything it touches—worldwide. That is why I chose to move from the historiographic (or merely anecdotic) problem of who participated in what group and where to a critical perspective on the logic of avant-gardism in this particular site of production. In this sense, it is true that futurism is "the one myth that unites the avant-gardes" (Eysteinsson 1990, 149), not because all aggressively embraced technological advances and the radical erasure of the past, but because they all strove to bring about some sort of change in culture and society.[1] In the peripheries, this demanded an investigation of how novelty is produced and valorized, not in terms of national institutions (when promoted or condemned by artistic circles, newspapers, museums, academia) but within a largely ungraspable scope of shifting geopolitical hegemonies and of the differential uses and ways of circulation of cultural production that legitimize, reproduce, or contest these hegemonies. I showed how in Latin America, addressing these problems entailed interrogating the constitutional incompleteness of modernity based on coloniality and the promises of emancipation at the individual, national, and continental level.

"The New Continent," Mexican poet Manuel Maples Arce wrote in 1923, "continues to be a literary blackmail of the vanguardist expositor and intrepid theorizer José Vasconcelos, a joke by Christopher Columbus, or a piece of news by the Associated Press" (Schneider 1997, 169). This compressed dictum illuminates many of the discussions with which I have characterized the Latin American avant-gardes: the intention to find a new locus of enunciation, without the modern desire for the new perpetuating colonial mechanisms of subjection or leading to redemptive new totalities. Between a continuity of subordinated positions in the world design and a shift of hegemony from Europe to the United States (of which the Associated Press is emblematic), the artist and critic has to forge his or her own ground.[2]

From the inception of the imagination of the world as a unified entity (with the encounter of what was to become "the New Continent"), the schemes of universal history implied a politics of time differentially distributed. When applied to the study of the modernizing impetus of the avant-gardes, this focus on modernity's longue durée and extended spatial sway restructures the opposition between tradition and novelty that supports the unidirectional idea of modernity. The question is no longer whether Latin Americans leaned more toward tradition than toward novelty, because both tradition and novelty were instrumental in trying to map out historical change. The main problem for a conceptualization of these artistic movements is not "tradition" and how Europeans and Latin Americans differentially employed it, because this was simply one factor in responding to a larger, more urgent, and thus more relevant problem of position. The avant-gardes mobilized tradition as a critical answer to the question of the place of Latin America within a larger modernity in which colonial projects, past and present, continue to be foundational.

I therefore have attempted to move from the vocabulary of elegy, where traditions survive and are consequently rescued by cultural heroes for a pantheon that is always nationally based, to the persistence of an epistemological predicament. Precisely at the point when European hegemony was imploding, tradition represented a burden for European dadaists, futurists, and surrealists, not simply because of a presumed longer history of the "old continent" but rather because the West was imagined as a self-contained continuity from the Greeks onward, with its epistemological superiority. Primitivist trends embraced by the European avant-gardes often and in various ways redoubled the abjection of "the rest" for which this primitivism attempted to compensate.

The loci of enunciation that the vanguards made available were not about receptivity and the incorporation of a (foreign) modernity to be ingeniously adapted to (traditional) cultural milieu. They were not, in sum, forms of mediation by which the national cultural import/export balance could be made to turn positive. Creative adaptations and transculturations, often loaded with a history of brutal impositions, had been common since the colonial period. In a 1925 newspaper article, Mário de Andrade used his tumultuous, contradictory style to unfold the multiple layers of the conundrum. He started by reproducing the readily available understanding of cultural circulation, only to move away from it to make clear that the vanguards sought to disrupt the recourse to creative adaptations: "And we imitated the European 'isms.' Two things differentiated our imitations from the former ones; we imitated the present and not an orientation founded in past eras. But sometimes even I rebel against calling our primitive modernizing movement an imitation. To follow a universal spiritual state of an epoch is more a fatal necessity than an aping gesture."

He thus interrogates the diffusionist premise of modernity in order to understand his own locus of enunciation on its own terms, not as a residual phenomenon. And after taking to task the understanding of the direction that history took, from Europe to a lagging America, an understanding that five centuries of metropolitan dependence had imprinted, compressing it instead into a single present in which the new art was bound to exist and, as a "fatal necessity" apprehend the present, he concludes: "I sent away all the European 'isms.' Guys, Europe is our Orient. Cut" (Schwartz 1991, 507). Thus, the author proposes for artistic and cultural production not just an autonomist cut to achieve a true national spirit, but a cinematic caesura, moving on to compose a different scene, one in which a radical redefinition of the geographical coordinates effects a compelling figuration of a literal mapping (Europe is actually to the east of America) with allegorical potency (Europe, like the Orient, is a powerful, imaginary object of desire). It is the vanguards' politics of situated universalism.

Consequently, the novels I have analyzed completely recast contemporary avant-garde futurism and primitivism—modes with which the avant-gardes intended to dislodge the unidirectional time of universal history, the sense of time that the peripheral avant-gardes opened up and exploded. The travel writings investigated these problems in the context of a presentation of everyday life. The discourses by which Latin Americans enacted the promise of inclusion in the modern world (from anthropology and folklore to migration and development) continually reemerged in writing that confronted them in their actuality and in their circulation. By taking different routes, both Mário de Andrade and Roberto Arlt arrived at certain sites (the abandoned railway, the train at a halt, the occupied house, the newsroom, the scene of ethnology, the scene of photography, etc.) that they appropriated as a situated vantage point from which the problems they confronted might be read within a world dynamic. Avant-gardists' writing of homecoming gave way to a historical pressure to narrow down, find closure, and leave behind the expansive insights gained by this perspective. A disappointment with the promises of modernity was processed through the disavowal of the cosmopolitan horizon of political action and aesthetic agency.

What these analyses show us is how and when the discourses of the Latin American avant-gardes maintained their radical vision. They avoided taking refuge in the parochial or reinvesting in national culture for the constitution of a new hegemonic order, and they did so not by treating the drive for cosmopolitanism as the happy embrace of the privilege of detachment, but by examining, as Vallejo did, the place of articulation from which they wrote.

It is possible to read as an undercurrent in this book an argument that speaks of developments from the 1920s to the 1940s in terms of the construction of the populist state. Mário de Andrade registered the historical change from a patronizing notion of folklore to a notion of the people with potential political agency, people who were to be incorporated in the machinery and the cultural policy of the Estado Novo that terminated with the aristocratic state in the 1930s.[3] Roberto Arlt, for his part, echoed in his writing the increasingly dominant role of mass media in the national imagination and a potential for social change that would come together with the advent of the Peronismo movement in the 1940s. This is exactly what the homecoming of the 1930s and 1940s was about, an ambiguous recognition of a new strategy of alliances that took up the symbols of nationality to bring about the sense of a national people while preserving the interior space of poetic spirituality that was being threatened by new political agents (Romero 1986, 374; Martín-Barbero 1993, 158–9). I waited this long to spell out this argument because it is not new, and because the clarity gained by emphasizing the constitution of citizenship, when combined with a reflection on the place of literature in this development, tends to uphold a narrative of achievement toward national self-realization. In this narrative of progressive inclusion, literature is subsumed by a role of hegemonic legitimization or accused a posteriori of co-opting political difference by sublimating it aesthetically. Insisting on the national frame of analysis, or even on a frame of comparative cultural historiography of Latin American countries, ends up occluding the cosmopolitan political sensibility that was present during these years and that is not contained within the narratives of the state—an intellectual trend that never ceased to be present from the time of the avant-gardes and that now speaks to our world.

Since I have claimed that avant-gardes are still read and thought about in Latin America, since I have implicitly defended the idea that the "historical" avant-gardes never ceased interrogating readers and audiences, it is only logical to conclude that I aspire to a reading of the avant-garde that helps us to understand our present. It is tempting to say that, because the language of novelty and survival is readily available, today the enterprise for which the avant-gardes stood is "still" current. It would be more precise to say that the most compelling cultural productions in Latin America today take up their intent. These productions advance a localized way of being that is unavoidably worldly, ineluctably modern as a struggle for agency or as an interruption of the constant reformulation of modernity—an interruption of the discourses that legitimate and make desirable a global dynamic that distributes, authorizes, and naturalizes inequality.

One of the main features of the avant-gardes on which the critics almost unanimously agree is the questioning of the place of the arts in society. In a way, I chose to stretch this very basic common understanding to an unexpected new extent. The avant-gardes unsettled the instituted sites of enunciation and explored the deadlocks wrought by the embrace of modernity —the ways in which modernity assigns positions within it and, complementarily, the parameters by which these positions are valued and measured as historical stages. If, in Latin America, they helped to foster the institutionalized sphere of the artistic, rather than shaking it up, without this making them more conservative than the Europeans (as had been repeatedly argued), it is because, as I have shown, they grappled with a different predicament than did the Europeans. They opened up the languages in which their paradoxical position in a changing world could be spelled out, and in some cases they explored hiatuses and imagined articulations that would disrupt and turn around the hegemonic discourses.

For more than twenty years now, postmodern criticism has issued a death certificate for the idea of the avant-garde, when it didn't defend it with a gloss of nostalgia. The survival of modernist aesthetic paradigms, with all the implications that these carry, implications of defiance, rupture, emancipation, and faith in its own social relevance, was conceivable only in forsaken enclaves of this planet where utopias still hold sway and modernity's enchanting promises are preserved by a state of naive underachievement and colorful, but bumpy, unevenness—say, in a Latin American country where there are still things to wait for modernity to deliver. In any case, the avant-gardes are history, so the critical voices say, for the parts of the world that really count and set the expectations for everything else that carries the labels of what is up-to-date and provide models of imitation. Pluralism, relativism, and multiculturalism have prevailed in advanced societies, while the wretched of the earth still endure their artistic upheavals, their prophets and saints, their undifferentiated realms where the arts merge with politics and faith, regarded by the theorists of the postmodern with a glance of nostalgic paternalism.

All of that seems to have changed in the cultural climate lately, and now postmodernism names a bygone era of indefensible, when not disingenuous, optimism. Some master narratives of modernity, those that favor the enforcement of a global design, are back with renewed vigor and the desire not to leave one's position to the fanciful interplay of deterritorialized flows seems to have caught once more the artistic and critical imagination. In truth, the narratives of the new and the idea of discovery have been utterly displaced, have partially lost their glitter, and have ceased to carry the initiative for the advance of history, while conquest and domination are revealed as obscenities that were always more uneuphemistically pronounced on the peripheries of the system. But the cosmopolitan impulses that gave the avant-gardes their reason to be do not cease to gain currency: to transform conditions of the present into opportunities for the exercise of aesthetic agency. That movement entails not sublimating these conditions but making visible their contemporaneity, disrupting what is presented as the regime of modern times.

NOTES

Chapter 1: Locating the Avant-Garde

1. For reasons of style, I will use the terms "vanguard" and "avant-garde" interchangeably.

2. Because Latin America was colonized mainly by powers outside the central narrative of European modernity, the region's place in relation to the West has always been problematic. This predicament is illustrated by the arrangement of disciplinary divisions, as Immanuel Wallerstein (1997) has shown. As a result, Spanish-speaking and Portuguese-speaking Latin America has fallen through the disciplinary cracks, and the recourse to anthropology to elaborate on its modernity (as I will discuss in the following chapters) is thus symptomatic. For more elaboration on the geopolitical division of disciplines, see Mignolo (2000a, particularly chapter 5).

3. I use quotation marks because, although the field of modernism has always been more or less cross-national, the inclusion of Latin America within the frame is always tenuous. I will address the topic of the constitution of the field and its Eurocentric assumptions more directly (particularly in chapter 2). A mere gesture of inclusion, effected by the generous stretching of the category to encompass the so-called Third World, doesn't really address the problem if the field is not reconceptualized as a cross-regional, dialogical clash at the juncture of a crisis of the European modernizing project.

4. Unruh draws on Roberto González Echevarría's *The Voice of the Masters* (1985) for her treatment of what Echevarría calls the organicist perspective on identity: Basically, the originality at the kernel of identity has its source in nature and the landscape as well as in the metaphors used to express this originality. This is not to be confused with the notion of an organic work of art, which I understand in Bürger's terms (1984) and which implies the idea of the work of art as an indivisible totality.

5. The school so characterized by Borges is *rubenismo* (for Rubén Darío). The author, with his characteristic sarcasm, gives this idiosyncratic name to *modernismo*—the trend in Hispanic American letters that appropriates certain fin-de-siècle European poetics for a Latin American sense of cultural autonomy. Rubén Darío is in many ways the founder, the most representative, and the best poet of this literary trend. Borges's text is one of the three introductions to the seminal *Indice de la nueva poesía americana*, an anthology of Hispanic American vanguardist poetry edited in 1926 by the Argentinean Borges, the Chilean Vicente Huidobro, and the Peruvian Alberto Hidalgo. Although with sections divided by

country, the anthology gives a sense of the cross-regional spirit that was pervasive among writers and artists of the vanguard movements.

Borges's tentative reference to 1922 is strangely precise. It is the year of the Week of Modern Art in São Paulo (which Borges might have learned about through the articles published in the magazine *Martín Fierro* in September 1925), which inaugurated in Brazil the idea of modern art. César Vallejo, though he despised the provocateur spirit of the vanguards, created the most originally experimental poetics of this time, publishing that same year *Trilce,* (included in his *Obra poética completa* [1986]), arguably the most important poetry book of the vanguard movements in Spanish. I will make more references to the Brazilian movement and the Peruvian poet, in chapters 4 and 6, respectively.

6. Unless otherwise noted, all translations, including this one, are my own. In this particular case, an English version of the book exists (*The Contemporary History of Latin America,* translated by John Charles Chasteen [Durham, N.C.: Duke University Press, 1993]), but the translation of this particular paragraph is partial and loses many nuances.

7. The expression comes from Andreas Huyssen's book *After the Great Divide* (1986). Huyssen takes it from Adorno. The categories of "mass" and "elite culture," as Fredric Jameson (1992) shows, should always be conceived together as dialectic opposites. In this sense, it can be argued that the avant-garde intended to unsettle this distribution of forces in the cultural field.

8. I chose the masculine here not only because the name of the group (and of the magazine that issued the manifesto), Martín Fierro, refers to a masculine character of the Argentinean foundational poem but also because the manifesto can be aligned with the spirit of virility typical of several avant-garde texts.

9. There are different compilations of Latin American avant-garde programmatic texts, of which the most complete is Jorge Schwartz's (1991), which is superbly annotated. See also Osorio T. (1988) and Verani (1990), both with useful introductions.

10. See Rodó's *Ariel* (first published in 1900). John Beverley (1999) has rightly argued that this position is continually refashioned in Latin American studies in trying to counterpoint globalizing trends. See his discussion of "neo-Arielism" (18–19).

11. Anderson (1998b) takes this suggestive phrase from Philippine author José Rizal's novel *Noli me tangere*. Rizal depicts a narrator who cannot avoid looking at a native garden without comparing it with a "normal" European garden.

12. I am resorting to the category of cognitive mapping as elaborated by Fredric Jameson, particularly in his book *Postmodernism, or, the Cultural Logic of Late Capitalism* (1991, 399–418). See also his 1999 piece "Cognitive Mapping."

13. I am not proposing new jargon to complicate the landscape of the "posts." I am merely pointing out the fact that perhaps because the fervor of these debates has subsided and explicit alignment with these labels is increasingly rare, their consequences have been already incorporated in every critical discussion.

14. Two English translations exist, but only of *Los siete locos,* the first part of the novelistic diptych. *The Seven Madmen,* translated by Nick Caistor (London: Serpent's

Tail/UNESCO, 1998) and *The Seven Madmen: A Novel,* translated by Naomi Lindstrom (Boston: D. R. Godine, 1984).

15. The English translation drops the subtitle: *Macunaíma,* translated by E.A. Goodland (New York: Random House, 1984).

Chapter 2: A Case for Geopolitics

1. It is still necessary to make the following clarifications when referring to non-European modernisms, though it might be tedious for some. *Modernismo* was introduced as a category by Rubén Darío in 1888, and *postmodernismo* was used later to characterize trends that formally and thematically broke from the harmonic structures and art-for-art-sake aesthetic common during the previous epoch. The label *modernismo*, as we will discuss later at great length, was also adopted by the Brazilian artistic avant-garde of the 1920s to name their own enterprise. I will use the terms in Spanish or Portuguese (they have the same spelling) when specifically referring to the Latin American movements, and I will reserve the use of the English terms "modernist" and "modernism" when the reference is geographically more vague. See also note 5 of chapter 1.

2. Angel Rama's article "Las dos vanguardias latinoamericanas" (1995), originally published in 1973, contains the fundamental turning point: Rehearsing the old accusation that Latin American art is a mere copy of metropolitan originals, Rama also highlights the existence of a different trend, one that responds in an original way to a Latin American crisis and therefore functions inside what he calls the "Latin American literary system" (147). The latter is represented, interestingly, by Roberto Arlt and César Vallejo, two authors with whom I am particularly concerned, but because they deconstruct the opposition taken by Rama. See also Nelson Osorio T., Beatriz Sarlo, and Wilson Martins, authors whose frame of analysis is the nation and/or the subcontinent as semiautonomous literary systems.

3. Here Alonso is referring in particular to Beatriz Sarlo's *Una modernidad periférica: Buenos Aires 1920 y 1930* (1988), a foundational study of a modernist cultural sphere.

4. For a discussion of the incorporation of modernist revolutionary tendencies into mainstream "late modernism," see Jameson (2002, part 3). Regarding the Latin American case, I am making reference to the continuous recycling of avant-garde products that have been recast in recent years as new plays, movies, artistic exhibitions, and performances. I draw on personal experience here—remarkable in its sheer randomness. I happened to be at a cultural center in Santiago, Chile, in the early 1990s when a large interactive installation drawing on Huidobro's texts was displayed; in the late 1990s in São Paulo, I was fascinated by a multimedia and interactive exhibit on Mário de Andrade's *Macunaíma*, staged at a neighborhood cultural center on the outskirts of the city; and in Buenos Aires, sometime after that, I saw a highly successful theatrical adaptation of Roberto Arlt's *Los siete locos*. Both Roberto Arlt's *El juguete rabioso* and de Andrade's *Macunaíma* were adapted for the big screen. I am sure the list could be extended to include São Paulo's prestigious art biennial featuring *antropofagia* as the convoking theme, for instance, if I could conduct a more systematic research of these translations and rewritings, which involve not only a

process of adaptation but also the enactment of a new reading. Given the sometimes informal character of these productions, which often are not publicized beyond the local cultural circuit, a systematic listing is almost impossible. It would be necessary to be there.

5. David Harvey (1990, 275) skillfully depicts these lines of imperial thought, which he calls, simply, "geopolitics": "Friedrich Ratzel in Germany, Camille Vallaux in France, Halford Mackinder in Britain, and Admiral Mahan in the United States all recognized the significance of command over space as a fundamental source of military, economic, and political power. Were there, they asked, strategic spaces within the new globalism of trade and politics, the command of which would confer favoured status upon particular peoples? If there was some Darwinian struggle for survival of the different peoples and nations of the earth, then what principles governed that struggle and what would its outcome probably be?" My use of the term "geopolitics" includes, but it is not limited to, Harvey's. A good survey of this geopolitical thought at the turn of the century is provided by Ó Tuathail (1996, particularly chapter 1).

6. See also James Clifford (1997), whose intellectual project involves turning around diffusionist visions of European expansionism as "celebrated, or deplored, as a simple diffusion outward—of civilization, industry, science or capital" (3). Anibal Quijano (1995 and 2000) makes a related argument.

7. I am presenting these positions merely as examples. They are authored by Xavier Abril, José Carlos Mariátegui, Evar Méndez, Evaristo Ribera Chevremont, and Arturo Uslar Pietri, respectively.

8. In English, of course, in the original. The Tupi constituted the largest of the indigenous peoples of the Amazonian basin.

9. There are many possible definitions of historicism. I am following Chakrabarty (2000) in my approach to the subject, but it can be said, too, that it is the process by which the past becomes available and the present is already historical and comparable to the past (Jameson 2002, 242–45)—a definition akin to Walter Benjamin's overly quoted "homogeneous, empty time" (1969, 261). Peter Osborne (1995), who most clearly defines the field, says that historicism might mean two different things: the proposed identity of truth and history (e.g., in Hegel) or the opposite idea (for the German objectivist school, which at the end of the nineteenth century opposed Hegel). In fact, Benjamin associated historicism with both the aforementioned schools and with the Enlightenment philosophy of progress. Historicism, Osborne proposes, is a response to the breakdown of tradition, an attempt to create a historical time-consciousness that parallels the empty time of progress. It is a compensatory reaction internal to the temporality of modernity that makes the construction of history as progress possible. But inasmuch as modernity always involves forgetting, the continuity with the past is only abstract in terms of its value as heritage and tradition (see chapter 4 of Osborne's compelling 1995 book *The Politics of Time: Modernity and Avant-Garde*).

10. See for example Walter Mignolo's *Local History/Global Designs* (2000a, 19). On the other hand, the South Asian case institutionalized the label of postcolonial critique in the academy.

11. For a more detailed account of the changing value of the term throughout its European history, see Osborne (1995); the essay "Modernity and the Planes of Historicity" by Koselleck (1977); Campagnon (1994, chapter 1); Gumbrecht (1992); and Jameson (2002, part 1, chapter 1). All draw on Hans Robert Jauss's "La modernité dans la tradition littéraire et la conscience d'aujourdui," in *Pour Une Esthétique de la réception* (Paris: Gallimard, 1978).

12. This brilliant article, which performs this idea of rewriting from its title, "Modernity Modernity," is not mentioned by Jameson, but it is a source of his evident speculations about the beginning of modernity (compare Meschonnic [1992, 413] with Jameson [2002, part 1, chapter 3]), as well as their idea of modernity as a linguistic shifter (419 of Meschonnic; 19 of Jameson).

13. Its first Spanish edition appeared in 1923. Among the contemporary critical readings of Spengler, we find that of José Carlos Mariátegui (1973, 89) and Arturo Uslar Pietri (1985). Roberto González Echevarría's *Alejo Carpentier, the Pilgrim at Home* (Ithaca: Cornell University Press, 1977) provides an essential account of the importance of Spengler for the Latin American cultural debates of the 1930s.

14. See Mignolo (2000), particularly chapter 4, and Quijano (2000).

15. See also Édouard Glissant's compelling *Poetics of Relation* (2000).

16. See Giovanni Arrighi (1998, 121) for a discussion of the reification of the center-periphery scheme.

17. Marinetti himself traveled to Brazil and Argentina to give a series of conferences. See particularly Schnapp and de Castro Rocha (1996), Osorio T. (1982), and Fabris (1994).

18. Drawing on Michael Hardt and Antoni Negri (who in turn draw on Michel Foucault), Alberto Moreiras (1998) differentiates between disciplinary projects (which base their power on fixating points of difference for the constitution of an identity) and control projects (which presuppose the flexible and re-programmable status of identity). Although Moreiras generally sustains that the former correspond to national ideologies whereas the latter respond to the cultural logic of globalization, I argue that flexible, fluid identities, and sites of contestation of the control that they operate, were imagined by the Latin American vanguards as they responded to an earlier globalization.

19. I don't see how the idea of heterogeneous temporalities, a common chestnut of cultural studies, would be able to surpass anthropological multicultural mapping.

20. See for example the Latin American subalternist founding statement, included in Beverley, Aronna, and Oviedo (1995).

21. The original reads, in part, "con las plumas o el *chiripá* que nos atribuye." The *chiripá* is a garment worn by gauchos over their pants.

22. For a postcolonial approach to modernity's libidinal charge, see Young (1995).

23. The young Malfatti exhibited her expressionist-informed paintings in São Paulo in 1917, to harsh critiques from the established cultural intelligentsia. The reception of the Argentinean Petorruti's cubist- and futurist-inflected art was similar.

24. The European bias of Anderson's Third World paragraph was already noticed by García Canclini (1989), although in different terms. García Canclini takes issue with the

all-encompassing category "Third World" and with the understanding of its cultural modernity as "a deferred and deficient echo of the center" (69).

25. According to Bender and Wellbery (1991, 3), "Mikhail Bakhtin borrowed the suggestive term 'chronotope' from Einstein's physics in order to designate the fusion of temporal/spatial structures and to define characteristic time/space formations in specific narrative genres such as the romance, the idyll, the folktale, the picaresque novel, and so forth. . . . Bakhtin's term is suggestive because it points to the diversity of prototypical cultural forms within which time assumes significance."

26. As Caren Kaplan (1997, 33) puts it, "Williams's perspectives on modern metropoles, then, demonstrate that an emphasis on mass displacement alone does not deconstruct a modernist trope. Nor, as Paul Gilroy has argued, does such an emphasis escape neoconservative affiliations. In order to destabilize the Euro-American myth of modernist exile, it is necessary to critique the formation of centers as well as peripheries as modernist productions."

27. I am using the term "tactical counternarrative" in the sense given it by Michel de Certeau. Whereas the strategic is based on place as a distinct field of vision and the establishment of a visual vantage point, the tactical is action with no option of grasping the whole. It is thus without a general plan and, therefore, based on opportunities and chance.

28. The pessimistic reading can be related to Gramscian critique and the position that Timothy Brennan (1997) has taken in recent debates about cosmopolitanism.

29. David Palumbo-Liu (1997) provides a solid critique of Bourdieu from a transnational viewpoint.

30. Wilson Martins (1970) has mapped out the Brazilian literary system at the stage of the emergence of the vanguard movements, and Beatriz Sarlo (1988) and Francine Masiello (1986) have performed excellent analytical panoramas of the Argentinean.

31. These reflections are of course inspired by Jacques Derrida's elaborations (1978) in the essay "Freud and the Scene of Writing."

32. I am referring of course to the Romantic dictum "Man is only completely human when he plays," stated by Friedrich von Schiller in his 1795 work *On the Aesthetic Education of Man*. Disinterestedness guarantees the working of an autonomous, free consciousness. See also Kant (2000) on the "free play of the faculties," first published in 1790.

33. Argentinean critics of Arlt, such as Elsa Drucaroff (1999, chapter 2) and Silvia Saítta (2000, 56–59), have shown convincingly that the myth of the proletarian journalist that the author cultivated doesn't correspond with his comfortable position in the workplace, where his success as an author exempted him from the rules governing other journalists. This is of course important, but rather than serving as an attempt to demystify Arlt, it sheds light on the author's effort to construct an artistic persona.

Chapter 3: Locating the Future in *Los siete locos*

1. The history of these contending groups has been told countless times. Suffice it to say here that the Florida group that issued the magazine *Martín Fierro* can be roughly characterized as more invested in liberal values, artistic individualism, and a defense of the in-

dependence of the cultural sphere, whereas the Boedo group tended more toward a social-realist aesthetic and internationalist and proletarian ethics. For a more detailed history and a fine analysis of the Argentinean literary milieu of the 1920s and 1930s, see Beatriz Sarlo's *Una modernidad periférica: Buenos Aires 1920 y 1930* (1988), and Francine Masiello's *Lenguaje e ideología: Las escuelas argentinas de vanguardia* (1986).

2. The argument of Arlt's novel resembles in many aspects that of Dostoyevsky's 1871 work *The Demons*. This doesn't seem to be the result of coincidence but, rather, of decisive imitation. But as Amícola (1994, 15–19) has pointed out, the aristocratic attack on liberalism and the defense of the religious dimension of the Slavic soul is nowhere to be found in Arlt. Quite the opposite, as I will demonstrate with my argument: Both the force of modernization and that of a possible revolutionary movement constantly undermine every spiritual and/or territorial niche that could serve as counterpoint.

3. For a discussion of the imperial geopolitical theories of the late nineteenth century (principally, those of Friedrich Ratzel and Halford J. Mackinder) and their visual displays, see Christopher GoGwilt (2000, especially chapter 1). His main argument is that the emergence of the field of geopolitics is related to the crisis of the model of civilization and *Bildung*, which constituted a set of cultural arguments for European superiority and universality.

4. Although not discussed in the novel, the Morgan family fortune is related in more than one sense to the geopolitical preoccupations that are present in it. J. P. Morgan's fortune was closely related to the construction of railroads in the United States. He died—as a good man of the nineteenth century—just before the outbreak of World War I, in 1913. His heir, J. P. Morgan Jr., continued to expand the family's fortunes, strengthening their banking interests by supporting British financial stability during the First World War and financing reconstruction in the war's aftermath. The story of the family fortune seems to echo the kind of shift in world power that is present in the novel.

5. Amícola (1994) stresses the role of the Astrologer as a propagator of wrong ideologies that thwart the genuine revolutionary process. "Astrology" and "fascism," the terms that appear in the title of his book, are to be related as two modes of inauthenticity: "fascism reveals itself as a countermarch in the not-always lineal historical progress" (50). Meanwhile (leftist) revolution is to be understood as adhering to a more lineal one. A classic book in Arlt criticism, Beatriz Pastor's *Roberto Arlt y la rebelión alienada* (1980) brings this division between true and alienated rebellion to its apotheosis: Every character is dissected according to his or her distance from the ideal of a revolutionary consciousness that is the master criteria for evaluation. Other critics, such as Sarlo, are more attuned to matters of representation and to the process of belief and making believe, which is not likely to be overcome by any historical progress, revolutionary or otherwise.

6. Neil Smith (2003) has argued in a brilliant book, that the U.S. constitutes its global political power by denying geopolitics, as if geopolitics were defeated after the era of European imperialism. The map functions throughout the novel as a constant reminder of what Smith argues is "the fact that global power is disproportionately wielded by a ruling class that remains tied to the national interests of the United States" (xix).

7. My use of the concept of deterritorialization is of course informed by the elaborations of Deleuze and Guattari, *Anti-Oedipus: Capitalism and Schizophrenia* (Minneapolis: University of Minnesota Press: 1977). But Immanuel Wallerstein (2003), among others, gives a far more precise rendition of what he calls "historical capitalism" as continually moving between territorializing and deterritorializing strategies, while Robert Young (1995) elaborates an explicitly Deleuzian version of the concept for colonial and postcolonial situation.

8. Note, for example, a very mediocre but nevertheless exemplary poem by the Uruguayan avant-gardist Juan Parra del Riego in his 1925 book iconoclastically titled *Himno del cielo y los ferrocarriles* (Hymn of the sky and the railroads). In the poem "Pampa Argentina," he proclaims: "I saw you from the train / I was coming from the side / where one can see America as a fruit under the sun." The train here is a place for reconciliation between the individual (who carries within himself the "bitter and dark ill of the cities" that the countryside would unsettle) and the American landscape.

9. See my discussion in chapter 2 of Perry Anderson's seminal article.

10. See, for example, Benedict Anderson's *Imagined Communities* (1996) and Timothy Brennan (1997).

11. The relationship between the railroad and national cohesion is everywhere throughout the nineteenth century (most famously in the work of Sarmiento). Subscribing to this consensus, a historian of the railroad in Argentina (Rebuelto 1994, 51) declares that the underlying reason for its construction was "not purely [the pursuit of] material advantages, as it was for the European countries that perfected the industry of transportation," but "a slow conquest of the Republic by the rail, that is to say, for civilization; and the international railroads that cross the frontiers are factors in the union with neighboring countries . . . of extreme importance for South American politics." More eloquently, Ezequiel Ramos Mejía (minister of public works in the era of the construction of railroads) declared at the inauguration of the Retiro train station in Buenos Aires that "everyone knows . . . that the railroad and the telegraph have been the main factors of our definitive organization and of the achieved civilization, even more so than in other countries where distance and the desert were not, as they were here, the main allies and accomplices of barbarism" (Rebuelto 1994, 88).

12. See Wallerstein (2003, chapter 4).

13. This last, more common vision of the political act that perpetuates the order of the visible is called by Rancière "the police." The thesis is developed in *Disagreement* (1999).

14. "The war imposed homogeneous time," points out Kern (1983, 288), who calls World War I, after Gertrude Stein, "the cubist war": simultaneity and perspectivism were paramount, the lack of a center key, "a composition [that of this war] of which one corner was as important as another corner" (Kern 1983, 288).

15. "The speculative returns, located in the very heart of the mechanical order," points out de Certau (1988, 113); and "How can the railroad system, with its intricate synchronization, serve as an emblem of randomness?" asks Gumbrecht (1997, 178).

16. The suburban enclave chosen by Arlt seems to be paradigmatic of a certain Argentinean nineteenth century as well. Temperley was founded by an Englishman (George Temperley, 1823–1900), who partitioned his own land in order to create a town bearing his name. With the zeal of a pioneer, he funded the construction of an Anglican church (Holy Trinity) and a train station, later making arrangements for the train to stop there. An indication of its continuing symbolic relevance is the fact that the Prince of Wales paid a visit to the Temperley station in 1925 (http://www.temperleyweb.com.ar, consulted March 7, 2005).

17. In fact, the narration of his life by Haffner mirrors the two-stage logic of the revolutionary plan, inasmuch as the first breakthrough period of adventures is followed by a reorganization of his life as based on rational decisions and conservative growth: "I have planned out my life like an industrialist. Every day I go to bed at midnight and get up at nine in the morning," he says (39).

18. Remedios de Escalada's industrial activity was inextricably related to the functioning of the railroad system. The workshops were dedicated exclusively to the fabrication and repair of railroad components. In 1923, they received the name that concomitantly names the town that was developed around the compound.

19. The other kind of a society of spectacle is the "diffuse form [that] is associated with the abundance of commodities, with the undisturbed development of modern capitalism. Here each commodity considered in isolation is justified by an appeal to the grandeur of commodity production in general—a production for which the spectacle is an apologetic catalog" (Debord 1994, 42).

20. Beatriz Sarlo (1988, 57) reads the inventor in terms of the disjunctive temporalities of daily life under capitalist production and consumption and the stroke of luck (*batacazo*): "the triumph of the inventor endows him, in a single shot, with fame, women, money." Ricardo Piglia (1986) instead touches upon the writer's own conception of literature and politics as a machine of make-believe.

21. For a discussion on the persistent feminization of the mass media public (a topic that goes back at least to *Madame Bovary*) and its connection to Adorno's anxiety about the loss of self, see Andreas Huyssen (1986, especially chapters 1 and 3).

22. There is, in fact, a certain homosexual tension, mixed with hatred, between Erdosain and Barsut.

23. The Mexican narrative of the 1920s is a good example of this trend, "idle fictions," to use Gustavo Pérez Firmat's apt expression, turned toward an exploration of the topography of subjectivity. See for example Arqueles Vela's 1926 *El café de nadie*; Xavier Villaurrutia's 1928 *Novela como nube*; and Salvador Novo's 1928 *Return Ticket*. Metafiction is explored more prominently, and in different ways, in *Fulano de tal* (1925) and *Libro sin tapas* (1929), by Felisberto Hernández. Also consider *El habitante y su esperanza*, the lyrical 1926 novel by Pablo Neruda; *Papeles de recienvenido y continuación de la nada* (1929), by Macedonio Fernández; and *Un hombre muerto a puntapiés* (1927), by Pablo Palacio.

24. The region plays a role at the end of *El juguete rabioso*, Arlt's 1926 novel, when it

is suggested that the protagonist, Silvio Astier, exhausted by the moral dilemmas and the travails he encounters in Buenos Aires, looks for solace in the mountain landscape of the Argentinean South.

25. See his *Fervor de Buenos Aires* (1923), *Luna de enfrente* (1925), and *Cuaderno San Martín* (1929).

26. In Argentina, "British capital became so routine an element of administrative life that municipal and provincial governments vied with the national state for funds on the London stock exchange," writes Tulio Halperín Donghi (1996: 189), referring to what he calls the "maturity of the neocolonial order"—roughly, 1880 to 1930.

27. Smith argues that the shift of the world hegemony from the European empires to the new constitution of world power under the U.S. and its allies, which begins after World War I, conceals its geopolitical intent and its roots in European geopolitics under the veil of universalizing notions of global liberalism.

28. A brilliant exception that nevertheless follows the tendency to endow Arlt with prophetic powers is Josefina Ludmer's interpretation of the novel. In conclusions that are compatible with my argument, Ludmer engages the prophetic not as individual vision but as an epistemological stance. We are in the presence, according to her argument, of a particular "Latin American cultural formation," one in which political representation is figured from the other side of a frontier in which everything—capitalism, socialism, anarchism, fascism, etc.—exists in a monstrous state, beyond binary oppositions that would grant a clear-cut differentiation. By untying the representations forged in the center of capitalism, the simultaneous existence of the incompatible in "the other side" (the peripheries) highlights unexpected familiarities across allegedly oppositional binaries. Therefore, the capacity to "announce the coup d'état of 1930" (Ludmer 2004, 382) is based, following Ludmer's complex argument, in this epistemological stance within global capitalism (381–85).

29. It is perhaps of relevance here that at the time Arlt was writing, the Argentinean movie industry was the strongest and most widely distributed in Latin America.

Chapter 4: *Macunaíma* in the Mouth of the Cannibal

1. *Antropofagia* was vindicated in the 1950s, for example, by the *poesia concreta* movement led by Haroldo and Augusto de Campos; in the 1960s by the *tropicalista* movement of young musicians, as well as by the *cinema novo* film trend (e.g., the 1969 Joaquim Pedro de Andrade film *Macunaíma* and the 1971 Nelson Pereria dos Santos film *Como era gostoso o meu francês* [How tasty was my little Frenchman]); in the 1990s, the most relevant art exhibit in Latin America, the Bienal de São Paulo (in its twenty-fourth edition), adopted the title *"Antropofagia: Releituras"* (Antropophagy: Rereadings).

2. São Paulo underwent a rapid process of industrialization and growth beginning in the early twentieth century. It became a magnet for immigration, both from the hinterlands of Brazil and from Europe.

3. *Macunaíma* was written in 1926 and 1927 and published in 1928.

4. Bibliographic information about what has been dubbed the "heroic" era of *mod-

ernismo, often idealized as the golden age of artistic agitation, abounds. See Randall Johnson (1999) for a good account (and a perceptive critical analysis) of the main trends of the movement. In his survey called *The Modernist Idea*, Wilson Martins includes a chapter about the festival called "Seven Days that Shook the Literary World."

5. It is clear that cannibalism is a constant in Western literature and thought. Besides the volume edited by Barke, Hulme, and Iversen (*Cannibalism and the Colonial World*. Cambridge: Cambridge University Press, 1998), an excellent discussion of the subject can also be found in Maggie Kilgour's *From Communion to Cannibalism: An Anatomy of Metaphors of Incorporation* (Princeton, N.J.: Princeton University Press, 1990). David K. Jackson (1987) usefully traces the contemporaneous relevance of the cannibal in the production of Marinetti, Cendrars, Apollinaire, Jarry, Picabia, and others.

6. A reading of Brazilian cultural history was exhibited at the Guggenheim in New York—Brazil: Body and Soul (curated by Edward T. Sullivan, October–May 2001). It was displayed as a historical trajectory starting with the Baroque and jumping almost immediately to artists associated with *modernismo* (Emiliano Di Cavalcanti, Tarsila do Amaral, etc.).

7. The most programmatic article by Haroldo de Campos in that regard announces this paradox in its title "The Rule of Anthropophagy: Europe Under the Sign of Devoration."

8. See chapter 2, note 5, for examples of these reevaluations. But *modernismo's antropofagia* has always had the potential of standing for the Latin American cultural situation, not only the Brazilian. One of the latest reincarnations of this potential in postcolonial theory is Roberto Fernández Retamar's "Caliban Speaks Five Hundred Years Later," in which he revisits his famous reading of Shakespeare's Caliban, this time in light of Oswald's elaboration. See *Dangerous Liaisons: Gender, Nation, and Postcolonial Perspectives*, eds. Anne McClintock, Aamir Mufti, and Ella Shohat (Minneapolis: University of Minnesota Press, 1997).

9. Fernando Ortiz, the Cuban intellectual who articulated the notion of *transculturación* in his *Cuban Counterpoint of Tobacco and Sugar* (1940), had ties to the Cuban *minorista* intellectual vanguard and to writers and artists (Nicolás Guillén, Wilfredo Lam, Federico García Lorca, Alejo Carpentier, etc.) and was profoundly informed by other vanguard trends. He was a pioneer in the anthropological reevaluation of Afro-Cuban cultures that made possible avant-garde negritude (whose most prominent example was Nicolás Guillén). In his 1940 treatise, Ortiz shows the role of colonial exploitation and modes of production in shaping what becomes most authentically national. The counterpoint between tobacco and sugar marks the place where Cuba is inscribed in the colonial and transnational market. Throughout this chapter, I will use "transculturation" in order to name a strategy of nationalization of difference, not to make a direct allusion to Fernando Ortiz. His performative decentering of metropolitan anthropological approaches for which culture can be singled out and objectified was also meant to provide a model for Cuban national culture. See Fernando Coronil's introduction to the English translation.

Mexican José de Vasconcelos, although not a vanguardist himself either, introduced a notion of hybridity in *The Cosmic Race* (1926) that can't be assessed without reference to the intellectual milieu of the Mexican revolution and the artistic vanguards that preceded him. Vasconcelos remained attached to a racial construct made up of heterogeneous but "Latin-dominant" mixes, prophetically posited as a way to embrace and supersede the variety of the Latin American racial stock.

10. Particularly *francesas,* French women. Reporting from Brazil, Lévi-Strauss (1974, 125) recalls that "brothels, most of them specializing in those *francesinhas* . . . together with French nuns, were the most active agents of French influence abroad in the nineteenth century."

11. See, for example, Santiago (1989, 76–80).

12. The debate around the novel's genre was already enacted by Mário, who referred to *Macunaíma* as a "history" and a "romance" (in an attempt to bring it close to popular tales, according to Cavalcanti Proença). The critic Gilda Mello e Souza classifies it as rhapsody, while other critics are more apt to see it as an epic. All these theories, which implicitly judge the novelistic structure against the canon of nineteenth-century realism, are as irreproachable as they are misguided. The novelistic genre has survived by incorporating genres, both those historically preceding it and those contemporary with it, as different mass-media expressions. Most importantly, these critical strategies are guided by a longing for an authenticity that would be found in the popular or the classic genres, an authenticity that is a value constantly undermined by the novel.

13. Freud's *Totem and Taboo* is also an intertext of the "Manifesto antropofágico."

14. Fredric Jameson's (1987) discussion on the allegorical quality of Third World narrative has triggered its own breed of critical response. I believe the debate (upon which I already touched in chapter 2, in reference to Yúdice's argument) is finally over. I am neither supporting Jameson's idea nor intervening in that particular discussion. The force of Jameson's conception is based on the possibility of reading the political into the "private" problems presented by realist novels. *Macunaíma*, with its protagonist "the hero of our people," already introduces itself as dealing with something other than a bourgeois individual. It is, no doubt, a national allegory. Its problem, if we are to put it in the terms of this polemic, is the impossibility of allegorizing the nation.

15. For this and other information on Mário's intellectual resources, the study of Telê Porto Ancona Lopes (1972) is fundamental. Lopes informs us that Mário read Frazer's influential treatise in an abbreviated French version, *Le rameau d'or*, translated by Lady Frazer (Paris: L. Orientaliste Paul Geutner, 1923). The connection between *bumba-meu-boi* and the vegetation cycle has already been pointed out by Gilda Mello e Souza in *O Tupi e o Alaúde* (São Paulo: Livraria Duas Cidades, 1979).

16. The dance, which concerns a cycle of death and resurrection, is performed in street festivals and carnival celebrations throughout Brazil. The different characters of the ritual incarnate Christian saints, cattle tenders, and a magic ox (*boi*). Besides the obvious Portuguese elements, the cult of the ox also has African roots. It is believed that it started as a play among African slaves in the Northeast. As it spread subsequently it incorporated other regional elements. Mário de Andrade annotated his version of *Le rameau d'or* with the fol-

lowing reminder to himself: "Show that the cult of the ox in the *bumba* has nothing to do with the ox of the solar cult or other silliness. It is the transformation of the vegetal cult into animal cult" (Lopez 1972, 90). The solar cults are central to Sir Edward Tylor's theses in *Primitive Culture*—which Mário also read in a French translation (Lopez 1972, 87).

17. See Raul Antelo's *Na Ilha de Marapatá: Mário de Andrade lê os hispanoamericanos* (Hucitec: São Paulo, 1986) for a comprehensive analysis of Mário's readings of his Spanish-language contemporaries.

18. Mário bitterly complains in a private letter to a friend: "When Oswald [de Andrade] was traveling through Europe and I had resolved to champion Brazilianness, not only to touch the problem more closely but also to call attention to it . . . and Oswald would write to me from there 'Come here to know what art is,' 'Here is where you find what we should follow' etc. . . . And I, due to my resolution, replied, 'It is only Brazil that interests me,' 'I deepened my face inside I peered into the virgin forest.' . . . Oswald comes back from Europe, invents Brazilwood . . . and I myself turned into Brazilwood in the eyes of everyone" (later published in *Macunaíma*, 497).

19. Proença (1987, 286); *Macunaíma*, 560 (glossary).

20. See Skidmore (1974) for a full-fledged analytical account of this development.

21. See Lilia Moritz Schwarcz's excellent 1993 study on race and the gaze, *O espetáculo das raças: Cientistas, instituições e a questão social no Brasil, 1870–1930* (São Paulo: Companhia das Letras).

22. The idea of racial democracy was introduced by Gilberto Freyre in his *Interpretação do Brasil* (1941), but its genesis can be traced back to the *modernistas*.

23. This is one of the important contributions of Roberto González Echeverría's theory of Latin American narrative in his *Myth and Archive* (1990). But *Macunaíma* disarranges González Echevarría's model. While the regional novel, which is the subject of the critic's historiography, borrows its discursive authority from anthropology, this modernist novel includes a repertoire of contrastive anthropological discursive strategies, which ultimately puts into question the authority of the science. This latter development González Echevarría identifies with postmodernism and ascribes to the narrative of Borges and García Márquez, among others. My point is that the avant-gardes were already questioning the makeup of anthropological authority.

24. For an analytical account of this inaugural trip, see Aracy Amaral (1970).

25. "The name Icamiaba comes from the region next to Mt. Icamiaba in the Amazon, where, according to the legend, the women warriors lived" (glossary for *Macunaíma*, 551). The Amazon got its name after Spanish conquistador Francisco de Orellana reported having been attacked by women warriors.

26. John Beverley (1999, 45) foregrounds the teleological quality of the narratives of transculturation.

27. This is one of the foundational myths of Brazilian nationality, according to DaMatta (1981), a tripartite scheme that obliterates the hierarchical racial ideology in the construction of identity by assigning to each group a place in human history (62–71).

28. What *Macunaíma* doesn't produce is an embodiment of a transcendental mixed

identity, as can be found in Nicolás Guillén's "Balada de los dos abuelos" (in his book *West Indies, Ltd.*, 1934), where poetic, subjective, and national unity are simultaneously achieved by the poetic voice that transcends historic differences between its white and black ancestry.

29. In *Les fonctions mentales dans les sociétés inférieures* (1916), which Mário probably read (although Lopez claims that Mário actually had access to this book only after he completed the novel). In the English edition (*How Natives Think* [Salem, N.H.: Ayer, 1984]) the mention to the Bororo parrot-man can be found on page 77. A good discussion of Lévy-Bruhl's influence in Anglo-American modernism can be found in David Spurr's "Myths of Anthropology: Eliot, Joyce, Lévy-Bruhl," *PMLA* 109, no. 2: 266–80.

30. My conclusions are related to what Maggie Kilgour (1990, 226) regards as the trajectory of cannibalism in Western thought, one of "increasing internalization, a movement toward a world in which everything is imagined as being 'inside.' This has certainly been the dream underlying the hope of the scientific mastery of nature, as well as various forms of imperialism." The impossibility of mastering the colonial position from inside the nation and its dream of autonomy is what is at stake in the novel.

Chapter 5: Leaving Home

1. I am indebted here to the project of subaltern studies in the sense used by John Beverley (1999: 16) when he states that "what subaltern studies makes visible is precisely the fissured character of the national narrative itself, the way it is intersected by other stories, other modes of production, other values and identities." I would argue, however, that a radical subalternist project would necessarily distance itself from the national perspective by which these "others" are silenced, not attempting to stitch the fissures for a reconstitution of the national body.

2. This self-reproducing national expansionism is one of the prevalent ideologies of Brazilian modernity. In *A pátria geográfica*, Vidal e Souza (1997) analyze several essays on the interpretation of Brazilian reality to highlight their geographical argumentation. One of the most interesting chapters in the evolution of this thought is the nationalist recuperation of the geographical argument during Getúlio Vargas's populist regime, which lasted most of the period from 1930 to 1954, expressed in essays that would become canonical, such as *Marcha para oeste* (March toward the west, 1943), by Cassiano Ricardo. *Modernismo* prepares the ground for this recuperation of the hinterlands, but it is also profoundly at odds with this nationalistic epic, and my interpretation highlights this latter side of the divide.

3. Until the end of the 1950s, several European travelers of different sorts (filmmakers, engineers, journalists, missionaries, etc.) kept claiming for themselves the title of precursors in a virgin land (see Ross and Hampton, 1993).

4. The two folders have different subtitles. The first, corresponding to the Amazonian travel, reads: *Travel through the Amazon to Peru, through Madeira to Bolivia, and through Marajó to the Point of Saying Enough!* This one obviously mimics and parodies the style of

earlier travelogues. The second folder, corresponding to the *sertão* trip, is entitled *Ethnographic Travel*, perhaps connoting an initially more serious intention, although this is rendered ambiguous within the context of the main title. All that is clear is that the author is attempting to construct a new space between already institutionalized ones.

5. See Weinstein (1983).

6. Mário calls this boy an "expert *tapujo*," a Tupi word that formerly signified a member of an enemy tribe but that came to be used in Brazilian Portuguese, particularly in the Amazonian region, for an integrated or pacified Indian.

7. Interestingly, not even this influx of capital made the Amazon region into an integral part of the national economy (Weinstein 1983, 230).

8. A concept that he elaborates in the second trip but that appears in his later studies of folklore. Mobile traditions are the ones in constant transformation, whereas fixed ones (such as neocolonial architecture) are purely decorative, institutionalized, and stagnant (see 1981, 254–55).

Mário de Andrade's legacy for Brazilian folklore studies is invaluable. Part of this legacy consisted of the material collected on these voyages, particularly the second one to the Northeast. Some of his studies in ethnomusicology were published during his lifetime, others constituted an always postponed project. His most famous unpublished book, to which he always referred in articles and conversations, was *Na pancada do ganzá*. Oneyda Alvarenga, in her preliminary study of the posthumously published *Os cocos* (which was planned by Mário as a section of *Na pancada*), affirms that from 1935 until his death, it was his post as director of the Department of Culture of São Paulo that prevented him from accomplishing his folkloric and literary projects.

9. Whose most conspicuous exponent in the Brazilian context of the late nineteenth century was Silvio Romero.

10. Jean de Léry, in his Historie d'un voyage fait en la terre du Brésil (History of a voyage made to the land of Brasil, 1578) describes some dramatic dances. Karl Friedrich von Martius, a native of Bavaria, traveled with Johann Baptist von Spix for three years in the late 1810s through the interior of Brazil (including the Amazon). Upon their return to Munich, they published their travelogue in three volumes that appeared from 1823 to 1831 (*Reise in Brasilien*). Besides gathering botanical and zoological samples, they collected native songs and depicted and described the customs and mores of different tribes in good naturalist fashion. In addition to this work, von Martius established the parameters for Brazilian historiography when he was awarded the first prize by the Instituto Histórico e Geográfico Brasileiro for his essay entitled "Como se deve escrever a história do Brasil" (How Brazilian history should be written, 1845). The piece "furnished the fundamental elements of imperial historiography: incorporation of the three races with an emphasis on the predominance of Portuguese over indigenous and African; attention to regional particularities, with regard to ultimate unity; intransigent defense of constitutional monarchy as guarantor of national unity; belief in a grand destiny" (Murilho de Carvalho 1999, 242).

11. It can be argued that Vladimir Propp was at the same time organizing the same puz-

zle differently, with a protostructuralist notion of a universal folklore. True, but it would have explained away concerns that Mário was wrestling with from a Latin American subject position.

12. *Coco* is both a dramatic dance and the music that accompanies it.

13. Mário planned, but never finished, a novel that included the character Chico Antônio. As late as August and September of 1943, Mário published a number of journalistic articles on Chico Antônio in his music column in *Folha da Manha*.

14. According to a web search engine for quotations (www.giga-usa.com, consulted on March 7, 2005), it is a "song of the French Soldiers in the Great War." It was written in 1914 by Louis Bousquet (lyrics) and Camille Robert (music). The web site translates: "When Madelon comes out to serve us drinks, / We always know she's coming by her song. / And every man he tells his little tale, / And Madelon is never too severe— / A kiss or two is nothing much to her— / She laughs us up to love and life and God— / Madelon, Madelon, Madelon" (January 21, 2004). The complete lyrics in their original French can be found at www.paroles.net (as of March 7, 2005). A character in e. e. cummings's novel *The Enormous Room* (1922), about the author's detention in a French prison, also sings the song.

15. I am inspired by Paul Gilroy's lead when, in his reconceptualization of modernity from the standpoint of one of its excluded narratives, that is, slavery, he points out the importance of the chronotope of the ship. See Gilroy (1993, chapter 1).

16. The construction of the railroad was carried out in two stages, from 1878 to 1879 and from 1907 to 1912. It was, as the historian of this enterprise puts it, one of the many workers' burial sites of the late nineteenth century, along with the Belgian Congo Railroad and the Panama Canal (Foot Hardman 1988, 129). Workers of nationalities as varied as Indian, Chinese, and Bolivian were recruited through international agencies. The many difficulties, along with very poor health conditions of the site, led to the complete abandonment of the project (including buildings and at least one locomotive) after eighteen months of work (131). More than twenty thousand workers from fifty different nationalities were imported for the second attempt, of whom around 20 percent died in work-related circumstances (139–40). The reasons for building this railroad were always more symbolic than economic, according to Foot Hardman's account. Moreover, rubber prices and the importance of that industry for Brazil diminished dramatically as soon as the project was finished in 1912.

17. Libero Badaró was an Italian-born physician who immigrated to Brazil and had a prominent career as an anti-imperial journalist. He was assassinated during an 1830 protest against the emperor Dom Pedro I. A São Paulo street now bears his name. It so happens that the art gallery where the polemical exhibit by the expressionist painter Anita Malfatti took place was located on this street, an event usually recognized as an antecedent of the 1922 Week of Modern Art. The Taunays were an important family of French academic painters that landed in Brazil. Nicolas Antoine Taunay went to Brazil in the early nineteenth century as part of a French artistic mission and became one of the founders and faculty members of the Imperial Academy of Fine Arts in Rio. Two of his sons, Felix and

Adrien, followed in his steps, the former joining the faculty of the academy and the latter a commissioned painter for different expeditions. Matarazzo was a well-known Italian businessman, especially prominent in the São Paulo industrial boom of the early twentieth century.

18. There was a remarkable revalorization in the 1990s of Arlt's journalistic production, with the release of many editions of his "Aguafuertes," some of them edited by literary critic Sylvia Saítta, who also wrote the first biography of the author (2000).

19. In his fundamental study of the politics of space in the city of Buenos Aires, Adrián Gorelik (1998) has noted that what once had been a flexible mechanism of producing citizenship by the dialectical implementation of the grid and the park came to a point of stagnation in the 1930s that he calls "modernization without reform." Mass culture, Gorelik points out, works in this reformulation of urban space by transforming citizens into spectators.

20. In this permanent questioning of its own grounds, this dialect of identification and defamiliarization, we can read Arlt's distancing from the picturesque chronicling of some antecessors (Fray Mocho, Payró, and from the mimetic realism of the socially *engagé* vanguard). Jens Andermann (2000), in a compelling comparison of Payró's and Arlt's travel writing, has made the point that the former was striving to incorporate the hinterlands into the repertoire of institutionalized discourses (128–50). Arlt's strategies, I argue, point directly to the task of these discourses.

21. From a critical perspective more interested in the fragmentation of the self, Francine Masiello's analysis (1986) of Argentinean avant-garde discourses reaches conclusions that are complementary to my own. Departing from the "self-protective elaboration of mythology in which Borges and Macedonio Fernández are engaged, which inscribe the subject in an enclosed discursive space," Arlt's opening of the discursive space and undermining of the authority conferred to the writer "announces the inexorable triumph of forces beyond the self" (229). Masiello locates this disruptive other logic in the audience.

22. Villa Crespo is a middle-class Buenos Aires neighborhood. The paragraph finishes with the untranslatable "buscara yacija en la casa infernal," "yacija" being a rarely used word that encompasses the meanings of "bed" and "grave."

23. The recurrent use of the term "spectacle" in the works of Arlt. This story, which begins "Maciel Island is rich in brutal spectacles," after several paragraphs of a continuing use of this same notion, ends up by pointing to the observer's will to forget "that sinister spectacle." The spectacular character of modern modes of production forms part of a complex that I will try to analyze later in this chapter. My intention for now is to connect the spectacular with the daily production of accounts and with the general function of journalism—which no doubt can be related to the pseudocyclical time of commodity as spectacle as elaborated by Guy Debord (1994), departing from Marx's notion of commodity fetishism as evoking the ritual circularity of religious rites. Within the unification of time that is linear and of an irreversible planetary scale, according to Debord, there exists a consumable time, a daily dose of spectacle that takes up and commodifies aspects of an abolished previous cyclical time. Although I don't share the philosophy of history implicit in

Debord's account (bourgeois time is for him more truly historical than the mythical times of the past and therefore rises above the irrationality of myth, since Judeo-Christianity is more "historic" than primitive religions), I find the notion of pseudocyclical time of great worth in characterizing the repetitive and recurrent character of the spectacular event, a "commodity [that] is presented as a moment of authentic life whose cyclical return we are supposed to look forward to" (112).

24. I find Susan Buck-Morss's succinct definition (1989, 219) of the complex Benjaminian notion useful here: "In the traces left by the object's after-history, the conditions of its decay and the manner of its cultural transmission, the utopian images of past objects can be read in the present as truth. . . . Benjamin was counting on the shock of this recognition to jolt the dreaming collective into a political 'awakening. . . .' The presentation of the historical object within a charged force field of past and present, which produces political electricity in a 'lightning flash' of truth, is the 'dialectical image.'"

25. In his study of space, Henri Lefebvre (2000) separates concrete space from abstract space. While abstract space names what is produced by a process of commodification and bureaucratization, concrete space names those elements of everyday life that, without being colonized by previous processes, take with them pieces and memories of other ways of spatial conformation. According to Edward Ball (Gregory 1994, 402), Lefebvre's intention is "to conceive everyday life in such a way as to retrieve it from its modern state of colonization by the commodity form and other modes of reification. A critique of the everyday can be generated only by a kind of alienation effect, insofar as it is put into contact with its own radical *other*, such as an eradicated past . . . or an imagined future."

26. Here I am using Mary Louise Pratt's concept (1992) that a "contact zone is an attempt to invoke the spatial and temporal copresence of subjects previously separated by geographic and historical disjuncture and whose trajectories now intersect." With this concept, Pratt attempts to challenge the perspectives that she calls "diffusionist," which put emphasis only on the outward diffusion of conquest and domination—an agenda that I share but attempt to pursue through different strategies. The "contact zone" tries to emphasize how subjects are constituted in relation, "in terms of copresence, interaction, interlocking understandings and practices, often within radically asymmetrical relations of power" (7).

27. See, for example, his *En el país del viento: Viajes a la Patagonia (1934)* (Buenos Aires: Simurg, 1997), which compiles his writings from his trip to the south.

28. See "Paris, Capital of the Nineteenth Century" in Walter Benjamin (1986); also Buck-Morss (1989, 81–82).

29. The "Aguafuertes fluviales" of June, July, and August 1933 remain unpublished in book form.

30. Arlt channels his annoyance by classifying typical travel subjects: the frustrated writer of means, the petty fugitive, the bored aristocrat, and so on.

31. Some of his chronicles focus on the social implications of the cinematographic spectacle, which he usually favors. The corpus dealing with film is compiled under the title *Notas sobre el cinematógrafo* (Buenos Aires: Simurg, 1997).

32. Jonathan Friedman (1995, 78–79) has shown how both positions depend on the anthropological concept of the cultural mosaic: "The practice of cosmopolitanism, common to the self-styled global ethnographer of culture, is predicated on maintaining distance, often a superiority to the local. . . . There was a time when cosmopolitans, as anthropologists, could pass themselves off as masters of otherness. This was a world of discrete cultures, the classical mosaic of relativism."

33. I won't touch upon his Spanish season at the time of the Republic, because it would deserve a whole chapter that would have to take into consideration the enormous corpus of the international and internationalist modernist writing on Spain. Moreover, Arlt's treatment of topics such as Galician migration to Argentina, Basque nationalist movements, and Andalusian Gypsies while he travels through these regions deserves a full-fledged analysis. Sylvia Saítta (2000, 189–91) points out that Arlt wanted to be at the forefront of the conflict in Spain as a foreign correspondent, but instead, "from his office in Buenos Aires, he had to settle for witnessing the world through cables and reports, from the sidelines, from the 'margin of the newswire' . . . one of the goals of his column was to flesh out the news that came from wires stripped of all their drama. . . . Just as he expands three lines with narrative, Arlt describes some of the photos that arrive at the newspaper office and elaborates the meaning that the images suggest. The descriptions of the photographs of what is happening elsewhere in the world, whether in the great cities or in the remote towns, allows Arlt to be a direct spectator of the events and not merely a resigned correspondent of war from far away." My argument differs from Saítta's useful remarks in that I tend to regard his strategy as something other than a compensation for the lack of presence. The Spanish *aguafuertes* are compiled in the volumes *Aguafuertes Gallegas* (Buenos Aires: Ameghino Editora, 1997) and *Aguafuertes Gallegas y Asturianas* (Buenos Aires: Losada, 1999).

I consulted the articles of the "Tiempos presentes" and "Al margen del cable" era in his original source of publication, the newspaper *El Mundo*, in the Biblioteca Nacional in Buenos Aires. A selection—based on what was contemporaneously reproduced by the Mexican newspaper *El Nacional* between 1937 and 1941—was recently published: *Al margen del cable: Crónicas publicadas en "El Nacional," México, 1937–1941* (Buenos Aires: Losada, 2003).

34. This is a recurring theme in Arlt's work, as seen already in the analysis of *Los siete locos*. In his chronicles, he had taken issue with the end of the voyage from the radically different perspective of the bourgeois interior. In a chronicle of March 15, 1930, the writer plays with "faded memories from postcards" of the "fin-de-siècle" to affirm that the interior décor of a pub anywhere can now replace an uncomfortable trip to London.

35. As we have already seen, falsification has an important place in Arlt's work. In an article published around this time (March 29, 1937), for example, Arlt recounts the biography of Lillian Valerie Smith, who spent much of her life posing as a British colonel. When her disguise was revealed and her identity as a woman and a civilian discovered, she began to fall down the social ladder until ending up as a "horrible human form, with horrible hair and an ugly nose." It is interesting that her fall does not produce a woman, but

rather an entity of no gender, thus suggesting a dose of falsification in all "authentic" identities.

Chapter 6: Cosmopolitanism and Repentance

1. See the prologue to *El reino de este mundo*. For a good sample of the contemporary discussions surrounding *lo real maravilloso* and its relationship to *realismo mágico*, see Parkinson Zamora and Faris (1995).

2. See, for example Mike Gonzalez and David Treece's *The Gathering of Voices*, an otherwise valuable contribution to Latin American poetic historiography but whose underpinning ideology, one that dominates many readings of the evolution of the Latin American avant-garde, is sufficiently illustrated by the title of the chapter devoted to the study of these movements: "Awakenings: The Slow Return to the Real."

3. An idea already suggested by Leo Spitzer (1945) in his seminal article on chaotic enumeration ("La enumeración caótica en la poesía moderna") as a multifaceted resource that may point to the diversity and unity of its constitutive elements.

4. I am using this pair of concepts—difference/diversity—as delineated by Homi Bhabha in *The Location of Culture* (1994). Diversity responds to a teleology that sublates difference into a totality (cultural relativism or pluralism), whereas difference intervenes by displacing and disrupting the dream of totality.

5. This feature of the disembodied perspective was delineated, with a very different sort of critique in mind, by Ortega y Gasset in *La deshumanización del arte* (1925).

6. Mihai G. Grünfeld compiled the excellent anthology of the Latin American vanguard poetry from which I am drawing, which brings together material that it is otherwise difficult, if not impossible, to access.

I find it necessary when dealing with poetry on more than an incidental basis to provide the original version in Spanish along with an English translation.

7. The genealogy of cosmopolitanism doesn't commence, of course, with the Enlightenment but in antiquity, with the Stoics, who opposed a Manichean division between city dwellers and barbaric peoples. On this subject, see Julia Kristeva (1991). Some authors have challenged this genealogy, which follows the European-centered hegemonic view of modernity. See, for example, Scott L. Malcomson (1998), who argues for a non-Western reading of cosmopolitanism: "As far as cosmopolitanism is concerned, I would venture that the rest of the world has almost nothing to learn from the West" (24).

Kant proposes his ideas about cosmopolitanism in "Idea of a Universal History with a Cosmopolitan Purpose" (1991a) and in "Perpetual Peace: A Philosophical Sketch" (1991b). In the first article he suggests that "we shall discover a regular process of improvement in the political constitutions of our continent (which will probably legislate eventually for all other continents) . . . We should observe how their inherent defects led to their overthrow, but in such a way that a germ of enlightenment always survived, developing further with each revolution, and prepared the way for a subsequent higher level of improvement" (52).

8. The two projects are logically linked, and not at odds with each other, as Walter Mignolo has argued (2000b). They are linked by the logic of providential, teleological his-

tory underpinning the cosmopolitan ideal. See Mignolo for an otherwise excellent discussion on the colonial logic of the cosmopolitan ideal and the possibility of a cosmopolitan thinking of colonial difference.

9. About the equalizing logic of the national form, see Benedict Anderson's article in *Cosmopolitics*, "Nationalism, Identity, and the World-in-Motion: On the Logic of Seriality" (1998a).

10. Sylvia Molloy (1988) discusses this debate (very underplayed by its protagonists) at length in her fascinating article "Ser y decir en Darío." In her reading of Rodó's critique of Darío, Molloy points out the ambiguity of the critique of the poetry as a disturbing "shameful pleasure" (36) involved in the act of reading, an enjoyment of the theatricality of Darío's writing while censoring its masquerade. Indeed, a moral regimentation of pleasure underpins this poetry of remorse, sometimes complemented by a theory of representation that attempts to control its exuberance.

11. What John Beverley (1999) has called appropriately 'neo-Arielism' (using of course Rodó's *Ariel* as a paradigm of a certain position in Latin Americanist debates) is a contemporary version of this same dilemma. Beverley makes reference to current positions in the academy that, in order to defend the Latin American intellectual tradition against postcolonial and subalternist theories, prefer not to interrogate this intellectual tradition reproduces subordination.

12. Significantly, a contemporaneous poetic elaboration on the prodigal son like Saint John Perse's *Exile* centers not on repentance but on the exiled condition as transcendental, while Andre Gide's *Retour de l'enfant prodigue* features an unresolved quarrel between individual freedom and the demand, exerted by parental law, to return home.

13. That homecoming and repentance form a foundational narrative of Latin American letters can also be asserted through a cursory examination of some nineteenth-century and twentieth-century novels. Among nineteenth-century cases are the sentimental novel *Maria* (1867) by Jorge Isaacs and the naturalist work *Sin rumbo* (1885) by Eugenio Cambaceres. In both, repentance and homecoming only prefigure the discovery that it is too late to recover what has been lost. It can be argued that the social base of the return of the avant-gardists is different: While the former novels are about a class of oligarchic landowners announcing its own defeat, the poetry of return of the 1940s must be read as part of the development of a national bourgeoisie pressured to find a new alliance with the populist state. The order to be restored is a capitalistic, flexible one, with the only patriarchal overtones being spiritual in nature. For this line of interpretation, *Rayuela* (Hopscotch, 1963) by Julio Cortázar is the great novel of return and recuperation that sums up the trajectory of the thirty years of literary production I am trying to reinterpret, from the completely skeptical cosmopolitan experience of the protagonist Oliveira to his return and recovery of a sense of community—albeit a very lax and transient one—that doesn't fail to bring about the stasis or death of the protagonist.

14. "Miramar" could be read as "mira mar," that is to say, "he looks at the sea"; while "Ponte Grande" means "grosse point."

15. See José Murilo de Carvalho (2001, chapter 2) for an analysis of "the most defining

event of Brasil's political history since independence" (89). According to David Rock (1994, 16), "under the Estado Nôvo (new state) established by Getúlio Vargas in 1937, Brazil . . . constructed a heavily regulated and increasingly centralized economy" that will be later linked, around 1945, to "the emergence of new popular movements and with attempts to promote greater social equality." Different economic and social measures were implemented in the 1930s and 1940s in other countries in Latin America (Mexico, Chile, etc.) in order to terminate the oligarchic rule.

16. Mário de Andrade's puzzling conference "The Modernist Movement" of 1942 could have figured in this survey. I decided not to include it because I already have analyzed his texts extensively. Let me say, however, that in his retrospective assessment of the movement, he accuses himself and his generation of having excessively concentrated on their own affairs while they were deceivingly proclaiming to be saving Brazil—of being ultimately self-centered, hypersensual, and individualistic. Even when, on the other hand, he regards his work as a "happy dedication to my time and my land" and the *modernista* movement as "a revolutionary spirit as necessary as the Romantic" and therefore a threshold to a new world civilization to come, he can't help but argue that all his endeavors were delusional: At the root of all the illness is perhaps the "sensual haughtiness of individualism" (Andrade 1979, 311, 309, 312). What we have in the conference is a major text of repentance and remorse, full of moral condemnation, but self-critical and with no final, nostalgic reconciliation—as is always the case in the work of Mário de Andrade. Thus, the text remains morally ambiguous. The explosive, joyful enthusiasm that he associates throughout the conference with the 1920s is neither suppressed nor accounted for in his remorse.

17. I am succinctly describing the trajectory that goes from his first poetry books *Veinte poemas para ser leídos en un tranvía* (1922) and *Calcomanías* (1925) to his later productions *Espantapájaros (al alcance de todos)* (1932), *Persuasión de los días* (1942), and *Campo nuestro* (1946). But *En la masmédula* (1954), his most radical poetic undertaking, which removed his discourse from any desire of reconciliation, was still to come. The poetic choices of this, his last book, which radically departs from the stance of *Campo nuestro* and reconsiders some of the author's most radical poetic criticism of modernity, probably helps to foreground the pervasiveness of the 1940s tone of repentance.

18. Historian David Rock (1994, 5) summarizes the main features: "Population growth and urbanization, the spread of popular nationalism, the acceleration of industrial development, the expansion of the interventionist state, and the emergence of populist movements stressing industrial development and social reform. Some of these conditions were present during earlier periods, particularly in the 1930s. In the 1940s, however, they rapidly intensified and started to emerge in conjunction with one another as part of a multilayered, reciprocal process of change."

19. For the notion of the "auratic," used in the sense of an attempt at recovery of a lost trace, see Alberto Moreiras (2001, chapter 7), where the author superbly interprets Pablo Neruda's "Alturas de Macchu Picchu," arguably the text of repentance and homecoming par excellence.

20. In that sense, Vallejo's cosmopolitanism can be related to Julia Kristeva's understanding of the concept. As defined in a nutshell by Amanda Anderson (1998, 284–85) in her brilliant article on the current debate about cosmopolitanism, "Kristeva's cosmopolitanism is defined both by detachment from provincial identities and by the therapeutic exploration of strangeness within and outside of the self."

21. I have respected the excellent translation by Eshleman and Barcia (Vallejo 1978), save for one modification. I changed the verb "to leave" in the first line ("the one who leaves you") to the expression "to move away from," since I believe that the openness of the Spanish "el que se aleja de ti" is better captured.

22. This uneven structure, masked as parallel, is also more noticeable with the modification of the translation: "To move away! To remain!" rather than "To leave! To remain!"

Chapter 7. Epilogue

1. As I argued in chapter 2, futurism is not absent from the Latin American avant-gardes. Although it usually does not receive favorable criticism and despite the ambivalent reception of Marinetti's movement, texts, and public persona, some poets did embrace technological novelty and even an exalted war rhetoric as the engine toward a sea change in society. See for example Kin Taniya (pseudonym for Luis Quintanilla), poet of the Mexican Estridentista group, or the Peruvian Alberto Hidalgo.

2. As stated at its Web site: "Founded in 1848, a year of revolution in Europe and therefore of great newsworthiness in the United States, The Associated Press is the oldest and largest news organization in the world." (http://www.ap.org/pages/about/history/history.html, as of March 7, 2005)

3. See note 15, chapter 6.

WORKS CITED

Adorno, Theodor W., and Max Horkheimer. 1998. *Dialectic of Enlightenment*. New York: Continuum.

Agamben, Giorgio. 1999. *The End of the Poem: Studies in Poetics*. Stanford, Calif.: Stanford University Press.

Agnew, John. 1993. "Representing Space: Space, Scale and Culture in Social Science." In *Place/Culture/Representation*, edited by J. Duncan and D. Ley. London and New York: Routledge.

Alonso, Carlos J. 1998. *The Burden of Modernity: The Rhetoric of Cultural Discourse in Spanish America*. New York: Oxford University Press.

———. 1990. *The Spanish American Regional Novel: Modernity and Autochthony*. Cambridge and New York: Cambridge University Press.

Amaral, Aracy. 1970. *Blaise Cendars no Brasil e os modernistas*. São Paulo: Martins.

Amícola, José. 1994. *Astrología y fascismo en la obra de Arlt*. 2nd ed. Rosario, Argentina: Beatriz Viterbo.

Andermann, Jens. 2000. *Mapas de poder. Una arqueología literaria del espacio argentino*. Rosario, Argentina: Beatriz Viterbo.

Anderson, Amanda. 1998. "Cosmopolitanism, Universalism, and the Divided Legacies of Modernity." In *Cosmopolitics: Thinking and Feeling beyond the Nation*, edited by P. Cheah and B. Robbins. Minneapolis: University of Minnesota Press.

Anderson, Benedict. 1996. *Imagined Communities. Reflections on the Origin and Spread of Nationalism*. 7th ed. London and New York: Verso.

———. 1998a. "Nationalism, Identity, and the World-in-Motion: On the Logics of Seriality." In *Cosmopolitics: Thinking and Feeling beyond the Nation*, edited by P. Cheah and B. Robbins. Minneapolis: University of Minnesota Press.

———. 1998b. *The Spectre of Comparisons: Nationalism, Southeast Asia, and the World*. London and New York: Verso.

Anderson, Perry. 1984. Modernity and Revolution. *New Left Review* 144: 97–113.

Andrade, Mário de. 1976. *Taxi e crônicas no Diário Nacional*. São Paulo: Livraria Duas Cidades/Secretaria da Cultura, Ciência e Tecnologia.

———. 1979. *Obra escogida: Novela, cuento, ensayo, epistolario*. Caracas: Biblioteca Ayacucho.

———. 1983. *O turista aprendiz*. 2nd ed. São Paulo: Livraria Duas Cidades.
———. 1984. *Os Cocos*. Preliminary study by Oneyda Alvarenga. São Paulo: Livraria Duas Cidades.
———. 1996. *Macunaíma o herói sem nenhum caráter*. Edited by T. P. A. Lopez. Paris: ALLCA XX/Fondo de Cultura Económica.
Andrade, Oswald de. 1971. *Memórias Sentimentais de João Miramar/Serafim Ponte Grande*. Vol 2 in *Obras Completas*. Rio de Janeiro: Civilização Brasileira.
Antelo, Raúl. 1986. *Na Ilha de Marapatá: Mário de Andrade lê os hispanoamericanos*. São Paulo: Hucitec.
Arlt, Roberto. 1981. *Obra completa*. Vol. 2. Buenos Aires: Carlos Lohlé.
———. 1986. *Los siete locos/Los lanzallamas*. Buenos Aires: Biblioteca Ayacucho/Hyspamérica.
———. 1998. *The Seven Madmen*. Translated by Nick Caistor. London: Serpent's Tail/UNESCO.
Arrighi, Giovanni. 1998. "Capitalism and the Modern World-System: Rethinking the Nondebates of the 1970's." *Review* XXI (1): 113–29.
Asturias, Miguel Angel. 1930. "Leyendas de Guatemala." In *Cuentos y leyendas*. Nanterre: Colección Archivos, 2000.
Augé, Marc. 1995. *Non-places: Introduction to an Anthropology of Supermodernity*. London and New York: Verso.
Badiou, Alain. 1992. "L'âge des poètes." In *La Politique des poètes. Pourquoi des poètes en temps de dètresse?* edited by J. Rancière. Paris: Éditions Albin Michel.
Bakhtin, M. 1981. *The Dialogical Imagination*. Austin: University of Texas Press.
Barker, Francis, and Peter Hulme, and Margaret Iversen, eds. 1998. *Cannibalism and the Colonial World*. Cambridge and New York: Cambridge University Press.
Bender, John, and David E. Wellbery, eds. 1991. *Chronotypes. The Construction of Time*. Stanford, Calif.: Stanford University Press.
Benjamin, Walter. 1969. "Theses on the Philosophy of History." In *Illuminations. Essays and Reflections*. Translated by Harry Zohn. New York: Schocken.
———. 1986. "Paris, Capital of the Nineteenth Century." In *Reflections. Essays, Aphorisms, Autobiographical Writings*. New York: Schocken Books, 1986.
———. 1998. *The Origin of German Tragic Drama*. Translated by John Osborne London and New York: Verso.
———. 2003. *The Arcades Project*. Translated by Howard Eiland and Kevin McLaughlin Cambridge, Mass.: Harvard University Press.
Berman, Marshall. 1988. *All that Is Solid Melts into Air. The Experience of Modernity*. New York: Penguin.
Beverley, John. 1999. *Subalternity and Representation: Arguments in Cultural Theory*. Durham, N.C.: Duke University Press.
Beverley, John, Michael Aronna, and José Oviedo, eds. 1995. *The Postmodernism Debate in Latin America*. Durham, N.C.: Duke University Press.

Bhabha, Homi K. 1994. *The Location of Culture*. London and New York: Routledge.
Blanchot, Maurice. 1981. *De Kafka a Kafka*. Mexico City: Fondo de Cultura Económica.
Borges, Jorge Luis, Alberto Hidalgo, and Vicente Huidobro, eds. 1926. *Indice de la nueva poesía americana*. Buenos Aires: Sociedad de Publicaciones El Inca.
Bradbury, Malcolm, and James Walter McFarlane. 1976. *Modernism: 1890–1930*. Harmondsworth, U.K., and New York: Penguin.
Brenkman, John. 1979. "Mass Media: From Collective Experience to the Culture of Privatization." *Social Text* (1): 94–109.
Brennan, Timothy. 1997. *At Home in the World: Cosmopolitanism Now*. Cambridge, Mass.: Harvard University Press.
———. 1990. "The National Longing for Form." In *Nation and Narration*, edited by Homi K. Bhabha. London and New York: Routledge.
Buck-Morss, Susan. 1989. *The Dialectics of Seeing. Walter Benjamin and the Arcades Project*. Cambridge, Mass.: MIT Press.
Bürger, Peter. 1994. *Theory of the Avant-Garde*. Minneapolis: University of Minnesota Press.
Calinescu, Matei. 1977. *Faces of Modernity: Avant-Garde, Decadence, Kitsch*. Bloomington: Indiana University Press.
Campagnon, Antoine. 1994. *The Five Paradoxes of Modernity*. New York: Columbia University Press.
Cândido, Antônio. 1970. *Vários escritos*. São Paulo: Livraria Duas Cidades.
Carpentier, Alejo. 1995. "On the Marvelous Real in America." In *Magical Realism: Theory, History, Community*, edited by L. P. Zamora and W. B. Faris. Durham, N.C.: Duke University Press.
Carrera Andrade, Jorge. 2000. *Antología Poética*. Mexico City: Fondo de Cultura Económica.
Chakrabarty, Dipesh. 2000. *Provincializing Europe: Postcolonial Thought and Historical Difference*. Princeton, N.J.: Princeton University Press.
Chambers, Iain. 1994. *Migrancy, Culture, Identity*. London and New York: Routledge.
Clifford, James. 1988. *The Predicament of Culture. Twentieth-Century Ethnography, Literature, and Art*. Cambridge, Mass.: Harvard University Press.
———. 1997. *Routes: Travel and Translation in the Late Twentieth Century*. Cambridge, Mass.: Harvard University Press.
Cosgrove, Denis. 2001. *Apollo's Eye. A Cartographic Genealogy of the Earth in Western Imagination*. Baltimore: Johns Hopkins University Press.
da Cunha, Euclides. 1980. *Los Sertones*. Trans. Estela dos Santos. Caracas: Biblioteca Ayacucho.
DaMatta, Roberto. 1981. "Disgreção: A fábula das três raças, Ou o problema do racismo à Brasileira." In *Relativizando: Uma introdução à antropologia social*. Petrópolis: Vozes.
Darío, Rubén. 1985. *Poesía*. Caracas: Biblioteca Ayacucho.
de Campos, Haroldo. 1986. "The Rule of Anthropophagy: Europe under the Sign of Devoration." *Latin American Literary Review* XIV (27): 42–60.

Debord, Guy. 1994. *The Society of Spectacle*. New York: Zone Books.
de Certeau, Michel. 1988. *The Practice of Everyday Life*. Berkeley and Los Angeles: University of California Press.
Deleuze, Gilles, and Félix Guattari. 1977. *Anti-Oedipus: Capitalism and Schizophrenia*. New York: Viking.
de Man, Paul. 1988. *Blindness and Insight: Essays in the Rhetoric of Contemporary Criticism*. Minneapolis: University of Minnesota Press.
———. 1993. *Romanticism and Contemporary Criticism. The Gauss Seminar and Other Papers*. Baltimore and London: Johns Hopkins University Press.
Derrida, Jacques. 1994. *Spectres of Marx*. London and New York: Routledge.
———. 1978. *Writing and Difference*. Chicago: University of Chicago Press, 1978.
Drucaroff, Elsa. 1999. *Arlt, profeta del miedo*. Buenos Aires: Catálogos.
Eagleton, Terry. 1970. *Exiles and émigrés: Studies in modern literature*. New York: Schocken Books.
Eysteinsson, Astradur. 1990. *The Concept of Modernism*. Ithaca: Cornell University Press.
Fabian, Johannes. 1983. *Time and the Other: How Anthropology Makes its Object*. New York: Columbia University Press.
Fabris, Annateresa. 1994. *O futurismo paulista. Hipóteses para o estudo da chegada da vanguarda ao Brasil*. São Paulo: Editora Perspectiva.
Finazzi-Agrò, Ettore. 1996. "As Palavras em jogo." In *Macunaíma: O herói sem nenhum caráter*, edited by Tele Porto Ancona Lopez. Paris: ALLCAXX/Fondo de Cultura.
Foot Hardman, Francisco. 1988. *Trem fantasma. A modernidade na selva*. São Paulo: Companhia das Letras.
Friedman, Jonathan. 1995. "Global System, Globalization and the Parameters of Modernity." In *Global Modernities*, edited by M. Featherstone, S. Lash, and R. Robertson. London and Thousand Oaks, Calif.: SAGE.
Gaonkar, Dilip Parameshwar, ed. 2001. On Alternative Modernities. *Alternative Modernities*. Durham, N.C.: Duke University Press.
García Canclini, Néstor. 1989. *Culturas híbridas: Estrategias para entrar y salir de la modernidad*. Mexico City: Grijalbo.
Gilroy, Paul. 1993. *The Black Atlantic: Modernity and Double Consciousness*. Cambridge, Mass.: Harvard University Press.
Girondo, Oliverio. 1994. *Obra*. Buenos Aires: Losada.
Glissant, Édouard. 2000. *Poetics of Relation*. Ann Arbor: University of Michigan Press.
GoGwilt. 2000. *The Fiction of Geopolitics: Afterimage of Culture, from Wilkie Collins to Alfred Hitchcock*. Stanford, Calif: Stanford University Press.
González, Horacio. 1996. *Arlt: Política y locura*. Buenos Aires: Colihue.
Gonzalez, Mike, and David Treece. 1992. *The Gathering of Voices: The Twentieth-Century Poetry of Latin America*. London and New York: Verso.
González Echevarría, Roberto. 1977. *Alejo Carpentier, the Pilgrim at Home*. Ithaca: Cornell University Press.

———. 1985. *The Voice of the Masters: Writing and Authority in Modern Latin American Literature.* 1st ed. Austin: University of Texas Press, 1985.

———. 1990. *Myth and Archive: A Theory of Latin American Narrative.* Durham, N.C.: Duke University Press, 1998.

Gorelik, Adrián. 1998. *La grilla y el parque: Espacio público y cultura urbana en Buenos Aires, 1887–1936.* Bernal, Argentina: Universidad Nacional de Quilmes.

Gregory, Derek. 1994. *Geographical Imaginations.* Cambridge, Mass., and Oxford, U.K.: Blackwell.

Grunfeld, Mihai Gheorghe. 1995. *Antología de la poesía latinoamericana de vanguardia, 1916–1935.* Madrid: Hiperión.

Gumbrecht, Hans Ulrich. 1997. *In 1926: Living at the Edge of Time.* Cambridge, Mass.: Harvard University Press.

Halperín Donghi, Tulio. 1996. *Historia contemporánea de América Latina.* Madrid: Alianza Editorial.

Harvey, David. 1990. *The Condition of Postmodernity: An Enquiry into the Origins of Cultural Change.* Cambridge, Mass., and Oxford: Blackwell.

Heller, Agnes. 1993. "On the Railway Station." In *A Philosophy of History in Fragments.* Oxford and Cambridge, Mass.: Blackwell.

Holanda, Sérgio Buarque de. 1982. *Raízes do Brasil.* 15th ed. Rio de Janeiro: José Olympio.

Huidobro, Vicente. 1948. *Ultimos poemas.* Santiago, Chile: Ahués.

———. 1963. *Obras completas.* Santiago, Chile: Zig-Zag.

———. 1972. *Poemas articos.* Santiago, Chile: Editorial Nascimento.

———. 1999. *Manifestos Manifest.* Translation by Gilbert Alter-Gilbert. Los Angeles: Green Integer.

Huyssen, Andreas. 1986. *After the Great Divide. Modernism, Mass Culture, Postmodernism.* Bloomington: Indiana University Press.

Jackson, Kenneth David. 1987. Primitivismo e vanguarda: O 'mau selvagem' do modernismo brasileiro. *Arquivos do Centro Cultural Portugues* 23: 975–82.

Jameson, Fredric. 1987. "World literature in an age of multinational capitalism." In *The Current in Criticism. Essays on the Present and Future of Literary Theory,* edited by C. Koelb and V. Lokke. West Lafayette, Ind.: Purdue University Press.

———. 1991. *Postmodernism, or, The cultural logic of late capitalism.* Durham, N.C.: Duke University Press.

———. 1992. "Reification and Utopia in Mass Culture." In *Signatures of the Visible.* London and New York: Routledge.

———. 1999. "Cognitive Mapping." In *Poetics/Politics. Radical Aesthetics for the Classroom,* edited by A. Kumar. New York: St. Martin's Press.

———. 2002. *A Singular Modernity: Essay on the Ontology of the Present.* London and New York: Verso.

Johnson, Randal. 1999. "Brazilian Modernism: An Idea Out of Place?" In *Reinscribing Cul-*

tural Modernity from Spain and Latin America. New York and London: Garland Publishing.

Kant, Immanuel. 1991a. "Idea of a Universal History with a Cosmopolitan Purpose." In *Kant: Political Writings.* Cambridge and New York: Cambridge University Press.

———. 1991b. "Perpetual Peace. A Philosophical Sketch." In *Kant: Political Writings.* Cambridge and New York: Cambridge University Press.

———. 2000. *The Critique of Judgment.* Translated by J. H. Bernard. Amherst, N.Y.: Prometheus Books.

Kaplan, Caren. 1996. *Questions of Travel: Postmodern Discourses of Displacement.* Edited by F. Jameson and S. Fish. Durham, N.C.: Duke University Press.

Kern, Stephen. 1983. *The Culture of Time and Space 1880–1918.* Cambridge, Mass.: Harvard University Press.

Keyserling, Count Hermann. 1927. *The World in the Making.* New York: Harcourt, Brace.

Kilgour, Maggie. 1990. *From Communion to Cannibalism: An Anatomy of Metaphors of Incorporation.* Princeton: Princeton University Press.

King, Anthony D. 1995. "The Times and Spaces of Modernity (or Who Needs Postmodernism?)." In *Global Modernities,* edited by M. Featherstone, S. Lash, and R. Robertson. London and Thousand Oaks, Calif.: SAGE.

Kirby, Kathlenn M. 1996. *Indifferent Boundaries. Spatial Concepts of Human Subjectivity.* New York and London: The Guilford Press.

Koch-Grünberg, Theodor. 1981. *Del Roraima al Orinoco.* Translated by F. D. Ritter. 3 vols. Caracas: Ernesto Armitano.

Koselleck, Reinhart. 1977. *Futures Past. On the Semantics of Historical Time.* Cambridge, Mass.: MIT Press.

Kristeva, Julia. 1991. *Strangers to Ourselves.* New York: Columbia University Press.

Larsen, Neil. 1990. *Modernism and Hegemony: A Materialist Critique of Aesthetic Agencies.* Minneapolis: University of Minnesota Press.

Lefebvre, Henri. 2000. *The Production of Space.* Oxford, U.K., and Cambridge, Mass.: Blackwell.

Levi-Straus, Claude. *Tristes Tropiques.* Translated by John and Doreen Weightman. New York: Penguin, 1974.

Lévy-Bruhl, Lucien. 1966. *The 'Soul' of the Primitive.* New York and Washington, D.C.: Frederick A. Praeger.

Lezama Lima, José. 1969. *La expresión americana.* Santiago, Chile: Editorial Universitaria.

Livingston, Robert Eric. 2001. "Glocal Knowledges: Agency and Place in Literary Studies." *PMLA* 116 (1): 145–57.

Lloyd, David. 1996. "Race under Representation." In *Culture/Contexture. Explorations in Anthropology and Literary Studies,* edited by E. V. Daniel and J. M. Peck. Berkeley and Los Angeles: University of California Press.

Lopez, Telê Porto Ancona. 1972. *Mario de Andrade: Ramais e caminho.* São Paulo: Livraria Duas Cidades.

———. 1974. *Macunaíma: a margem e o texto*. São Paulo: Hucitec.
Lyotard, Jean-François. 1991. *The Inhuman. Reflections on Time*. Stanford, Calif.: Stanford University Press.
Ludmer, Josefina. 2004. *The Corpus Delicti: A Manual of Argentine Fictions*. Pittsburgh: University of Pittsburgh Press.
Malcomson, Scott L. 1998. "The Varieties of Cosmopolitan Experience." In *Cosmopolitics. Thinking and Feeling beyond the Nation*, edited by P. Cheah and B. Robbins. Minneapolis: University of Minnesota Press.
Mariátegui, José Carlos. 1969. *Siete ensayos de interpretación de la realidad peruana*. Havana: Casa de las Américas.
———. 1973. *José Carlos Mariátegui en sus textos*. Vol. 2. Lima: Peisa.
———. 1989. *Invitación a la vida heróica*. Lima: Instituto de Apoyo Agriario.
Martín-Barbero, Jesús. 1993. *Communication, Culture and Hegemony: From the Media to Mediations*. Communication and Human Values. London and Newbury Park, Calif.: SAGE.
Martins, Wilson. 1970. *The Modernist Idea: A Critical Survey of Brazilian Writing in the Twentieth Century*. Translated by J. E. Tomlins. New York: New York University Press.
Masiello, Francine. 1986. *Lenguaje e ideología: Las escuelas argentinas de vanguardia*. Buenos Aires: Hachette.
Mendieta, Eduardo. 1998. "Modernidad, posmodernidad y poscolonialidad." In *Teorías sin disciplina: Latinoamerianismo, poscolonialidad y globalización en debate*, edited by S. Castro-Gómez and E. Mendieta. Mexico City: Miguel Angel Porrúa; and San Francisco: University of San Francisco.
Mello e Souza, Gilda de. 1979. *O tupi e o alaúde*. São Paulo: Livraria Duas Cidades.
Meschonnic, Henri. 1992. "Modernity Modernity." *New Literary History* 23 (2): 401–30.
Mignolo, Walter D. 2000a. *Local History/Global Designs. Coloniality, Subaltern Knowledges and Border Thinking*. Princeton: Princeton University Press.
———. 2000b. "The Many Faces of Cosmo-polis: Border Thinking and Critical Cosmopolitanism." *Public Culture* 12 (3): 721–48.
Molloy, Sylvia. 1988. "Ser y decir en Darío: el poema liminal de *Cantos de vida y esperanza*." *Texto Crítico* 14 (38): 30–42.
Moreiras, Alberto. 1994. "Pastiche Identity, and Allegory of Allegory." In *Latin American Identity and Constructions of Difference*, edited by Amaryll Chanady. Minneapolis: University of Minnesota Press.
———. 1998. Fragmentos globales: Latinoamericanismo de segundo orden. In *Teorías sin disciplina. Latinoamericanismo, poscolonialidad y globalización en debate*, edited by S. Castro-Gómez and E. Mendieta. Mexico City: Miguel Angel Porrúa; and San Francisco: University of San Francisco.
———. 2001. *The Exhaustion of Difference: The Politics of Latin American Cultural Studies*. Durham, N.C.: Duke University Press.
Moretti, Franco. 1986. "The Moment of Truth." *New Left Review* (159): 39–48.

———. 1996. *Modern Epic. The World-System from Goethe to García Márquez*. London and New York: Verso.

Murilho de Carvalho, José. 1999. "Brasil: Nações imaginadas." In *Pontos e bordados: Escritos de história e política*. Belo Horizonte: UFMG.

———. 2001. *Cidadania no Brasil: O longo caminho*. Rio de Janeiro: Civilização Brasileira.

Ó Tuathail, Gearóid. 1996. *Critical Geopolitics. The Politics of Writing Global Space*. Minneapolis: University of Minnesota Press.

Osborne, Peter. 1995. *The Politics of Time: Modernity and Avant-Garde*. London and New York: Verso.

Osorio T., Nelson. 1982. *El futurismo y la vanguardia literaria en América Latina*. Caracas: Centro de Estudios Latinoamericanos Rómulo Gallegos.

———. 1985. *La formación de la vanguardia literaria en Venezuela (antecedentes y documentos)*. Caracas: Biblioteca de la Academia Nacional de Historia.

———, ed. 1988. *Manifiestos, proclamas y polémicas de la vanguardia literaria hispanoamericana*. Caracas: Biblioteca Ayacucho.

Palumbo-Liu, David. 1997. Introduction: Unhabituated Habituses. In *Streams of Cultural Capital: Transnational Cultural Studies*, edited by D. Palumbo-Liu and H. U. Gumbrecht. Stanford, Calif.: Stanford University Press.

Pastor, Beatriz. 1980. *Roberto Arlt y la Rebelión Alienada*. Gaithersburg, Md.: Hispamérica.

Pellicer, Carlos. 1996. *Poesía Completa*. Vol. 1. Mexico City: UNAM/Ediciones del Equilibrista.

Pérez Firmat, Gustavo. 1982. *Idle Fictions: The Hispanic Vanguard Novel, 1926–1934*. Durham, N.C.: Duke University Press.

Piglia, Ricardo. 1986. "Sobre Roberto Arlt." In *Crítica y Ficción*. Santa Fé, Argentina: Universidad Nacional del Litoral.

Pratt, Mary Louise. "Fieldwork in Common Places." In *Writing Culture. The Poetics and Politics of Ethnography*, edited by James Clifford and George E. Marcus, 27–50. Berkeley, Los Angeles and London: University of California Press, 1986.

———. *Imperial Eyes. Travel Writing and Transculturation*. London and New York: Routledge, 1992.

Proença, Manuel Cavalcanti. 1987. *Roteiro de Macunaíma*. Rio de Janeiro: Civilização Brasileira.

Puig, Manuel. 1976. *El beso de la mujer araña*. Barcelona: Seix Barral.

Quijano, Anibal. 1995. "Modernity, Identity, and Utopia in Latin America." In *The Postmodernism Debate in Latin America*, edited by John Beverley, Michael Aronna, and José Oviedo. Durham, N.C.: Duke University Press.

———. 2000. "Coloniality of Power, Eurocentrism, and Latin America." *Nepantla: Views from the South* 1 (3): 533–80.

Rama, Angel. 1982. *Transculturación narrativa en América Latina*. Mexico City: Siglo Veintiuno.

———. 1995. "Las dos vanguardias latinoamericanas." In *La riesgosa navegación del escritor exiliado*. Montevideo: Arca.

Rancière, Jacques. 1994. "Discovering New Worlds: Politics of Travel and Metaphors of Space." In *Traveller's Tales,* edited by George Robertson, Melinda Mash, Lisa Tickner, Jon Bird, Barry Cutis, and Tim Putnam. London and New York: Routledge.

———. 1999. *Disagreement.* Minneapolis and London: University of Minnesota Press.

———. 2002. "On the Aesthetic Revolution." *New Left Review* (14): 133–51.

Rebuelto, Emilio. 1994. "Historia del desarrollo de los ferrocarriles argentinos." In *Los ferrocarriles en la Argentina 1857–1910,* edited by E. Schickendantz and E. Rebuelto. Buenos Aires: Fundación Museo Ferroviario.

Rincón, Carlos. 1995. "The Peripheral Center of Postmodernism." In *The Postmodernism Debate in Latin America,* edited by J. Beverley, M. Aronna and J. Oviedo. Durham, N.C.: Duke University Press.

Rock, David. 1994. Introduction. In *Latin America in the 1940s: War and Postwar Transitions,* edited by D. Rock. Berkeley and Los Angeles: University of California Press.

Romero, José Luis. 1986. *Latinoamérica: Las ciudades y las ideas.* Mexico City: Siglo XXI.

Ross, Peter, and Blanche Hampton. 1993. "Don't Trust the Locals. European Explorers in Amazonia." In *Literature and Travel,* edited by Michael Hanne. Amsterdam and Atlanta, Ga.: Rodopi.

Rowe, William. 1996. *Hacia una poética radical. Ensayos de hermenéutica cultural.* Rosario, Argentina: Beatriz Viterbo/Mosca Azul.

Saítta, Sylvia. 2000. *El escritor en el bosque de ladrillos: Una biografía de Roberto Arlt.* Buenos Aires: Sudamericana.

Santiago, Silviano. 1989. *Nas malhas da letra: Ensaios.* São Paulo: Companhia das Letras.

Sarlo, Beatriz. 1988. *Una modernidad periférica: Buenos Aires 1920 y 1930.* Buenos Aires: Nueva Visión.

———. 1992. *La imaginación técnica: Sueños modernos de la cultura argentina.* Buenos Aires: Nueva Visión.

———. 1993. *Jorge Luis Borges: A Writer on the Edge.* London and New York: Verso.

Schnapp, Jeffrey T., and João Cezar de Castro Rocha. 1996. "Brazilian Velocities: On Marinetti's Trip to South America." *South Central Review* 13 (2–3): 105–56.

Schneider, Luis Mario. 1997. *El estridentísimo, o, una literatura de la estrategia.* México City: Consejo Nacional para la Cultura y las Artes.

Schwarcz, Lilia Moritz. 1993. *O espetáculo das raças: Cientistas, instituções e questão social no Brasil 1870–1930.* São Paulo: Companhia das Letras.

Schwartz, Jorge. ed. 1991. *Las vanguardias latinoamericanas: Textos programáticos y críticos.* Madrid: Cátedra.

———. 1993. *Vanguardia y cosmopolitismo en la década del veinte. Oliverio Girondo y Oswald de Andrade.* Rosario: Beatriz Viterbo.

Schwarz, Roberto. 1992. *Misplaced Ideas: Essays on Brazilian Culture.* London and New York: Verso.

Skidmore, Thomas E. 1974. *Black into White: Race and Nationality in Brazilian Thought.* New York: Oxford University Press.

Smith, Neil. 2003. *American Empire: Roosevelt's Geographer and the Prelude to Globalization.* Berkeley and Los Angeles: University of California Press.

Sommer, Doris. 1999. *Proceed with Caution, when Engaged in Minority Writing in the Americas.* Cambridge, Mass.: Harvard University Press.

Spengler, Oswald. 1962. *The Decline of the West.* New York: The Modern Library.

Spitzer, Leo. 1945. *La enumeración caótica en la poesía moderna.* Translated by R. Lida. Buenos Aires: Facultad de Filosofía y Letras de la UBA/Instituto de Filología.

Spurr, David. 1994. "Myths of Anthropology: Eliot, Joyce, Levy-Bruhl." *PMLA* 109 (2): 266–80.

Taylor, Charles. 2001. "Two Theories of Modernity." In *Alternative Modernities*, edited by Dilip Parameshwar Gaonkar, 172–96. Durham, N.C.: Duke University Press, 2001.

Unruh, Vicky. 1994. *Latin American Vanguards: The Art of Contentious Encounters.* Berkeley and Los Angeles: University of California Press.

Uslar Pietri, Arturo. 1985. "La vangurdia: Fenomeno cultural." In *La formación de la vanguardia literaria en Venezuela (Antecedentes y documentos),* edited by Nelson Osorio T. Caracas: Academia Nacional de la Historia.

Vallejo, César. 1978. *The Complete Posthumous Poetry.* Translated by Clayton Eshleman and José Rubia Barcia. Berkeley and Los Angeles: University of California Press.

———. 1986. *Obra poética completa.* Caracas: Biblioteca Ayacucho.

———. 1987. *Desde Europa: Crónicas y artículos (1923–1938).* Lima: Fuente de Cultura Peruana.

Vattimo, Gianni. 1988. *The End of Modernity: Nihilism and Hermeneutics in Postmodern Culture.* Baltimore: Johns Hopkins University Press.

———. 1992. *The Transparent Society.* Baltimore: Johns Hopkins University Press.

Verani, Hugo J. 1990. *Las vanguardias literarias en Hispanoamérica (manifiestos, proclamas y otros escritos).* Mexico City: Fondo de Cultura Económica.

Vidal e Souza, Candice. 1997. *A pátria geográfica: Sertão e litoral no pensamento Social brasileiro.* Goiânia: Universidad Federal de Goiás.

Wallerstein, Immanuel. 1997. "The Time of Space and the Space of Time: the Future of the Social Science." *Political Geography* 17 (1): 71–82.

———. 2003. *Historical Capitalism and Capitalist Civilization.* London and New York: Verso.

Weinstein, Barbara. 1983. *The Amazon Rubber Boom 1850–1920.* Stanford, Calif.: Stanford University Press.

Williams, Raymond. 1996. *The Politics of Modernism: Against the New Conformists.* London and New York: Verso.

Young, Robert J. C. 1995. *Colonial Desire: Hybridity in Theory, Culture and Race.* London and New York: Routledge.

Yúdice, George. 1992. "Postmodernity and Transnational Capitalism in Latin America." In

On Edge: The Crisis of Contemporary Latin American Culture, edited by G. Yúdice, J. Franco, and J. Flores. Minneapolis and London: University of Minnesota Press.
———. 1999. "Rethinking the Theory of the Avant-Garde from the Periphery." In *Modernism and Its Margins: Reinscribing Cultural Modernity from Spain and Latin America*, edited by A. L. Geist and J. B. Monleón. New York and London: Garland Publishing.
Zamora, Lois Parkinson, and Wendy B. Faris, eds. 1995. *Magical Realism: Theory, History, Community*. Durham, N.C.: Duke University Press.

INDEX

"Actual Number 1" manifesto, 141
Adorno, Theodor, 66, 151, 155
aesthetics: and the avant-garde, 70; *lo real maravilloso*, 137; and modernity, 12, 14, 34, 166; and native values, 141, 144; as subject position, 42–43, 46–48, 116
Agamben, Giorgio, 159
Alencar, José de, 100
alienation, 59–61
All That Is Solid Melts into Air (Berman), 32
allegory, 84–85, 88–90, 152–53
Alonso, Carlos, 14, 21–22, 153
Altazor o un viaje en paracaídas (Huidobro), 148
Amaral, Aracy, 107
Amaral, Tarsila do, 116, 140
Amauta (magazine), 35
Amazon, 109, 111–18
Anderson, Amanda, 41
Anderson, Benedict, 7, 37
Anderson, Perry, 6–7, 8, 32–36
Andrade, Mário de, 9–11, 30; authorial voice of, 110–11; and folklore, 183n8; *Macunaíma*, 41–46, 77–105; on *Macunaíma*, 84; self-criticism of, 163–64, 190n16; travel writing of, 107–23
Andrade, Oswald de, 10, 13, 18–19, 26, 40, 44, 78, 89, 94, 107, 140, 146–47
anthropology: cultural relativism and, 93–94, 187n32; and Western superiority, 24. *See also* ethnography
anthropophagy: and colonialism, 182n30; *Macunaíma* and, 44–46, 77–81, 83, 103–4; originality and, 79–80; recurrences of, 178n1; resistance and, 28; significance of, 78
Antônio, Chico, 118–19
Antropofágico (O. Andrade), 78
Aragon, Louis, 7
Argentina, in Arlt's journalism, 123–35
Arguedas, José María, 28, 95
Ariel, 7
Arlt, Roberto, 8–11, 41, 164; as author/journalist, 46–48, 174n33; economic observations of, 126–31; as journalist, 123–24, 131–32; literary place of, 49–50; *Los siete locos/Los lanzallamas*, 49–76; and Spain, 187n33; spectacle in writings of, 185n23; travel writing of, 123–35
Associated Press, 162
Asturias, Miguel Angel, 9, 30, 81
Augé, Marc, 23
authenticity, 10, 91, 137, 144, 153, 159; and genre, 180n12; and the political, 62, 66, 69, 175n5; and subjectivity 56, 68, 187n35; systems of, 115–18; and time, 86
autonomy, anthropophagy and, 79–80
avant-gardes: author/artist as theme of, 71; concept of, 16, 161–62; cosmopolitan versus native origins of, 12–14; critical capacity of, 22, 28, 152–53, 164; cultural currency of, 14–15, 165–67, 171n3; derivative character of, 17–18; European, 1–2; evolutionary model of, 12–13; as global, 27; Latin American, 1–11; mass culture and, 7; and modernity, 19; nostalgia concerning, 15; old regime and, 34; and

205

the people, 165; regionalism versus, 23, 28, 139; remorse of, over cosmopolitanism, 136, 145–46, 149–51, 153, 157, 190n16; and revolution, 35; role of art as theme of, 70; subjectivity as theme of, 70. *See also* modernity
"Aviso a los turistas" (Huidobro), 26

Badaró, Líbero, 121, 184n17
Badiou, Alain, 158
Bakhtin, Mikhail, 36
Bandeira, Manuel, 99
bandeirantes, 109
Baudelaire, Charles, 68
Benjamin, Walter, 11, 77, 127–28, 133
Berman, Marshall, 32
El beso de la mujer araña (Puig), 69
Bhabha, Homi, 97, 99
Blanchot, Maurice, 157
Boedo group, 49, 175n1
Bopp, Raul, 99, 107
border thinking, 159
Borges, Jorge Luis, 4, 49, 77, 89, 124, 125, 169n5
Bourdieu, Pierre, 41
Bradbury, Malcolm, 39
Brazil: Andrade's travel writing about, 108–23; anthropophagy and, 78–81; frontier of, 109–10, 182n2; *Macunaíma* and, 77–105; race in, 92–93, 99
Brazilian avant-garde. See *modernismo*
"Brazilwood manifesto," 6
Buarque de Holanda, Sérgio, 87
Buenos Aires, Argentina, 124–29
bumba-meu-boi, 85, 180n16
Bürger, Peter, 3, 38

Caliban, 7
Calinescu, Matei, 16
Campo nuestro (Girondo), 150
Campos, Haroldo de, 79
Cândido, Antônio, 89
cannibalization. *See* anthropophagy
Cardoza y Aragón, Luis, 29, 140

Carpentier, Alejo, 137
Carrera Andrade, Jorge, 145
Cendrars, Blaise, 94, 99, 107, 110, 147
Chakrabarty, Dipesh, 32
chronotopic criticism, 36
ciranda, 116
cities: avant-gardes and, 139–40; cosmopolitanism and, 139–40; Latin American modernism and, 38–39; in *Macunaíma*, 98; modernity and, 5; simultaneity and, 38. *See also* Buenos Aires, Argentina
Clifford, James, 40, 86, 106, 115
coco, 118, 120, 184n12
collage, 3, 43, 77, 81, 107, 140
colonialism: anthropophagy and, 78–79, 182n30; in *Macunaíma*, 100–105; modernity and, 16; nationalism and, 23–24; opposition to, 4. *See also* conquerors
Columbus, Christopher, 162
commodity fetishism, 128
community, alternate narratives of, 30
conquerors, 108–9
Conrad, Joseph, 58–59
contact zones, 127, 186n26
"Contra el secreto profesional" (Vallejo), 12
cordial man, 87
Cosgrove, Denis, 52
cosmopolitanism: anthropology and, 94, 187n32; and cities, 139–40; critical, 40–41; history of, 188n7; and internationalism, 149; Latin American writers and, 146–60; meanings of, 139; and nativism, 12–14, 136, 138, 141–46, 150–51, 165; in 1920s, 139; rejection of, 137–38; remorse over, 136, 145–46, 149–51, 153, 157
costumbrismo, 124
critical capacity of Latin American avant-gardes, 22, 28, 152–53, 164. *See also* resistance
cultural relativism, 93–94
Culturas Híbridas (García Canclini), 30
culture, place and, 23

Cunha, Euclides da, 98, 110

dadaism, 78
DaMatta, Roberto, 99
Darío, Rubén, 13, 32, 144, 149, 169n5, 171n1
De Man, Paul, 91, 152, 153
Debord, Guy, 63, 66, 68, 185n23
The Decline of the West (Spengler), 22, 55
defamiliarization, 39
The Demons (Dostoyevsky), 175n2
Derrida, Jacques, 50
Diário Nacional (newspaper), 44, 115, 119
Diderot, Denis, 112
difference, cosmopolitanism and, 142–44
Don Segundo Sombra (Güiraldes), 129
Dostoyevsky, Fyodor, 175n2

Eagleton, Terry, 39
economy. *See* market economy
Einstein, Albert, 57
elite culture, 5
Eliot, T. S., 86
Enlightenment, 20–21
Espantapájaros (Girondo), 150
ethnographic surrealism, 86
ethnography, 110–14. *See also* anthropology
Europe: cosmopolitanism and, 141; cultural tours of, 88–89; Latin America versus, 2–4, 22, 164. *See also* European avant-gardes
European avant-gardes: Latin American versus, 1–2; and origin of modernity, 21; and primitivism, 24
extraordinary, 62–66

Fabian, Johannes, 24, 94
flânerie, 125
folklore, 113, 118–19, 183n8
Ford (company), 123
Frank, Joseph, 36–37
Frankfurt School, 71
Frazer, James George, 85–86, 112
futurism, 28–29, 33, 161–62, 191n1

Gaonkar, Dilip Parameshwar, 91–92
García Canclini, Nestor, 8, 28, 30, 33, 115
García Lorca, Federico, 29
geopolitics: Andrade's *Macunaíma* and, 43; capitalism versus national sovereignty, 55; concept of, 15–16; imperialism and, 172n5; and maps, 52–55; and subjectivity, 53
Girondo, Oliverio, 10, 13, 24, 31, 89, 107, 140, 150–51, 153
globalization, 15, 23
The Golden Bough (Frazer), 85
González Echevarría, Roberto, 114, 137, 169n4
González Tuñón, Raúl, 124
Guillén, Nicolás, 30, 81, 140
Güiraldes, Ricardo, 89, 129
Gulliver's Travels (Swift), 112
Gumbrecht, Hans Ulrich, 37

Halperin Donghi, Tulio, 4
Hegel, Georg, 102
Heidegger, Martin, 23
Heller, Agnes, 128
heteroglossia, 36–37
Hidalgo, Alberto, 140
historicism, 31, 107, 142, 172n9
Horkheimer, Max, 151, 155
Huidobro, Vicente, 10, 13, 26, 34, 38, 107, 140, 147–50, 161
hybridity, 3, 28, 80–81, 97, 180n9

identity: avant-gardes and, 30; constitution of, 3–4; Vallejo and, 155–60
indigenous culture: avant-gardes and, 12–14, 114; cosmopolitanism and, 136, 138; modernity and, 18–19, 130–31; and nation, 114–17; and tradition, 113, 115
Interlunio (Girondo), 150
internationalism, 149
Iracema (Alencar), 100
irony, 153

Jameson, Fredric, 8, 31, 32, 36, 71
Jimmy (informant), 119–20
João VI, 121
Joyce, James, 37
Judeo-Christian temporality, 1
El juguete rabioso (Arlt), 66

Kant, Immanuel, 40, 142, 188n7
Kern, Stephen, 57, 59
Keyserling, Hermann, 22, 95
Kirby, Kathleen, 53
Koch-Grünberg, Theodor, 43–44, 77–78
Koselleck, Reinhart, 62

Laforgue, Jules, 18
Lanuza, González, 89
Larsen, Neil, 79, 103
Latin America: versus Europe, 2–4, 22, 88–89, 141, 164; global place of, 1–2; immigration and migration in, 39; modernity in, various meanings of, 17–19; traveling writers and, 107, and U.S. foreign policy, 75. *See also* national identities
Latin American literary history, 136–60
Latin American Vanguards (Unruh), 3
Lautremont, Comte de (Isidore-Lucien Ducasse), 18
Lefebvre, Henri, 186n25
Lery, Jean de, 117
Lévy-Bruhl, Lucien, 26, 102
Leyendas de Guatemala (Asturias), 9
Lezama Lima, José, 87, 159
Livingston, Robert Eric, 151
Ludmer, Josefina, 178n28
Lyotard, Jean-François, 73

macumba, 98–99
Macunaíma, o herói sem nenhum caráter (M. Andrade), 9, 41–46, 77–105; allegory in, 88–90; anthropophagy and, 78–81, 83, 103–4; colonialism in, 100–105; genre of, 180n12; hybridity in, 97; interpretations of, 83–85; modernist role of, 77; modernity in, 91–105; plot summary of, 81–83; sadness of, 83; symbolism in, 84–91; transculturation in, 94–98, 103–4
magic realism, 137
Malfatti, Anita, 34
"Manifesto Martín Fierro," 6
Maples Arce, Manuel, 13, 107, 140, 162
maps, 52–55
Mariátegui, José Carlos, 13, 26, 35, 136, 137–38
Marinetti, Emilio Filippo Tommaso, 28–29, 173n17
market economy: anthropophagy and, 80; Latin American avant-gardes and, 6–7; postmodernism and, 20
Marti, José, 24
Martín Fierro (magazine), 49, 124, 174n1
Martín-Barbero, Jesús, 63
martinfierristas, 56
mass culture, 5
mass media, 62–66, 70–72
Matarazzo (businessman), 121, 185n17
McFarlane, James Walter, 39
Memórias sentimentais de João Miramar (O. Andrade), 40, 146
Mendieta, Eduardo, 24
Meschonnic, Henri, 21
metafiction, 70
Mexican muralists, 9, 81
Mignolo, Walter, 8, 31, 159, 172n10, 173n14
Minas Gerais, Brazil, 108–9
mobile traditions, 113, 115, 118–20
modernismo: Andrade's self-criticism concerning, 190n16; anthropology and, 93; anthropophagy in, 28; Brazilian, 9, 86–89, 116, 182n2; cosmopolitanism-nationalism polarity in, 146–47; definitions of, 171n1; Hispanic-American, 7, 13, 141, 169n5; and primitivism, 24–25; self-consciousness of, 79; and temporality, 97–99; transculturation and, 98–99; and travel, 108–10. *See also* avant-gardes
modernity: alternative, 91–92; avant-gardes

and, 19; conditions of, 33–36; critique of, 1–2; cultural versus acultural theories of, 91–92; desire for, 32; diffusionist model of, 16; Latin American, 17–19; New World and, 18; performativity of, 21; postmodernism and, 19–20; promise of, 18; space and, 36–37; temporality and, 20–22; trains and, 56–57; as unaccomplished, 32–34; universality of, 2, 18. *See also* avant-gardes
Moraes, Raimundo, 44
Moreiras, Alberto, 87
Moretti, Franco, 36–37, 62, 66
Morgan, J. P., family, 175n4
El Mundo (newspaper), 123
muralists, Mexican, 9, 81
music, 116, 118–19

national identities: Andrade's *Macunaíma* and, 41–46; colonialism and, 23–24; cosmopolitanism and, 141–46, 150–51, 165; ethnography and, 114; *Macunaíma* and, 80–81, 83–91; and modernity, 21; post–World War I, 3–4; *testimonio* and, 30–31. *See also* indigenous culture
Neruda, Pablo, 13, 107
new: and discovery, 22; futurism and, 28–29; historical conditions for, 161–62; spatial conception of, 7–8; two types of, 7–8
Nicaraguan avant-garde, 7
North Pole, 132–33
novela de la tierra, 23

Odyssey, 145, 151
originality, 79–80
origins, critique of, 159–60
Ortiz, Fernando, 179n9
Osborne, Peter, 172n9
Osorio T., Nelson, 17–18

Pau Brasil (O. Andrade), 78
Pellicer, Carlos, 143–44
people: Andrade's *Macunaíma* and, 43; avant-gardes and, 165; and mass media, 63; and modernity, 91–92, 118. *See also* popular
performance, 117
periphery, as theme in *Los siete locos/Los lanzallamas*, 70–76
Petorruti, Emilio, 34
Piglia, Ricardo, 70
Poe, Edgar Allan, 18
popular, 9, 43, 83, 85, 87, 99, 118–19, 138
Portal, Magda, 35, 107, 151
positionality, of avant-gardes, 5–6, 19
postcolonialism, 8, 10, 15, 25, 41, 81, 102, 104, 139; and *antropofagia*, 45
postmodernism: Latin American avant-gardes and, 19–20; market economy and, 20; modernity and, 19–20, 166–67
Pound, Ezra, 29
Prado, Paulo, 107
Pratt, Mary Louise, 16, 186n26
primitivism: and critique of reason, 94; Latin Americans and, 24–26; versus linear history, 24, 94; meanings of, 94
"The Process of Literature" (Mariátegui), 137–38
Proença, Manuel Cavalcanti, 100
progress, 1, 16, 21, 73
Puig, Manuel, 69

race, 92–93, 99
railroads. *See* trains
Rama, Angel, 95, 138
Ramalho, João, 90
Rancière, Jacques, 54, 58
lo real maravilloso, 137
regional novel, 23, 28, 102, 139
resistance, 27–28, 72–76. *See also* critical capacity of Latin American avant-gardes
revolution, 35, 57–58, 62, 64–65
Rimbaud, Arthur, 18
Rincón, Carlos, 20
Rivera, Diego, 140
Robbins, Bruce, 153
Rodó, José Enrique, 7, 144

Rokha, Winétt de, 140–41
Romero, José Luis, 5
Rosa, Guimarães, 95
Rowe, William, 158
ruins, 88, 101, 104, 126–28
Rulfo, Juan, 95

Saítta, Sylvia, 187n33
"Santiago ciudad" (Rokha), 140–41
Sarlo, Beatriz, 74, 124
scenes of writing: Andrade's *Macunaíma*, 41–42; Arlt's *Los sietes locos/Las lanzallamas*, 46
Schwartz, Jorge, 139–42
Schwarz, Roberto, 25
The Secret Agent (Conrad), 58–59
Serafim Ponte Grande (O. Andrade), 146–47
serial novels, 63
sertão, 23, 109–10, 118
Os sertões (Cunha), 98, 110
Shlovsky, Viktor, 39
Los siete locos/Los lanzallamas (Arlt), 8, 41, 46–48; extraordinary in, 62–66; maps in, 52–55; periphery as theme in, 70–76; perspectives on modernity in, 66–69; plot summary of, 50–52; resistance in, 72–76; sociopolitical context of, 50; subjectivity and role of art as themes in, 70; time in, 55–62
simultaneity, 37–38
Solar, Xul, 140
Sommer, Doris, 120
space: concrete versus abstract, 186n25; Latin American avant-garde and, 1–8; modernism and, 36–37; in *Los siete locos/Los lanzallamas*, 72–73
Spain, Arlt and, 187n33
spectacle, 62–63, 66, 68, 185n23
Spengler, Oswald, 22, 55, 95
Spix, Johann Baptist von, 183n10
subjectivity: as avant-garde theme, 70; geopolitics and, 53; mass media and, 63; modernity and, 26–27; Vallejo and, 155–60; weak, 67, 69

Supplément au voyage de Bougainville (Diderot), 112
surrealism, 78, 80, 112, 137
Swift, Jonathan, 112
symbol, 84–91, 152–53

Taunay, Nicolas Antoine, 121, 184n17
Taylor, Charles, 92
temporality: avant-garde concept and, 16; circular, 85–86; futurism and, 28–29; homogenization of public time, 57–59; lack of, in Latin America, 28; Latin American sense of, 1–2, 25–26; in *Macunaíma*, 91–105; *modernismo* and, 97–99; modernity and, 20–22; primitivism and, 24; revolutionary time, 57–58; in *Los siete locos/Los lanzallamas*, 55–62, 73; subjectivity and, 26–27
testimonio, 30–31
Theory of the Avant-Garde (Bürger), 3
time. *See* temporality
Torres García, Joaquín, 140
"Tourist Advisory" (Huidobro), 26
tradition: indigenous peoples and, 113, 115, 118–20; Latin American art and, 28–30, 162–63; modernism and, 13, 20, 163
trains, 26–27, 56–59, 121–22, 128
transculturation, 80–81, 94–98, 103–4, 138, 179n9
travel writing, 106–35; Arlt in Argentina, 123–35; M. Andrade in Brazil, 108–23
tropical civilization, 95–96
O turista aprendiz (M. Andrade), 110

Ultimos poemas (Huidobro), 149
Ulysses, 145, 151
United States, in *Los siete locos/Los lanzallamas*, 52–55
universality: Arlt and, 130–35; critical cosmopolitanism and, 40–41; European avant-gardes and, 2, 18
Unruh, Vicky, 3, 169n6

Vallejo, César, 10, 12, 13, 153–60
vanguards. *See* avant-gardes

Vasconcelos, José, 95, 143, 162, 180n9
Vattimo, Gianni, 1, 66
Verde-Amarelo, 146
Viagem etnográfica (M. Andrade), 110
virgin land, 95–96
Von Martius, Karl Friedrich, 117, 183n10

Wallerstein, Immanuel, 37
The Waste Land (Eliot), 86

Webb, Percy, 134–35
Week of Modern Art (1922), 42
Whitman, Walt, 18
Williams, Raymond, 38–39
World War I, 3

Yrigoyen, Hipólito, 50
Yúdice, George, 8, 27–31